Strategy-Specific
Decision
Making

William G. Forgang is a professor of business and economics at Mount Saint Mary's College in Emmitsburg, Maryland. He teaches undergraduate- and MBA-level courses in managerial economics and business policy, and consults in the areas of strategic planning and staff development. The author lives with his wife, Nancy, in Gettysburg, Pennsylvania.

Strategy-Specific
Decision Making

A Guide for
Executing
Competitive
Strategy

William G. Forgang

M.E.Sharpe
Armonk, New York
London, England

Library of Congress Cataloging-in-Publication Data

Forgang, William G., 1946–
    Strategy-specific decision making : a guide for executing competitive strategy / William
G. Forgang.
    P. cm.
    Includes bibliographical references and index.
    ISBN 0-7656-1288-7 (alk. paper)
    1. Decision making. 2. Strategic planning. 3. Management. I. Title.

HD30.23.F683 2004
658.4′03—dc22   2003060489

Printed in the United States of America

The paper used in this publication meets the minimum requirements of
American National Standard for Information Sciences
Permanence of Paper for Printed Library Materials,
ANSI Z 39.48-1984.

∞

BM (c)   10   9   8   7   6   5   4   3   2   1

Contents

List of Figures and Tables

Tables

Preface

This book is directed toward those who want to be effective decision makers, to be part of a cohesive management team, and to contribute to the success of their firm. For readers in an academic setting, the immediate decision-making challenges may involve guiding a hypothetical firm in a strategic management simulation. However, these readers will soon join the ranks of those who make decisions that affect real firms, real people, and real money. The goals of this book are to help decision makers: (a) define problems, (b) evaluate alternatives, (c) take action to execute effectively their firm's competitive strategy, (d) explain their decisions, (e) earn the trust and confidence of others, and (f) achieve superior performance.

Making a business decision is similar to taking a photograph. For a photographer, a clear lens and accurate measures of light and distance are essential ingredients for achieving the desired outcome. In contrast, a defective lens and inaccurate measurements blur images and provide false information. The photographer is unable to focus upon the most important features of the intended picture and assess the options. Questions arise. Is the welcome sign to some exotic vacation resort included in the frame? Is the whole family in the picture? Will the picture come out clear or fuzzy? Will those in the photograph be pleased? One cannot be sure.

Taking photographs through a cloudy lens is filled with risk, stress, and uncertainty. The hazards are compounded if the photographer's work affects friends, family, or business associates. Where others are affected, a photographer seeks advice before taking and selecting a picture. Though the consultation is essential, it also heightens the stress. Different people have different aspirations for the photograph, and if the lens is cloudy, individuals see different things. Their recommendations differ. The one taking the picture is exposed. If the photograph comes out poorly, the photographer is likely to hear, "I told you so!"

Similar issues arise with business decision making. One's view of a problem or opportunity is distorted if the lens is cloudy. Imprecise images make it difficult to diagnose problems, options are hard to assess, and outcomes are difficult to predict. Consultation with colleagues or teammates in a class exercise adds stress. Different people see different things and make divergent recommendations. In the absence of a clear lens, several recommendations appear sensible. Debate is heated because no one is "wrong." But everyone cannot be right!

The analogy between management decision making and photography is, however, imperfect. Photographers enjoy many benefits not available in business. Unless a photograph is time sensitive, several pictures can be taken, and the cost of each photograph is low. The best picture is selected *after* viewing the outcomes. If disagreements persist, those with different tastes and preferences choose their own photograph. In contrast, business decision makers take action *before* viewing the outcome. Furthermore, many business decisions are costly to reverse. All members of the organization must abide by the single managerial choice and cannot select a different decision based upon their preferences. Under these circumstances, business decision makers are exposed and ripe targets for finger-pointing and second-guessing.

This book provides business decision makers with the tools to create a clear lens. Their firm's competitive strategy filters options and allows each manager across a firm and over time to apply common decision-making criteria. A decision maker's consistent application of a clear strategic lens reduces the stress of making decisions, facilitates communicating the logic of one's choice, earns the respect and confidence of coworkers, and im-

proves the execution of the firm's strategy. In the classroom strategy-specific decision making guides students' decisions, effectively executes their mock firm's strategy, and leads to well-reasoned reports. One outcome is a high course grade. Another outcome is that students become confident and insightful decision makers who are poised for success in the workplace.

The journey through this book is not easy, but neither is the journey to strategy-specific decision making. The reader is encouraged to work through the book carefully, to think about each of the case studies, to reflect upon the exercises, and to apply the lessons to their own experiences or simulation exercise. Work slowly; be patient. Decision-making methodology is not quickly incorporated into an individual's or an organization's thinking, but the long-term rewards are significant.

William G. Forgang

Acknowledgments

Many special friends and colleagues helped me complete this project. In particular Professors Charlie Beitz, Don Butt, Kirk Davidson, Karl Einolf, John Hook, Stephen Rockwood, Tom Ryan, and Ray Speciale created a hard-working and good-humored office environment conducive to completing lengthy and stressful projects.

Dan Smith, Rodger Mitchell, and the staff at Capstone Management Simulations influenced this book. Their Internet-based simulation, Capsim, is a rich teaching and learning exercise. The spirited discussions in my business strategy courses that rely upon Capsim prompted this book.

The editorial staff at M.E. Sharpe was professional and responsive. I enjoyed working with them. In particular, I thank Esther Clark, Lynn Taylor, Angela Piliouras, and Daphne Hougham, who were very helpful.

Throughout this project, my wife, Nancy, provided tireless encouragement and support, and she spent countless hours editing drafts. Her patience and faith are remarkable.

A Note to Instructors, Students, and Managers

This book is directed toward two audiences—students and managers. These current and future decision makers share common needs. Both seek to improve their decision-making skills, build successful careers, and strengthen the competitiveness of their current (or future) employers. Both also seek to communicate effectively the logic of their actions to earn the trust and confidence of their colleagues.

In an academic setting, this book is appropriate for advanced undergraduate or MBA students in a business-policy course. The practical decision-making focus differentiates this book from the contemporary group of cumbersome, case laden, and theoretical texts. In particular, it is designed for capstone business-strategy courses that utilize a simulation to enliven and enrich the learning experience. The decision-making focus complements a simulation by guiding students to develop a competitive strategy for their company; to make decisions in product design, production, human resources, marketing, management, and finance that will implement that strategy; and to explain the logic of their actions in terms of their firm's competitive strategy. The book's relatively small size and affordable price also make it attractive as a supplement to a computer-based strategic management simulation.

One very effective simulation is the Capstone Business Simulation (www.capsim.com) offered by Management Simulations, Inc.[1] This powerful Internet-based simulation places students and developing managers in decision-making roles in hypothetical and competitive manufacturing firms. The simulation challenges the learner to design a competitive strategy for a multiple products firm and to make decisions that execute the strategy. Students and developing managers experience the interdependence of functional areas of operation, learn the importance of consistent and commonly focused decisions, create a decision-making lens, and become accountable for the consequences of their decisions.

In a business setting, this book should be studied *prior to* the firm's annual strategic planning cycle. This sequence allows the firm to clarify its competitive strategy and develop a cohesive management team that consistently executes the strategy. Additionally, this book supports orientation programs that acquaint newly hired or promoted managers with their firm's strategy and the processes of making operating decisions to execute the strategy.

How to Use This Book

When using a simulation in an academic course or management development program, the first few class periods are difficult. Students and developing managers are often overwhelmed by the responsibility to learn quickly about strategic management *and* the simulation at the same time. But there is no luxury of time to digest the vast amount of information in small bites. At the start of a course or training program, a big gulp is required to prepare for the first round of decisions. There is no substitute for hard work, but the initial investment pays off. The rewards include favorable simulation results, and the workload dramatically eases after crossing the initial learning hurdle.

The format of this book helps the reader prepare for the first round of decisions. It can be read quickly. After a quick pass through the book, the reader is urged to concentrate on the Instructor's and Student's Simulation Guide, located in the appendix. Part A of the Guide, Presimulation Activities, is comprised of questions that bridge the concepts of strategic management with a simulation and prepare the readers for their first set of decisions. The questions direct the reader to the relevant text pages, allowing the Guide to be used as a reference tool. Instructors may ask for written replies to these questions or use them to direct class discussion.

Part B of the Simulation Guide, Postsimulation Activities, includes questions to diagnose the outcomes of each round of the simulation. These questions also include references to the relevant text pages. Readers may use these questions to prepare for class. Instructors may use the questions to prompt discussion or as written assignments. Part B also includes a suggested outline for written assignments, following each round of a simulation or at key milestones.

Pedagogical Features

Several sections and features of this book support both readers and instructors.

- *Gelle's Building Products* is a cohesion case. It is presented prior to chapter 1 and referred to throughout the book in text boxes to highlight key themes.
- *The Instructor's and Student's Simulation Guide,* in the appendix, provides instructors with exercises and discussion questions.
- Each chapter includes discussion questions and exercises that apply decision-making methodology to personal experiences or to the challenge of running a firm in a simulation. Some exercises appear twice: within a chapter and again in the Guide. Within chapters, the exercises prompt responses when text information is fresh in the reader's mind. When repeated, readers can revise their answers after completing their study of strategy-specific decision making.
- *Case studies*, located in the appendix, may be used as written assignments or as examples for class discussion.
- *Key themes and terms* are summarized at the end of each chapter.

The reader is encouraged to take each step in sequence and to apply the newly learned principles diligently. The learning opportunity for individual readers and their organizations is valuable and a leveraged result of the effort and thought applied to the exercises. Do not rush. Relax, and enjoy the opportunity to consider problems and solutions in a strategy-specific context.

Note

1. *Capstone: A Business Simulation* (Northfield, Ill.: Management Simulations, 2003) (www.capsim.com).

Cohesion Case: Gelle's Building Products

Before proceeding to chapter 1, please:
1. Read the Gelle's Building Products case study.
2. Write the memo requested at the end of the case.
3. Save your replies. You will be asked to review and revise these replies in the appendix.

John Chudovas is seated at the head of a conference table, flanked by his immediate and disgruntled staff. John knows they are frustrated by recent events, and their mood is reflected by the absence of the usual good-natured bantering. Each is looking for John to solve the problem.

The hastily scheduled meeting has only one agenda item: the firm's accounts receivable policy. John, the chief operating officer, is being forced to make a decision that ordinarily is made at a lower level. However, the newly hired vice president for finance and accounting, Sandy Koopmans, has recommended a change in policy, and senior staff members have objected.

Because of the lack of consensus, John has called this meeting. His goals are to discuss the situation and to make a decision, if not build a consensus.

Gelle's Building Products

Gelle's Building Products manufactures metal-based, vinyl-coated home construction and renovation materials. The products include storm doors, screen doors, windows, dormers, storage sheds, frames and braces for sun decks and Florida rooms, decorative fencing, and swimming pool cabanas. The common element is the decorative, low-maintenance, and weather-resistant vinyl coating over a strong and durable metal base.

Gelle's sales in fiscal 2002 totaled $22 million. Over the prior ten years the annualized rate of growth in sales averaged 3.6 percent.

Gelle's sells primarily to small family-owned construction and home repair companies throughout the mid-Atlantic region. The marketplace is intensely competitive. There are several producers of similar products, and there are many home builders and remodelers, each of whom has a favored supplier of materials. Further, large home products retailers create obstacles for Gelle's, whose size is insufficient to capture much shelf space.

John Chudovas

John has been the chief operating officer at Gelle's Building Products for almost a dozen years. Over this period Gelle's financial performance has been solid but not spectacular. John has earned the reputation of being a very diligent and dedicated worker. He is appreciated throughout the organization because he listens attentively and allows those on the front line to do their job. However,

John is not averse to stepping into the fray, mediating disputes, and making a decision.

The current controversy over the firm's accounts receivable policy irritates John. He believes that details are best handled at the operational level. However, given that Sandy Koopmans is a new employee and emotional memos have been circulated, John feels his involvement is essential.

In his customary style John opens the meeting by allowing each participant to explain their position and recommendation. John permits open discussion only after everyone has had an opportunity to speak.

The Recommendations

Sandy Koopmans, Vice President of Accounting and Finance: Currently, our accounts receivable are just below $1 million. Over the last year the receivables have grown 12.4 percent, whereas sales have increased only 4.1 percent. Last year our average collection period was about sixty days. Now the average collection period is about 128 days. I was surprised when I discovered this because my department did not change any policies, and low interest rates and the strong housing market should have reduced and not lengthened the receivables. I talked to some of the slower paying accounts on the telephone, and it appears that sales personnel are making inappropriate promises, such as accepting slower payment times.

The $1 million in receivables over an additional sixty days at 9 percent interest costs us about $15,000 per year. With our margins already thin, this added cost is deplorable. Furthermore, last week I attended our trade association conference in Chicago. During one of the sessions a CPA from one of the large public accounting firms indicated that for our industry the average collection period is approximately fifty days. We're not even close to the industry standard, and each additional day

in collection costs us money. While $15,000 may not sound like a lot, it is a sum that could go directly to our profit-sharing plan. For our employees, the dollar amount is meaningful.

I recommend we make clear to our customers that our payment policy is sixty days from shipment and that we impose a 1 percent per month finance fee. To be fair, we must permit no exceptions. Further, because of our impending need for cash given the planned replacement of the coating machine, we should notify each delinquent account that receivables over one hundred days will be forwarded to a collection agent.

Kirk Davis, Vice President of Manufacturing: We make good products. Our products are durable, easy to install, and require little maintenance even under the most adverse climatic conditions. Our end users never see our products warp, weather, or need paint. People understand that they must pay for what they buy. When I buy something, I understand finance charges. I agree with Sandy! Collections are not our problem. They should not pass their cash flow problems back to us.

Rebecca Green, Vice President of Marketing and Public Relations: My view is that we are discussing the wrong topic. Our collection policy is not a big deal one way or the other. Our customers understand paying bills. No doubt our easy credit terms may help some of our accounts. After all, every business has an occasional cash-flow problem. But our buyers want products delivered in a timely manner. Right now, the duration of time from our receipt of an order to delivery is thirty-one to thirty-eight days.

If we really want to improve our financial performance, our operations and customer service must be upgraded to better serve our buyers. I suggest cutting the time from receipt of an order to delivery to a maximum of ten days. Let's do everything we can to speed up manufacturing and shipping and, for now, ignore the payment policy.

Among the things I want to do is change our production scheduling. Currently, we schedule to achieve the longest possible production runs. And we do not make any deliveries to an account until their order is complete. If an account has ordered several different items, they wait until the production schedule cycles through all of our products. Finished products sit for extended periods on our loading dock. While long production runs and full truckloads lower our costs, these practices slow deliveries. We are not serving our customers effectively because our operations restrict their ability to serve their buyers.

Let's not let Sandy's preoccupation with finance charges distract us from more important issues.

Terrence O'Shea, Vice President for Sales and Service: The sales staff isn't doing anything inappropriate. We work with small family-owned businesses. In turn, they work with middle-class families. Both our buyers and the end users of our products have periodic cash-flow difficulties. Accommodating their needs is vital for building and sustaining relationships with our customers.

Our customers choose our products partially because of our payment flexibility. This does not disparage our products. Our products are high quality, but so are the products of many of our competitors. The contractors we work with do quality work, but they have many competitors. Our collections practices make us attractive relative to other materials producers because our customers can extend more favorable credit terms to their customers.

In my ten years and more than $150 million in gross sales, the uncollected accounts are less than 1 percent of total sales. The number of customers we have lost to competitors can be counted on one hand. We should be proud of this record. Our service to customers is the basis of our repeat business and favorable word-of-mouth promotion.

Sandy is right. There is an implicit interest cost associated with the aging of receivables. But there has been no change in the behavior of our sales force. There are no improper promises being made. The lengthening of the receivables is something we have experienced on a cyclical basis before. It is not a cause for concern. Rather, the goodwill results in repeat business, more than making up for the minor interest expense. With all due respect to Sandy, she has been part of Gelle's for only six weeks. I am sure she is doing what she was taught in business school. But she does not understand what has made this company successful. Let's not try to fix what's not broken.

John Chudovas, Chief Operating Officer: In spite of what each of you has said, at this point, I'm not sure why we haven't been able to solve the problem. I need time to think. Let's meet next week at the same time.

End-of-Case Exercise

To be completed prior to reading chapter 1.

1. Write a memo to John Chudovas. What should he do? Why? What should he tell his staff?
2. Develop a list of qualities that describes leaders. Evaluate John Chudovas as a leader.

Save these memos. Later, you will be asked to review and revise them.

Strategy-Specific Decision Making

1
Managing by Competitive Strategy

This book is directed toward individuals and organizations that seek to become superior performers, and the route to that success involves *strategy-specific decision making*. For the individual, success results from their applying a strategic lens to make consistently correct decisions, to explain effectively those decisions to others, to guide colleagues along a similarly directed decision-making path, and to contribute to their firm's exceptional performance. For the organization, success is a result of the careful *design and execution*[1] of their competitive strategy.

Getting Started

The management literature is filled with excellent theoretical and practical books about the design of a firm's strategy, sources of competitive strength, and the processes of strategic planning. But there are wide gaps in the literature. One gap occurs because strategists do their work and leave the details of implementation to functional area specialists in, for example, finance, marketing, and human resources.[2] But those professionals do not begin their work from the perspective of strategic management. Rather, functional area specialists pursue discipline-specific topics, thereby creating a gap between the design and the execution of a firm's strategy.

A second gap results from the rapidly growing use of computer-based business-strategy simulations in the classroom and in management development workshops. The transition from textbook and case study analysis to complex simulations offers many instructional benefits. Students and developing managers learn how to design and implement a competitive strategy; they acquire a holistic view of a company by experiencing the dependencies between functional area decisions; they sharpen decision-making and communication skills; and the immediate feedback from the results of their decisions adds excitement and accountability to the classroom. However, text materials to support the simulations have not advanced as rapidly as the technology.

A third gap is the difference between aspiration and achievement. A performance gap can be attributable to a poorly *designed* or a poorly *executed* strategy. A strategy can be poorly designed for several reasons. For example, a firm incurs the costs to differentiate its product from rivals, but what they thought was the unique feature of its product is not important to potential buyers. Or a strategy is poorly designed if the product or service is unusually vulnerable to existing or new competitors, technological change, political instability, or changing social norms. Also, a strategy can be poorly designed for a particular firm. Consider a business that has a creative idea that meets buyer expectations. However, their equipment is old and improperly configured for the new product. The firm is financially unable to replace their equipment. There is a mismatch between the company's abilities and strategy. For this firm, the competitive strategy is poorly designed.

A strategy is poorly executed if managers make inconsistent and incomplete decisions, and if their firm does not offer the product features, service, or price as intended. For example, consider a manufacturer whose competitive strategy emphasizes the durability of its product. The product is engineered for a long and useful life, but the procurement manager purchases material inputs on the basis of price. Procurement decisions are inconsistent with the engineering design, and the firm's products are not as durable as intended. Similarly, a price-conscious producer properly designs its products, and its procurement practices are appropriate given the strategy. The firm wisely invests in training to improve productivity and lower unit labor costs. But it fails to automate its manufacturing facility and does not capture this opportunity to reduce labor costs. Their cost strategy is poorly executed because decisions are not complete.

This book seeks to fill the three gaps. First, tools are developed to define and assess the *design* of a firm's strategy. Next, functional area decisions are examined from the perspective of *implementing* the firm's competitive strategy, which is the lens to evaluate options and guide decisions that *execute* the firm's strategy. Finally, the use of a strategy lens improves decision-making skills, closes the gap between aspirations and achievement, and yields individual and organizational success.

Strategic Management: Design and Execution

The goal of strategic management is superior and sustained financial performance, and the strategic management process is comprised of two stages. The *design* stage determines the way in which a firm intends to differentiate its good or service from rivals. In this stage a firm makes choices to gain a competitive advantage over rivals. In the *execution* stage decisions in the functional areas of operations implement the company's strategy.

Figure 1.1 maps these stages.

Design Stage

The design stage of the strategic management process shapes a firm's competitive strategy. For a single product or narrow group of products, a firm's competitive strategy refers to the weighted mix of price, product qualities and features, and service that differentiates its product from those of rivals. In most industries several different weighted mixes of these issues are possible. For example, rival manufacturers of an intermediate-stage product differently emphasize technical features, reliability, access, delivery time, after-sale service, age, and price. Within this industry, different strategies are successful. Buyers' needs, expectations, and abilities to pay are not homogeneous, allowing different sellers to concentrate on specific market segments by pursuing different competitive strategies.

Explicitly choosing a strategy is necessary because components of value often conflict with one another, imposing trade-offs. A trade-off occurs when a decision to improve one component of value limits another. A firm's decision to produce the most technically proficient product incurs high R & D and materials costs and thus is unable to be the lowest-priced seller. There is a trade-off between technical sophistication and price as ways to attract and retain buyers. Similarly, a vehicle manufacturer whose products are designed for safety is unable to be the industry leader in fuel efficiency. Technology limitations and production costs prevent even the most aggressive and ideal-

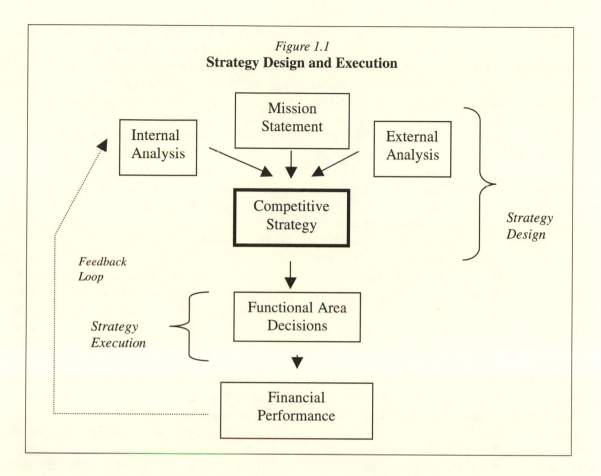

Figure 1.1
Strategy Design and Execution

istic firms from being the industry leader in all aspects of value at the same time.

Choosing a strategy prioritizes the elements of value and guides decision makers. Consider a hotel that decides to emphasize luxury service and accommodations. The hotel's management recognizes it cannot be the luxury service leader and the lowest-priced seller. The strategy based on luxury services dictate choices in staff size, training, furniture selection, food service, communications technologies, and marketing. The strategy guides decisions and limits the range of debate by clearly establishing priorities and the criteria to assess options.

Exercise 1.1

1. For your firm, one with which you are familiar, or the firm in your simulation, list the alternative ways in which one product can be differentiated from rivals.
2. Indicate the relative importance of the differentiators to a particular group of buyers.
3. What trade-offs exist between the differentiators?

A similar exercise is provided in the Instructor's and Student's Simulation Guide, question 1.

Mission Statement

The design stage of the strategic management process begins with a mission statement (see Figure 1.1). Mission statements are examined more carefully in chapter 3, but this stage of the discussion requires two considerations. A firm's mission statement: (a) identifies the products or services offered and (b) reflects the price, product features and qualities, and service that are intended to capture a competitive advantage.

Identifying a firm's good or service is not as simple as it sounds. For example, consider a neighborhood diner. Is it just a place that serves inexpensive meals? Or is it a place where friends, civic leaders, and business people meet while also having a meal? Different visions of the diner lead to different operating decisions. For example, a low-cost diner limits beverage refills to save money and to turn over their tables to new customers. In contrast, the diner that is a place for people to meet, willingly refills beverages and makes other decisions that encourage patrons to linger.

In every organization decision makers must know how their firm intends to compete against rivals. One set of decisions is made in a manufacturing firm that wants to be the industry's technical leader, whereas different decisions are made by a business that competes on ease of use of the product, and other decisions are made by a low-price seller. Decision makers who consistently make and explain their choices in terms of the firm's strategy earn the trust and confidence of their colleagues, while those who explain one decision on ease of use and another on costs create confusion and invite second-guessing.

The challenges of drafting a mission statement are most easily understood when considering the start-up phase of a business. An individual who plans to open a restaurant must have a vision that includes interior design, food preparation, and service. The business concept is expressed in the mission statement and guides the firm's choice of product features, service, menu items, ingredients, location, decor, hiring, and level of service. However, before the owner assumes the risk of opening, for example, an elegant French restaurant, internal and external analyses provide reality checks to prevent an unwise investment.

Internal Analysis

Internal analysis (see Figure 1.1) evaluates the firm's ability to implement the strategy. It identifies strengths and weaknesses that affect its ability to carry out the mission. Internal analysis assesses the prospective French restaurant owner's ability to finance the start-up costs, attract and retain appropriate personnel, manage operations, prepare and serve meals, and sustain the effective execution of the strategy over time.

A firm's strengths and weakness are assessed three ways: (a) relative to its strategy, (b) relative to its rivals, and (c) reassessed periodically. First, because different competitive strategies require different tools, equipment, financial capabilities, and skills, the assessment of a company's capabilities is completed relative to the needs to execute their particular strategy. For example, a manufacturer who competes on the basis of state-of-the-art products requires different machinery from a manufacturer who competes on the basis of relatively lower prices.

Second, because strategic management seeks a competitive advantage, the assessment of a firm's capabilities is completed relative to competitors' capabilities. For example, an accounting firm employs certified professionals. The company meets industry certification requirements and is proud of its staff. But it does not achieve an advantage over rivals who employ professionals with similar credentials. An advantage is gained by doing more accurate work, by completing work more quickly, or by providing a higher degree of courtesy and convenience to the client.

Finally, because the strengths and weaknesses of a firm and its competitors change over time, internal analysis is a recurring process. Changes come as firms differently invest in R & D, both in terms of dollars and focus, and in the development of their labor, facilities maintenance, support of distributors, or account management. Also, buyer expectations modify after a while, and competitors differently anticipate these changes. As a result, the effectiveness of the design and execution of an organization's strategy is not constant over time, and a firm's strengths and weaknesses must be reassessed periodically.

External Analysis

External analysis (see Figure 1.1) evaluates conditions outside the firm's doors and beyond its control but that affect its success. External analysis examines social, political, economic, regulatory, technological, and competitive environments as conditions within which the company produces and sells its products and that affect the firm's success. Favorable forces (rapid market growth, high contribution margins, and few competitors) create opportunities. Unfavorable external forces (slow growth, aggressive governmental regulations, intense rivalries, and vulnerability to technological change) pose threats.

External analysis is a reality check that prevents a firm from pursuing a competitive strategy in an excessively hostile environmental. When adverse environmental conditions exist, external analysis guides the firm toward more attractive marketplace opportunities. For ex-

ample, a small-town family-owned hardware store diverts assets to a new business rather than unwisely challenging a newly opened home products superstore.

External analysis is an ongoing task. Marketplace conditions change over time for many reasons, including the entry of new corporations and products, a product moving into the mature stage of its life cycle, the development of substitute products, changes in the competitive strengths of rivals, business cycle swings, and changing demographics, technology, or social attitudes. As a result, the wisdom of a firm's strategy relative to its external environments is periodically reassessed.

Competitive Strategy

The competitive strategy (see Figure 1.1) for a firm's single product or narrow group of products is defined by the particular mix of price, product qualities and features, and service that differentiate it from rivals. The firm's competitive strategy defines its decision lens and its route to attract and retain buyers and realize superior financial performance. A business commits to a strategy after determining its ability to execute it (strengths and weaknesses), and assessing the attractiveness of the marketplace (opportunities and threats). Internal and external analyses put the firm on a realistic path to gain an advantage over rivals and realize superior return. However, its weighted mix of price, product features and qualities, and service is not achieved by issuing orders to employees. The strategy is executed through management decisions.

Execution Stage

The execution stage of the strategic management process translates the firm's vision and aspirations into reality. The execution stage is comprised of decisions made every day, at all levels of an organization, and in all functional areas of operation. For example, managers select from alternative product designs, equipment, employee reward systems, marketing options, and prices; then the composite of these decisions determines the firm's strategy. Like the photographer who needs a clear lens and accurate measurements, decision makers need similar tools. The effective execution of a company's strategy requires a clear lens to filter options and make decisions.

The design and execution stages of the strategic management process provide reality checks that address three questions: (a) Can we do it? (b) Does it make sense? (c) Does anyone care?

Can We Do It?

This question coincides with the internal assessment. This assessment of the firm's skills, resources, and products is completed relative to its strategy and to rivals to determine its ability to capture and sustain a competitive advantage. It is important to emphasize two comparisons. The first is the firm's resources and skills relative to the requisites of implementing their strategy. Can the organization actually do what it intends? A yes answer is not sufficient; being good is not enough. Winning results from being better. Therefore, the second comparison is between a firm's abilities and those of rivals.

Does It Make Sense?

External analysis examines the sensibility of the firm's strategy relative to its external environments. Marketplace conditions determine if the strategy makes sense, and the critical variables include the number and strength of rivals, the rate of market growth, industry supply, and the vulnerability of the strategy to swings in the business cycle or shifts in consumer tastes, tax and regulatory policy, technology changes, and the threat of the introduction of new goods. Consider, for instance, a builder of beachfront homes. The firm has extraordinary skills and a track record of meeting buyer expectations. However, if the government eliminates the mortgage interest deduction for second homes or limits waterfront construction for environmental concerns, the builder will not succeed. The sensibility of the strategy is determined by the degree to which the company is vulnerable to its external environments.

Does Anyone Care?

This question focuses on buyer needs and determines if the firm's strategy is sufficiently important to buyers. This issue involves the buyers' assessment of a firm's mix of price, product features and qualities, and service. For example, a firm offers a technically proficient product that is equivalent to rivals. To gain a competitive advantage, this firm incurs costs to bring upgrades to market more quickly than competitors can. But in this market buyers are slow to upgrade their needs and will not pay a higher price for the most current product. Buyers are not attracted by the organization's pace of product introduction, and thus the firm does not recover the higher costs of reducing the cycle development time.

Financial Performance

Figure 1.1 indicates that a firm's financial performance is the lagged result of the design and the execution of a firm's strategy. As a lagged consequence, a firm's financial performance may be favorable because (a) it effectively designs and executes its strategy or (b) because rivals are ineffective with their strategic decisions, or (c) some combination of the two. Correspondingly, a firm's financial outcome may be disappointing because it (a) poorly designs or executes its strategy, (b) because rivals are effective, or (c) some combination of the two.

To guide future decisions, it is important to determine the reasons for financial success or disappointment. A firm whose financial success is based upon unusually favorable market conditions or ineffective rivals is vulnerable. The favorable circumstances may not be long lasting. The current financial success can be used to strengthen the execution of the firm's strategy to prepare for less favorable market conditions. In contrast, a company's disappointments may be attributable to a contested market and the effectiveness of rivals. These conditions force a complex decision. Is it appropriate to continue on course and face strong rivals, to change strategy, or to redeploy assets to new markets?

Feedback Loop

Figure 1.1 includes a feedback loop from financial performance to internal analysis. This connection highlights the fact that a firm's financial performance in one period affects its internal strengths and weaknesses in the following period. For example, a financially successful firm invests in R & D, training, capacity expansion, or marketing initiatives to build an infrastructure that supports its success in ensuing periods. This feedback loop results in a favorable cycle when financial success in one period strengthens the company's competitive abilities in future years. Alternatively, a cycle of decline begins when fi-

nancial stresses in one period prevent a firm from effectively executing its competitive strategy in the following period.

Exercise 1.2

1. For your firm, one you are familiar with, or your firm in a simulation exercise, evaluate the strengths, weaknesses, opportunities, and threats for each product.
2. This exercise should be completed after each round of decisions.

Strategy-Specific Decision Making

This book emphasizes the execution stage of the strategic management process by focusing on strategy-specific decision making. The decision-making methodology applies the firm's competitive strategy as a lens to evaluate decision options, to make consistent and complete decisions, and to explain the logic behind one's actions. Figure 1.2 displays the process of filtering options through a strategy lens and the decision option that most effectively executes the strategy passing through the lens.

Consider a marketing manager for a manufacturing firm who identifies several ways to improve sales, including a price reduction, an increase in the number of outside sales personnel, quicker deliveries to distributors, increased advertising, and increased training for those who interact with end users of the product. Each option is promising. None of the ideas are "bad." But budgets are limited, and decisions that allocate limited financial resources must be made. Further, the marketing manager's ideas must be evaluated relative to other options, including the manufacturing manager's eagerness to upgrade the product. How is one to choose?

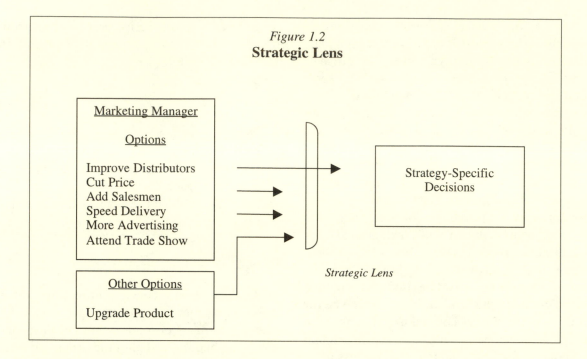

Figure 1.2
Strategic Lens

Gelle's Building Products: Conflicting Advice

John Chudovas received conflicting advice from his staff regarding the accounts receivable issue.

Sandy Koopmans urged a stricter collection policy. Terrence O'Shea disagreed. Rebecca Green believed the wrong issue was being discussed. She wanted to focus attention on the firm's delivery schedule.

Each staff member offered a different but reasonable recommendation. How is John to decide?

Figure 1.2 indicates that all options are filtered by a firm's strategic lens. Only the most favorable option effectively executes a firm's strategy and passes through the lens. Because this manufacturer emphasizes ease of access to a low-priced and standardized product, the strategy lens guides the mar-keting manager to improve distribution channels. The other options are rejected because they are not the most effective ways to implement the strategy. In contrast, a competitor who emphasizes state-of-the-art products relies upon a different strategic lens. Upgrading the product is the option that passes through the strategic lens.

Gelle's Building Products: What Is the Strategy?

At Gelle's, several different value-creating elements are discussed, including the quality of the products, favorable credit terms, and speed of delivery. Members of John Chudovas's staff disagree about the relative importance of these variables. The disagreements indicate that they do not commonly understand their firm's competitive strategy. The firm lacks a lens to assess the accounts receivable policy.

The benefits of strategy-specific decision making go beyond making one wise marketing decision. The same lens guides decisions across functional areas of the firm and over time. Product design, procurement, and human resources practices, for example, apply the same lens, leading to consistent decisions that effectively execute the company's strategy and lead to superior returns.

Strategic Management, Trade-offs, and Decision Making

A firm's competitive strategy for a single product or narrow group of products involves the weighted mix of price, product features and qualities, and service that distinguishes it from rivals. Choosing a mix of these issues is difficult because decision makers must weigh trade-offs.

Students face trade-offs, too. The time spent reading this book precludes other activities, including studying for other courses or going to the movies. Operating area managers also face trade-offs. Funds spent on one budget item cannot also be spent on other activities; people or machines assigned to one task cannot simultaneously do another; and policies that reward one behavior cannot also reward other actions.

Trade-offs

Strategic managers respond to trade-offs between components of value. For example, given known production methods and materials, increases in vehicle safety are achieved at the expense of fuel economy. Similarly, a decision to be a luxury leader in the hotel industry precludes being the market's low-priced seller. A restaurant's decision to offer speedier service limits its menu, serving style, and ability to customize products. In each example a decision to emphasize one element of value precludes or limits another. No seller can outperform rivals in all dimensions of value. A choice involving the specific weighted mix of elements that creates value must be made, and the choice involves managing the trade-off between components of value.

Consider a fast food producer who decides to emphasize speed of service to compete against rivals. In making this choice, the restaurant does not dismiss the importance of the taste of the food, nutritional content, service, or cleanliness. Rather, the restaurant seeks to provide speedier service while meeting buyer expectations in terms of the other components of value.

> ### Gelle's Building Products: Complete and Consistent Decisions
>
> Gelle's cannot offer favorable credit terms without making complementary decisions. For example, Gelle's must have a sufficient line of credit with its financial institution, minimize inventories, pay higher-level employees monthly rather than weekly, and invest any surplus cash overnight to earn interest income.

Following the decision to emphasize speed, the effective execution of the competitive strategy requires appropriately selected menu items, recipes, cooking systems, and serving procedures. The firm sells a standardized product. Heat lamps, precooking, assembly, and sale from a finished goods inventory contribute to the execution of the firm's strategy. But upon choosing a speed-focused competitive strategy (and, in turn, its equipment and systems) this firm surrenders some ability to customize its products. In contrast, a rival's strategy emphasizes customized products. It employs different tools and equipment and surrenders speed in favor of customization.

> ### Gelle's Building Products: Functional Area Dependencies
>
> Rebecca Green urges reducing the time from receipt of an order to delivery. Rebecca could be correct. But this shift in competitive emphasis cannot be undertaken without assessing the firm's tools, equipment, and capabilities relative to the proposed strategy. For instance, is the manufacturing equipment conducive to short production runs and rapid conversions to other product lines?

Both firms design their operations and equipment in accord with their competitive strategy, and their decisions limit flexibility. The speed-focused firm encounters problems trying to accommodate the demands of a customized product buyer. A customized sandwich cannot be sold from a finished goods inventory; therefore, efforts to satisfy a special request necessitate deviating from established procedures. Working outside of usual routines and systems is disruptive. The inefficiencies can be costly, and the profitability of the transaction must be questioned. The seller may be better off not having customers who fit poorly with established procedures.

Further, in trying to adapt to the particular needs of a custom product buyer, the execution of the speed-based strategy is weakened. Those waiting in the line are dissatisfied because the speed of service is reduced while employees deviate from their routines to serve a custom-focused buyer. Also, despite the best efforts to meet a customized request, the product may be inferior to the one offered by the custom-focused rival. The cooking procedures, recipes, and range of selections based on speed are less appropriate when producing a customized product. The custom-focused buyer is not fully satisfied and is reluctant to repeat the purchase. In contrast, the custom-focused seller has tools, equipment, menu items, and procedures that constrain its ability to compete successfully on the basis of speed.

> ### Gelle's Building Products: Evaluating the Trade-offs
>
> Challenging John Chudovas is the trade-off between an easy credit policy and stringent collections practices.
>
> Sandy Koopmans argues that the firm should employ collections practices common in their industry. Terrence O'Shea's position is that stricter collections will reduce service to the buyer. Koopmans and O'Shea do not commonly evaluate the trade-off because there is no consensus regarding the firm's competitive strategy.

The trade-off between speed and customization occurs at the margin. The issue is not speed *or* customization. Rather, in the absence of new technologies, incremental improvements in one variable coincide with incremental losses in the other. The trade-offs between elements of value allow different firms to pursue different strategies. For example, auto manufacturers place different emphases on style, fuel efficiency, safety, and performance.

A sandwich restaurant faces a trade-off between speed and customization, but the trade-off is not rigid. Some flexibility exists. The speed-focused restaurant is able to offer some customization without any significant compromise of its operations. It may, for example, preassemble some sandwiches without onions but can easily add them upon request. Each firm must understand the limits of its flexibility to meet buyer requests. The speed-focused firm places at risk the effectiveness of the execution of its strategy when serving custom-focused buyers.

A large number of custom-focused buyers and a wide range of custom requests eventually disrupt established processes, slow operations, and (ultimately) weaken the firm's competitiveness.

A business that serves diverse buyer needs with one set of processes risks becoming a weak competitor. The speed-focused restaurant that customizes products on demand becomes a weak competitor in both the speed and customized market segments. It is the leader in neither speed nor customization. This seller is improperly straddling markets because it fails to recognize the limitations imposed by its tools, systems, and personnel.[3] It cannot successfully serve a customer base too diverse relative to its resources and systems.

Many firms fail to recognize the trade-off between components of value. Some companies do not acknowledge the constraints imposed by their tools, systems, and personnel. For example, the self-confidence of some entrepreneurs leads them to believe any buyer request can be met! Other firms, in their eagerness to make sales, deny the constraints. Young or struggling businesses find it especially difficult to turn away any customer. Other firms are unwilling to commit to a competitive strategy. They pursue all buyers and apply an unclear strategic lens by assessing the trade-offs differently. But not recognizing the trade-offs between components of value has adverse effects. It results in a poor mix of customers; it blurs a firm's marketplace identity; it clouds the messages to employees, confuses performance expectations, raises costs, and prevents personnel from developing particular expertise.

Trade-offs and Operating Decisions

The design stage of the strategic management process involves responding to trade-offs, noting that components of value often conflict with one another. The execution stage of the strategic man-

agement process imposes other trade-offs that require managers to make decisions. For example, every organization allocates scarce financial and personnel resources among alternative uses. A senior-level manager struggles to choose from competing requests to upgrade equipment, improve the marketing, or increase training. In turn, functional-area managers allocate budget and personnel among competing options. Marketing managers (see Figure 1.2) must choose among options that enhance the service of individual accounts, improve distribution channels, increase print advertising, or upgrade electronic marketing capabilities. These resource allocation decisions require evaluating the opportunity cost of each action, and the decisions determine the effectiveness of the execution of the firm's strategy.

Trade-offs and Operating Policies and Practices

Another trade-off arises when selecting among alternative policies and practices. For instance, consider a firm that adopts a compensation policy to reduce disparities between employees. Reducing disparities has merit, but it is achieved at the expense of weakened rewards for either seniority or performance. A policy to promote from within offers employees opportunities for advancement, but the company loses the ability to hire new talent with varied experiences. Similarly, a policy to provide employees with a specific number of training hours per year builds skills and employee morale, but these gains accrue at the expense of fewer dollars for marketing or salary improvements. In each of the examples, the opportunity cost of any policy must be assessed. Which option is the most appropriate, given the firm's strategy?

Because operating policies affect the execution of the firm's strategy, a strategy lens is needed to guide decision making. For example, a firm's ability to compete on the basis of sustained and enduring relationships between front-line personnel and customers is determined by careful hiring, training, promotion, and reward policies that support the execution of the strategy. For this company, it is important to define the vesting period for the firm's pension fund in accord with competitive strategy.

Making Strategy-Specific Decisions

Responding to trade-offs and making decisions is a fundamental responsibility of managers, one they cannot evade. Even nonactions are decisions—marketing choices occur even if the manager fails to prepare a budget. Similarly, promotion decisions are made whether or not formal policies are in place. Strategy-specific decision making helps managers make purposeful choices rather than allow actions to occur by default, political pressure, or convenience.

Consider a manufacturing firm that is evaluating alternative quality management initiatives. Each initiative has a different primary effect: one lowers production costs, another reduces product development time, another improves product durability, and yet another reduces manufacturing defects. Each outcome is appealing, but budgets are finite and a choice must be made.

Estimates of the costs and benefits of the options depend upon a firm's strategy. For example, if the business competes on the basis of price, cost reductions are savings that also enhance the execution of the firm's strategy. Alternatively, reducing product development cycle times strengthens the competitive position of the manufacturer who competes on the basis of contemporary products. Cost reduction and reduced cycle time are favorable for all companies, but the relative importance of the gains depends upon the firm's strategy. In the absence of a clear strategic lens,

the costs and benefits of the alternatives cannot be properly estimated.

Strategy-specific decision making applies a firm's competitive strategy as a lens to assess options, weigh opportunity costs, and make a choice. However, the difficulty of applying a decision-making lens is directly associated with the *distance* from the decision to the execution of the strategy and the *number of areas affected.*

Distance

The distance between a particular decision and the execution of the firm's strategy refers to the number of cause-effect connections that comprise the distance. Greater distance makes the relevance of a strategy-specific decision-making lens less clear to the manager and to those who are affected by a decision. But it does not diminish the importance of a strategy-specific decision.

Suppose a manufacturing firm competes on the basis of customized products. This firm is unable to anticipate accurately its materials needs, so it holds very modest raw materials and parts inventories. The company relies upon a just-in-time inventory system, making the timely receipt of raw materials and parts essential. Within the firm, timely delivery requires effective communications between the sales force, procurement, finance, and manufacturing. The prompt payment of invoices for purchased materials is not simply a finance and cash management issue. Rather, it earns the cooperation of their vendors and contributes to the execution of the firm's strategy. The cause-effect linkages between the prompt payment of invoices and the execution of the firm's customization strategy define the distance. Though several cause-effect connections are involved, the management of the accounts payable is an essential ingredient in the execution of the firm's strategy.

Number of Areas Affected

Within an organization, all functional area managers face trade-offs. A manufacturing manager must choose between the length of the production run and unit costs. A finance manager must choose the duration of their payables and vendor relationships over opportunities for short-term interest income. A shipping manager must decide between speed of delivery and costs. A procurement manager must choose among vendors based upon the qualities of purchased items, price, range of products offered, return policy, and certainty of delivery. These decisions are made at the same time by different individuals in different parts of the organization. Yet individual decisions interact and determine the effectiveness of the execution of the firm's strategy.

The effective execution of the firm's strategy requires each functional area manager to apply a common decision-making lens to assess trade-offs and make decisions. For example, a manufacturer's decision to compete on the basis of the durability of its product requires consistent decision making in product design and engineering, manufacturing, and procurement. Decisions must be consistent and complete. Parochial concerns of individual departments and different goals cannot be tolerated. They weaken the execution of the firm's strategy. The larger the number of operating areas and the larger the number of decisions that must be coordinated add stress on management; however, everyone who contributes to the execution of the strategy must be commonly directed. The difficulties of coordination do not minimize the importance of strategy-specific decision making.

Not surprisingly, decision makers frequently receive conflicting advice, and stress levels rise with the diversity of opinions. The decision makers are exposed and targets of second-guessers.

However, the complexities and strains of decision making are reduced if managers consistently weigh trade-offs by applying the firm's competitive strategy as a decision-making lens. The strategy lens clarifies the options, helps weigh the opportunity costs, and communicates the logic of the decision.

Exercise 1.3

1. Identify and discuss a problem that involves the management of a trade-off. Refer to your employer or to your firm in a case study or management simulation.
2. Identify at least two different recommendations. Why do the recommendations differ? Discuss how a clear lens clarifies this problem and leads to a solution.

Strategic Leadership: A First Glance

Strategic leaders possess a multitude of skills, and the nature of strategic leadership is examined more carefully in chapter 9. However, this introductory section highlights two characteristics. First, strategic leaders are visionary.[4] Strategic leaders recognize a firm's strengths, weaknesses, opportunities, and threats and creatively design an effective competitive strategy. The second characteristic is the ability of strategic leaders to execute the strategy by focusing upon the details of a firm's operations.[5]

A complex organization cannot rely upon a single strategic leader. Vision and decision-making skills are needed at all levels of an organization. Though firms do not choose a competitive strategy through democratic practices, all must understand the strategy and link the details of their day-to-day activities and decisions to the requisites of strategy implementation.[6]

Summary

This opening chapter introduces the reader to key ideas that are developed in the following chapters. The *design* stage of the strategic management process leads to the definition of a firm's competitive strategy. The strategy specifies the particular weighted mix of price, product features and qualities, and price that differentiates a product or service from rivals. The *execution* stage of the strategic management process implements the strategy through the multitude of decisions that are made across a business and over time. Strategy-specific decision making relies upon filtering options through a strategic lens, and strategy-specific choices effectively execute the firm's strategy.

Key Themes and Terms

Competitive Strategy:

A firm's competitive strategy for a single product or narrow group of products is defined by the particular mix of price, product features and quality, and service that distinguishes its good or service from those of rivals. (See pages 5–7.)

External Analysis:

External analysis assesses the political, social, technological, and economic environments within that the firm operates and which affect the firm's financial performance. (See page 7.)

Internal Analysis:

Internal analysis assesses a firm's resources and skills relative to the requisites of implementing the firm's strategy and relative to rivals. (See pages 6–7.)

Strategic Management:

Strategic management is comprised of the decisions that *design* and *execute* a firm's competitive strategy. (See pages 3–5.)

Strategy-Specific Decision Making:

Strategy-specific decision making applies the firm's competitive strategy as the lens to evaluate alternative courses of action. (See pages 9–14.)

Trade-offs:

A trade-off occurs when one action precludes or limits other options. Strategic management includes responding to several trade-offs in *designing* and *executing* a firm's strategy. (See pages 11–14.)

Discussion Questions

1. What is meant by the term "competitive strategy?"
2. Does every business have a competitive strategy?
3. Is it necessary for a firm to have a common thread running through all of its operations?
4. Is it possible for a firm to be the industry's lowest-priced seller and offer the most technologically advanced product?
5. What is a trade-off? What is the role of a decision lens to evaluate the gains and the opportunity costs?
6. Why do firms scan their external environments? What do they look for?
7. What do firms examine when assessing their internal abilities? What factors make it difficult for firms to assess their internal strengths and weaknesses?
8. What does it mean to make consistent decisions over time and across an organization?
9. Why is it important for all employees to share a common view of their firm's strategy?
10. Consider the role of a strategic lens in guiding managerial decisions. How does the concept of a decision-making lens apply to your personal life?

End-of-Chapter Exercises

1. Provide an example of a trade-off in one area of operation in your firm. List the benefits and costs and explain how a strategy lens prioritizes arguments.
2. Obtain the mission statement for any well-known organization: Use the Internet or obtain a copy of the firm's annual report. Evaluate the mission statement in terms of the criteria established in this chapter.
3. Select a well-known firm and consider the following:
   a. Its competitive strategy. How does it differentiate itself from rivals?
   b. What must this firm do extremely well to execute its strategy?
   c. What environmental factors represent opportunities and what factors are threats?
   d. What factors over time may affect this firm's success?
4. Refer to Case 1, Nancy's Women's Shoppe, at the end of this book (page 159). Summarize the strengths, weaknesses, opportunities, and threats. Based upon this analysis, provide advice to Nancy.
5. Think of a difficult personal decision you have to make. Establish priorities and apply a decision lens. Is the choice easier to make?

Notes

1. Larry Bossidy and Ram Charan, *Execution: The Discipline of Getting Things Done* (New York: Crown Business, 2002), p. 34.

2. Robert M. Grant, *Contemporary Strategic Analysis*, 4th ed. (Malden, Mass.: Blackwell Publishing, 2001), p. 2.

3. Michael Porter, "What Is Strategy?" *Harvard Business Review* 74 (November–December 1996): 4.

4. Peter Drucker, *Management: Tasks, Responsibilities, and Practices* (New York: Harper Collins, 1974), pp. 611–12.

5. Bossidy and Charan, *Execution: The Discipline of Getting Things Done.*

6. Chuck Martin, *Managing for the Short Term* (New York: Doubleday Books, 2002).

2

Competitive Strategy

Chapter 1 introduces the design and execution stages of the strategic management process. This chapter develops three important ideas. First, a distinction is made between a firm's corporate level and lines of business strategies. Next, the value proposition defines a company's line of business strategy. Finally, the Cycle of Success is presented as a holistic model of a firm to facilitate strategy-specific decision making.[1]

Line of Business and Corporate-Level Strategies

Differentiating between a firm's corporate-level strategy and its line of business strategies focuses decision makers. A line of business strategy refers to the particular weighted mix of price, product features and qualities, and service for a single or narrow group of products that differentiates it from its rivals. A firm with multiple product groups has a particular mix of those features for each group and a corporate-level strategy that defines the intended relationship between the product groups. Corporate-level strategies are explored more carefully in chapter 8, but this brief introduction allows the reader to design lines of business strategies within a larger corporate context. Three generic corporate-level strategies are discussed: (a) conglomerate, (b) hygienic, and (c) leveraged strategies:

Conglomerate relationships are the weakest corporate-level strategy. Consider the owner of a small-town diner. The business is profitable, and the cash flow exceeds family and reinvestment needs. The "surplus" could be invested in financial instruments, a second diner could be built on the opposite end of town, a catering business could be opened, or a business unrelated to food preparation and service started. After considerable study, the owner purchases a tanning salon franchise. The two businesses, the diner and tanning salon, serve different clientele and do not share tools or equipment. The unrelated lines of business comprise a conglomerate corporate-level strategy. Each business attracts and retains buyers with its own weighted mix of price, product features and qualities, and service. With the exceptions of common ownership and potential tax and cash-flow benefits, the businesses are distinct and separate entities.

A hygienic corporate-level strategy offers opportunities for higher returns by capturing efficiencies through the multiple product groups. A lawn and garden care firm owns out-of-doors maintenance equipment. Rather than allow its costly tractors to sit idle during the winter, it diversifies into snow removal. The increased asset utilization reflects a hygienic corporate strategy. The efficient use of its assets boosts earnings in a way unavailable to an organization with a conglomerate corporate-level strategy. However, the efficiencies do not occur automatically. The lawn and garden firm must make strategy-specific decisions to implement its hygienic corporate strategy. If the company succumbs to the temptations of acquiring summer and winter equipment, its corporate strategy degenerates to a conglomerate relationship.

Exercise 2.1

1. Consider your firm, one you are familiar with, or one in a case study or simulation. Discuss the corporate-level strategy options.
2. For each corporate strategy option discussed, identify the decisions that execute the corporate strategies.

A similar exercise is provided in the Instructor's and Student's Simulation Guide, question 2.

Leveraged relationships offer additional opportunities to boost returns. Consider again the lawn and garden firm. During the summer months it cares for the lawns and gardens of high-income households. Their timely, courteous, and accurate service earns trust, confidence, and repeat business. Upon diversifying to snow removal, the firm's existing clients purchase the winter services. Buyers benefit by relying upon one trustworthy out-of-doors maintenance firm. For the seller, profits are bolstered by the efficient use of assets (hygienic corporate strategy) and by extending its skills and reputation into a new business (leveraged relationship). Similarly, a technology company develops the ability to upgrade products and introduce new ones very quickly, and this skill is leveraged by bringing each of its multiple product groups to market faster than rivals. The benefits of a leveraged corporate strategy do not occur automatically. The firm must make strategy-specific decisions to assure that critical skills are developed and improve the competitive strength of each product.

The Value Proposition

The value proposition (see equation below) defines a firm's line of business competitive strategy by specifying the product's price, features and qualities, and service.[2] The value proposition is the ratio of benefits extended to buyers over the life of the good or service relative to the direct and indirect costs. The benefits in the numerator are separated into results and process quality, and the costs in the denominator are separated into price and the cost of acquisition. Before proceeding to explain the value proposition, the reader is reminded to focus on the operational definitions of the terms to avoid confusion with the everyday use of some words.

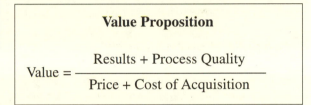

$$\textbf{Value Proposition}$$

$$\text{Value} = \frac{\text{Results} + \text{Process Quality}}{\text{Price} + \text{Cost of Acquisition}}$$

The components of the value proposition are explained below:

Results

Among the benefits received by a purchaser are results. An individual who is sick and goes to the doctor expects a proper diagnosis and treatment. No amount of bedside manner compensates if the desired results are not realized. For complex, multifeatured goods, the specific mix of results is important. For a new automobile, results include miles per gallon, safety, acceleration, handling, style, and dependability. Given the limitations of acceptable production costs, time, and design capabilities, no vehicle outperforms others on all of these qualities. Improving one result imposes a trade-off on another. For example, greater safety is achieved at the expense of reduced gas mileage. Certainly, over time, new technologies permit improvements in both qualities simultaneously. Given available technologies, the trade-off among competing benefits cannot be avoided.

The results associated with a vehicle are determined by the manufacturer's decisions. However, the results may be the outcome of conscious choices *or* an unintended consequence of inconsistent decisions made by poorly directed employees. For instance, a manufacturer of lawn and garden equipment may choose to emphasize ease of use, durability, product size, strength, or reduced smoke emissions. Being the best in the industry at all of these aspects of results is not possible. Technological limitations or prohibitive costs constrain even the most idealistic manufacturer.

Gelle's Building Products: Product Features or Service?

Terrence O'Shea believes the firm's products are good but that competitors offer similarly capable products. He believes there is no relative advantage from results. He sees the relatively easy credit policy as an important component of the firm's value proposition.

Consider a manufacturer who is uncertain about its mix of intended results. Design efforts sometimes pursue durability, while at other times they emphasize low weight or the ease of use. Procurement alternates between purchasing lightweight, low-cost, and durable material inputs. The inconsistencies manifest themselves in several ways. Production problems arise as parts and materials do not mesh; products are prone to breakdowns, and marketing messages are mixed. Consumers are confused and frequently disappointed. Employees are disoriented by the lack of consistent direction. They grow frustrated by inconsistent decisions and

become unsure how to handle their own responsibilities. Employees question the judgment and decision making of their managers and peers. Ultimately, the lack of strategic focus frustrates buyers and employees. Employee retention, buyer repurchase rates, and the firm's financial performance suffer. In contrast, a manufacturer who consistently and deliberately chooses a mix of results directs its engineering designs, procurement, manufacturing, and marketing without ambiguity.

Process Quality

Buyers receive more than the results associated with a product and frequently prefer one vendor because of intangibles. Process quality refers to the favorable aspects of completing a transaction and includes the ease, courtesy, and convenience of making a purchase. The responsiveness of a retail clerk or switchboard operator contributes to the value received by a buyer. The favorable location of a business, its ability to abide by promised schedules, its prompt return of phone calls, or the professionalism of front-line personnel are examples of process quality.

Gelle's Building Products: Internal Debate

There is disagreement among John's staff about the relative importance of results and process quality.

Kirk Davis, vice president of manufacturing, emphasizes results. His view is that buyers like the products because they are attractive, easy to install, and require little maintenance. Rebecca Green believes the key process quality variable is delivery time.

In an industry in which many competitors offer products with similar results, a firm may gain an advantage through superior process quality. An accounting firm whose technical capabilities are equivalent to rivals can out-perform competitors by offering a more convenient and attractive location and more responsive and personable professionals. A physician whose diagnostic skills are equivalent to others has a relatively more successful practice by providing more timely service, quicker response to phone calls, or superior bedside manner.

Results and process quality interact. The physician who takes the time to talk to patients (process quality) can more accurately diagnose problems and prescribe proper treatment (results). The CPA firm that learns a client's business (process quality) provides better consulting and tax advice (results). The teacher or corporate trainer who determines an individual's learning style (process quality) achieves superior learning (results). The numerator of the value proposition is not a simple summation; rather, results and process quality can be multiplicative. But the favorable interactions between results and process quality are not realized because of managerial aspirations. They must be carefully managed and are the result of strategy-specific decisions. For example, the CPA firm must hire, train, and motivate the professional staff to engage in consulting services.

Price

The denominator of the value proposition includes the purchase price and financing charges, as well as the costs of operating and maintaining the product over its expected useful life. A low-price strategy is a source of competitive advantage in markets where buyers know what they want to purchase and are not attracted by service amenities. Some buyers are attracted to warehouse grocery stores, choosing lower prices over breadth of selection and amenities.

Firms who lack results or process-quality advantages often have no alternative to price competition and discounting. When a good or a service are defined by an industry standard, rivals become indistinguishable. For example, financial statement audits by CPA firms are commodity-like. Under such circumstances price competition becomes increasingly important. However, to carry out a low-price strategy successfully, a firm must hold a cost of production advantage over rivals. Otherwise their low price translates to lower profits.

> **Gelle's Building Products: Payment Schedule**
>
> The ease of payment is both a price variable and a process quality variable. Easy payment schedules lower the financing cost for the purchaser (price). But Gelle's management of accounts payable also provides convenience (process quality) that allows buyers to extend similar options to their customers.

Process quality, results, and price may interact. For example, a building supply and home repair retailer relies upon front-line personnel to help customers make the right purchase (results and price) by teaching (process quality) them how to complete projects. The favorable interactions among results, process quality, and price enhance the value proposition extended to buyers and strengthen the firm's competitiveness relative to rivals. But these favorable interactions are not easily achieved. Front-line personnel must be properly selected, trained, and rewarded to achieve these favorable interactions, and important strategy-specific decisions include staff size, staff selection, rewards, marketing messages, and return of merchandise policies.

Cost of Acquisition

Buyers often incur costs beyond the sticker price, finance charges, and operating costs for a good or service. Waiting in line, experiencing poorly maintained facilities, working with rude or ill-equipped front-line personnel, and being forced to work within the seller's schedule or systems may sometimes impose dollar costs but are always unpleasant. Costs of acquisition are the inverse of process quality and include the inconvenient and nuisance aspects of completing a transaction. Costs of acquisition make buying difficult and unpleasant and weaken a firm's competitiveness.

Gelle's Building Products: Delivery Time

Rebecca Green, vice president of marketing and public relations, believes the slow deliveries (cost of acquisition) are a problem. She wants to speed up the delivery time; however, trying to remove costs of acquisition is expensive. Shorter production runs raise manufacturing cost, and less than full truckload deliveries raise shipping costs.

Firms do not purposefully create costs of acquisition. Rather, they are a consequence of other management decisions and may be expensive to remove. For instance, efforts to keep human resource costs low may result in poorly trained front-line personnel who cannot answer customer questions. A retailer's decision to limit Saturday hours imposes costs of acquisition. Buyers must shop when the store is open at the convenience of the seller. Similarly, the choice of an information system affects the ability of sales personnel to examine relevant data about a customer. Systems and people can be selected, designed, and trained to avoid and reduce acquisition costs, but eliminating acquisition costs can be expensive.

Results, process quality, price, and the cost of acquisition comprise the seller's intended value proposition. Figure 2.1 is the value proposition for a neighborhood coffee shop. The detailed example reflects a value proposition that is *intended, theme-based, and weighted.*

Intended Value Proposition

The value proposition in Figure 2.1 reflects the mix of the components of value the coffee shop intends to deliver to its customers. The coffee shop emphasizes process quality; the seller intends to offer a comfortable setting within which to enjoy a cup of coffee and freshly baked goods. However, the value proposition actually extended to buyers may differ if the owner ineffectively executes the competitive strategy—for example, by purchasing a second-class heating and air-conditioning system and uncomfortable furniture. The choices are driven by the owner's need to save money. As a consequence of those decisions, the intended comfort and service are not extended to customers.

Gelle's Building Products: Debating the Value Proposition

John Chudovas's staff disagrees on the relative weights in the firm's value proposition.

Kirk Davis places a heavy relative weight on results. The products are durable, easy to install, and require minimal maintenance.

Rebecca Green wants to put more emphasis on process quality through timely delivery.

Terrence O'Shea believes that ease of payment (price and process quality) is the crucial component of value for buyers.

Because the intended and actual value propositions may differ, firms must monitor the effectiveness of the execution of their strategy, and chapter 4 builds a performance monitoring system. For example, the coffee shop owner (see Figure 2.1) needs to monitor the actual levels of comfort and service.

Theme-Based Value Proposition

The value proposition in Figure 2.1 expresses themes by grouping similar items. Comfort is a

Figure 2.1
Theme-Based and Weighted Value Proposition: Neighborhood Coffee Shop

	% Total	Subtotal	Subtotal
Results	30%		
Selection			
Coffee blend selections			20%
Usual items			25%
Fresh, homemade baked items			25%
Attractive presentation of food			20%
Other			10%
Process Quality	45%		
Service		40%	
Speed			30%
Friendliness			50%
Special orders			20%
Comfort		60%	
Furniture			40%
Temperature			30%
Noise			30%
Price	15%		
Menu prices			75%
Beverage refills			25%
Cost of Acquisition	10%		
No checks			5%
No credit card			5%
Limited hours			45%
Parking limited/dark			45%
	100%		

theme comprising room temperature, noise levels, and the furniture. The themes describe the firm's competitive strategy, prompt employees to devise other ways to meet objectives, help employees understand their daily tasks, guide individual behaviors, and reduce the necessity of strict rules and policies. For example, the freshness theme makes clear that it is improper to inventory unsold baked goods for sale the next day. Even if the policy is not written down, strategically directed employees make the right decision.[3]

Weighted

The value proposition displayed in Figure 2.1 weights the elements of value to express their relative importance. The weights total 100 percent and indicate that the neighborhood coffee shop intends to compete primarily on the basis of process quality. The results, including food and beverage selections, are also important and account for 30 percent of the (intended) value extended. Price is relatively unimportant, and the firm recognizes that its location and some of its operations impose costs of acquisition.

The relative weights in the value proposition express priorities. The priorities provide a means to evaluate trade-offs, and guide the allocation of personnel, budgets, and time. For example, the value proposition for the coffee shop (see Figure 2.1) suggests that budget requests to improve the comfort of the room or food and beverage selections are higher priorities than reducing menu prices or improving the lighting in the parking lot.

Exercise 2.2

1. Ask several of your colleagues at work or teammates in a case study or simulation exercise to construct a theme-based and weighted value proposition for each of the products sold.
2. Compare the answers. Are the answers substantially different? If so, what are the implications for the firm? How should the leadership of the organization respond?
3. Discuss the management implications and challenges of your response to part 2.

Exercise 2.2 is important. The responses indicate if employees or teammates in a school project or exercise similarly understand the firm's competitive strategy. Substantial disagreements in the replies suggest that people may apply their own strategic lens when making decisions and evaluating the decisions of colleagues. The end results are likely to be inconsistent decisions, internal strife, second-guessing across the organization, a poorly executed value proposition, and a weak competitive position in the marketplace.

The Cycle of Success

The Cycle of Success (see Figure 2.2) provides a holistic view of the firm and facilitates the application of a firm's strategy as the decision-making lens. The Cycle of Success consists of four integrated triangles that link the firm's strategy with the expectations of its target buyers, the design and integration of its operations, the necessary skills and attributes of employees, and the organizational culture. The critical message of the Cycle of Success is that the firm's strategy permeates all of its actions, and the firm's competitive strategy is a lens through which options are assessed and decisions made.

Before examining the Cycle of Success, it is important to make two points. The Cycle is: (a) a means of analysis by providing a holistic view of the firm and facilitates the application of the firm's strategy as the lens through which options are assessed and decisions made, and (b) a process, not a solution. There is no simple means to impose this system of thinking on a firm, and it is improper to think that companies either employ this analytic perspective or do not. Rather, firms and individuals experience degrees of compliance with the methodology. However, those firms and individuals—by their own choices—who learn to rely upon the decision-making methodology reap the benefits of strategy-specific decision making.

The Cycle of Success is easily understood by examining the four triangles shown in Figure 2.2.

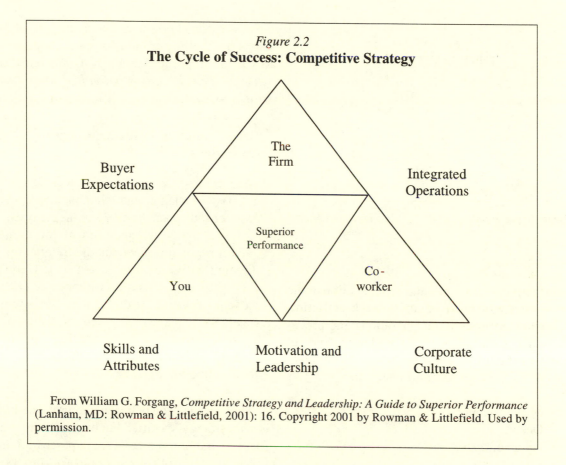

Figure 2.2
The Cycle of Success: Competitive Strategy

The Firm

Buyer Expectations

Integrated Operations

Superior Performance

You

Co-worker

Skills and Attributes

Motivation and Leadership

Corporate Culture

From William G. Forgang, *Competitive Strategy and Leadership: A Guide to Superior Performance* (Lanham, MD: Rowman & Littlefield, 2001): 16. Copyright 2001 by Rowman & Littlefield. Used by permission.

Triangle 1: The Firm

Triangle 1 in the Cycle of Success refers to the firm (see Figure 2.3).

The three edges of the triangle are: the firm's competitive strategy, its integrated operations, and buyer expectations.

Competitive Strategy

The competitive strategy refers to the weighted mix of results, process quality, price, and cost of acquisitions through which the firm seeks to achieve an advantage over rivals. A firm's strategy is deter-mined in the design stage of the strategic planning process and is implemented in the execution stage.

Integrated Operations

This corner of the triangle (see Figure 2.3) of the cycle follows the reasoning of Michael Porter.[4] A firm outperforms competitors by offering a relatively more attractive value proposition to its buyers based upon product characteristics, service, or price. However, success is not derived solely from the strategic concept reflected in the intended theme-based and weighted value proposition. The strategy must

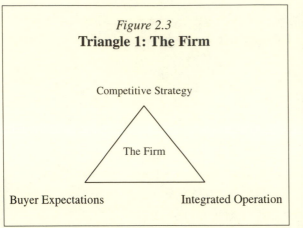

Figure 2.3
Triangle 1: The Firm

Competitive Strategy

The Firm

Buyer Expectations   Integrated Operation

be effectively executed, and the execution of the firm's strategy must occur through activities. Activities are individual operations and procedures that accumulate to the production and delivery of the firm's good or service. Several activities for a neighborhood bistro are:

- Menu selection
- Decor
- Hours of operation
- Size of staff
- Procurement practices
- Cooking systems
- Pricing

The activities listed above occur at all food service businesses. However, because different firms offer different value propositions, each designs activities in accord with its competitive strategy. A hamburger restaurant that emphasizes speed of service designs cooking and serving procedures different from the rival that emphasizes customized sandwiches. Debates regarding the design of activities are resolved by evaluating alternative systems in terms of the requisites of implementing the value proposition. For example, the

custom-focused producer rejects the use of heat lamps and selling from a finished goods inventory. It is inappropriate given its customization strategy. *The design of individual activities is strategy-specific!*

Gelle's Building Products: Integrated Operations

The accounts receivable decision at Gelle's does not exist in isolation, and John Chudovas's success depends upon the scope of his analysis.

The effective execution of the firm's value proposition depends upon commonly directed activities. For instance, if Gelle's easy payment schedule is important in the value proposition, it drives other decisions. Inventory management practices, debt management, and accounts payable must be aligned with the cash-flow implications of their collection practice.

The coordination between individual activities is also strategy-specific.[5] For example, the speed-focused hamburger restaurant places an individual at each work station: one takes orders and collects the money, one works the fryer, the next places the meat on a bun, and another adds the standardized condiments. The work stations do not communicate with each other, though a manager assures the work flow and finished goods inventory is appropriate given the volume of customers. In contrast, the customized sandwich shop operates as a job shop rather than an assembly line. Tasks are specialized and extensive communication is required between the order taker and the multiple stages of assembly of the sandwich. The fryer must know if an order is to be well done or medium, the sandwich assembler must know which condiments to apply, and the compiler of the order must identify each sandwich and properly group the side dishes and beverages. The flow of information within a firm and the coordination of its separate functions are strategy-specific.

The design and coordination of operating policies and practices are critical elements of strategy-specific decision making. This leads to:

Managing by Competitive Theme!

Doing the Right Things!

The concepts of *managing by competitive theme* and *doing the right things* are displayed in Figure 2.4. The figure refers to a speed-focused (process quality) restaurant. Reading from the left side of the figure, managers make decisions that shape activities, including cooking procedures, menu items, inventory management, tools and equipment, and training. The execution of the speed-focused value proposition occurs through strategy-specific decisions that design and implement specific activities.

The speed-focused firm depicted in Figure 2.4 does not operate with tunnel vision. Speed is not its only concern, evidenced by the weights assigned to results (taste and selection). This weighted mix of value complicates decision making because some decisions intended to reduce the time-to-service end up harming the taste of the product. Also, incremental improvements in speed have diminishing effects on value creation and come at increasingly higher price tags. Reducing the time from the placement of an order to delivery from ninety seconds to sixty seconds may be important to buyers. But, a further reduction to fifty seconds is proportionately more costly and of lesser importance to buyers. Despite these cautions, the weighted value proposition guides decision making by clarifying priorities.

Gelle's Building Products: Lack of Strategic Perspective

Gelle's is a troubled organization. John Chudovas is faced with a problem larger than the debate over the accounts receivable.

The disagreement over the receivables policy is a manifestation of the lack of agreement over the weighted value proposition. If John mandates a clear policy, the underlying disorder is not solved. The uncertainty over the value proposition will vent itself on other issues. A similar debate could emerge over Rebecca Green's interest in accelerating delivery time, a proposal to raise the technical capabilities of the products, or to change prices.

With the lack of common perspective, Gelle's is at risk. Decisions may not be consistent, weakening the execution of the firm's strategy.

In a small restaurant, the design of activities (see Figure 2.4) and associated decisions are the responsibility of a single manager. However, in more complex organizations, the activities and decisions cross lines of operational authority. For example, speed results from actions taken by directors in human resources (hiring), manufacturing (work flow), and finance (purchasing). Managing by competitive theme assures that decisions made by different people in different departments are consistent with executing the firm's value proposition.

The logic displayed in Figure 2.4 distinguishes between "Doing the Right Thing" and "Doing Things Right." The latter statement describes managers whose skill set is limited to generally accepted business practices and who focus on control systems and efficiency. In contrast, strategic leaders assess options in terms of the requi-

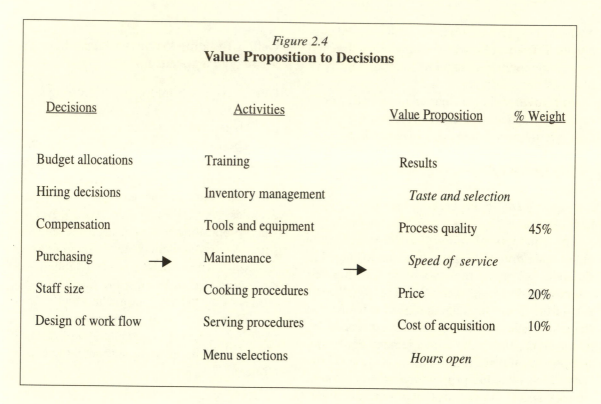

Figure 2.4
Value Proposition to Decisions

Decisions	Activities	Value Proposition	% Weight
Budget allocations	Training	Results	
Hiring decisions	Inventory management	*Taste and selection*	
Compensation	Tools and equipment	Process quality	45%
Purchasing	Maintenance	*Speed of service*	
Staff size	Cooking procedures	Price	20%
Design of work flow	Serving procedures	Cost of acquisition	10%
	Menu selections	*Hours open*	

sites of implementing the firm's strategy. Strategic leaders do the right thing as determined by the firm's strategy.

Buyer Expectations

The third edge of Triangle 1 (see page 26) refers to buyer expectations. As sellers approach a market with their value proposition, so do buyers. Each buyer, given different tastes and ability to pay, assesses alternate vendors and seeks the best fit. The fit determines the firm's Type I Buyers, those whose value proposition closely aligns with its offering. Firms who enjoy a high percentage of Type I Buyers also enjoy high customer loyalty, repeat purchases, and positive word-of-mouth recommendations.[6]

Gelle's Building Products: Do the Right Thing

Sandy Koopmans's eagerness to shorten the collection period is an example of doing things right. She argues that sound business practices should be in place.

In contrast, Terrence O'Shea wants to do the right thing. He wants to align the accounts receivable with the firm's competitive strategy.

A precise definition of the Type I Buyer is important for a firm. The most obvious advantage is that it drives external communications. A firm's marketing decisions maximize its exposure among their Type I Buyers who receive focused marketing messages. Despite these advantages, many firms fail to define their Type I Buyer. A seller may not recognize the differences between buyer groups or may be unwilling to narrow their target buyer group in order to cast the widest net. But the failure to define the Type I Buyer has adverse consequences.

Consider a hotel that believes its location, rooms, recreational opportunities, and food service meet the needs of every guest. However, this simplistic view fails to recognize that travelers are not homogeneous. Those with small children have different needs, for example, than senior citizens or businesspersons. Yet those who choose the hotel share common areas (lobby, restaurant, hallways, and recreational facilities), systems, and procedures. For example, the swimming pool can accommodate children at play or adults for lap swimming; dining areas can comfortably accommodate young families or business executives. Trying to serve and satisfy different sets of guests at the same time is problematic.

In contrast, a more focused hotel builds a value proposition for senior citizens. Given its target buyers, important themes in the value proposition commonly guide employees and their decisions. Decisions involving the layout of rooms, selection of furniture, design of recreational venues, the landscape of the grounds, parking areas, temperature of the water in the pool, front-desk services, entertainment, and food service are commonly directed to serve the senior traveler and execute the firm's strategy.

The definition of the Type I Buyer is not rigid. As a firm enjoys some flexibility in the mix and relative weights in their value proposition, some differences in buyer needs can be accommodated. For instance, different buyers choose a particular vehicle for different reasons. Some purchase a car because of its price; others because of the styling, gas mileage, or location of the dealer. Similarly, some senior couples enjoy a family resort, taking pleasure in watching children play. Production

methods also offer some flexibility, allowing, within limits, different buyers to be served somewhat differently. However, the range of buyer expectations that can be effectively served by a particular business has limits. The firms must recognize that some buyers fit poorly with their tools, systems, and personnel. A firm that serves buyers who hold dissimilar expectations risks creating an adverse cycles of low buyer satisfaction, low rates of repeat purchase, poor employee morale, and high turnover of buyers and employees.

Triangle 2: You

The second triangle in the Cycle of Success (see Figure 2.5) relates to you! The starting point is buyer expectations. Meeting buyer expectations occurs through the selection of equipment, operating systems, personnel training, and reward practices. The second corner of this triangle is the skills and attributes required to implement the firm's value proposition. The argument is simple: Different strategies require different skills and attributes of employees.

Skills and Attributes

Because different strategies require different skills and abilities, employees are not perfectly mobile between firms with different competitive strategies, even if the job descriptions are the same. For example, the buyer for a department store that specializes in inexpensive clothing needs different skills and attributes than a buyer for a high-end merchandiser. Strategy-specific hiring, promotion, and reward systems require agreement upon the firm's strategy, specification of the essential skills and attributes for the position based on the strategy, and consensus on how to identify those traits in job candidates and employees. Prior agreement on these issues allows the firm to present strategic themes in its recruiting announcements and job

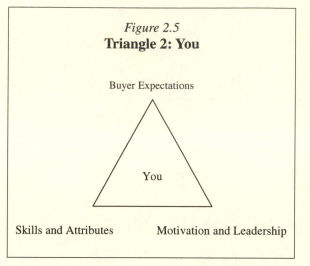

Figure 2.5
Triangle 2: You

Buyer Expectations

You

Skills and Attributes   Motivation and Leadership

descriptions. The firm benefits from applicant self-selection, and the range of disagreement over which candidate to select is reduced.

Gelle's Building Products: Type I Employees

John Chudovas's staff is hardworking and dependable. However, Sandy Koopmans could be uncomfortable working for a firm that does not impose a strict payment policy.

For example, a community college emphasizes the career applicability of its curriculum. In turn, it seeks teachers who have contemporary experience in their discipline, and this practical knowledge outweighs academic degrees and scholarly achievement. The strategy-specific criteria are a lens that filters job applicants. The lens reduces the range of debate and raises the likelihood of getting the right person in the right position. Still, hiring decisions are difficult. After all, different people see and interpret interview responses differently, and hiring always involves risks of an uncertain future. But any disagreements that re-

main after the application of a strategy-specific lens are healthy tensions within a firm.

Strategy-specific hiring attracts and retains Type I Employees who are comfortable with the dictates of implementing their firm's competitive strategy. Type I Employees carry out their tasks in alignment with the firm's strategy and do not moan about wanting to work elsewhere where tasks are done differently. They share a common decision-making lens that reduces the frequency and intensity of non-strategy-specific debate. As a firm benefits from a high proportion of Type I Buyers, it similarly benefits from a high proportion of Type I Employees. The higher the proportion of these employees, the greater the likelihood of high levels of retention, morale, referral of new employees, and the effective execution of the strategy.

Type I Employees are not "yes men." Those who simply choose not to question analyses and do not offer alternative views fail to contribute to healthy debate. They do understand their firm's strategy and are comfortable working within the dictates of the strategy. They do not engage in unhealthy debate because they uniformly apply a strategic lens. Type I Employees question an organization's assumptions and conventional wisdom; they consider the implications of an uncertain future and apply their disciplinary perspectives. They strive to make the organization stronger within the context of its strategy.

Motivation and Leadership

This corner of the triangle bridges each individual to the rest of the firm. Some individuals hold leadership roles that coincide with shaping motivation and reward systems, hiring, coaching, and training. However, everyone in an organization influences the behavior of colleagues. At all levels of the firm, there are opportunities to lead by example, and good natured "nagging" builds an organizational culture consistent with the execution of the company's strategy.[7]

Triangle 3: Coworkers

The third triangle (see Figure 2.6) refers to all employees and seeks a confluence among leadership and motivational practices to build an organizational culture that supports the requisite design and coordination of internal processes.

An organization's culture shapes employee behaviors. Some organizations create a culture that supports creative expression in product development; others enjoy a culture of customer service; and others take pleasure in a common mind-set wrapped around a commitment to precise, error-free work. In contrast, where no common strategic lens exists, organizations fragment. Different employees hold different values, and a common culture does not emerge. Internal strife arises as groups question the work and decision making of colleagues; employees become disgruntled and regress to "going through the motions."

The concept of strategy-specific motivation and leadership places considerable responsibility on managers at all levels of the firm and on all employees. While senior-level managers have the opportunity to shape an organization's competitive strategy, implementation responsibilities trickle down to all levels of the firm. Each level of management and each employee helps to align behaviors with the requisites of executing the firm's strategy.

Triangle 4: Superior Performance

The fourth triangle, Superior Performance (see Figure 2.7) results from the convergence of the three other triangles. The firm that carefully articulates its competitive strategy and successfully

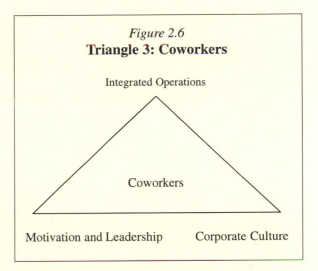

Figure 2.6
Triangle 3: Coworkers

Integrated Operations

Coworkers

Motivation and Leadership   Corporate Culture

executes its strategy outperforms less-focused rivals. A competitive strategy is successfully executed when properly directed toward the Type I Buyer and when the organization's tools, systems, process, and employees complement the strategy.

The successful execution of the competitive strategy requires strategic leaders at all levels of the firm. Strategic leaders are those who articulate the firm's strategy and who remain focused on the consistent execution of the strategy.[8] By thinking holistically, they link diverse activities to the execution of the firm's value proposition. By being obsessive, strategic leaders align operating policies and practices with the requisites of implementing the strategy. By being teachers, strategic leaders enable coworkers to align their responsibilities and behaviors with the execution of the firm's strategy.

Strategy-Specific Decision Making

The Cycle of Success is a holistic model of the firm. It links the execution of the firm's strategy to the design of its specific operations, policies, and practices, and it coordinates functional areas of the enterprise around common requirements dictated by

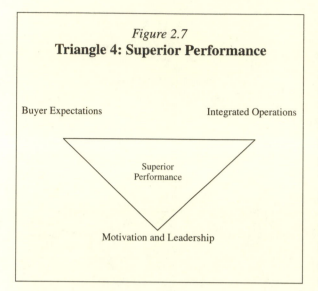

Figure 2.7
Triangle 4: Superior Performance

Buyer Expectations   Integrated Operations

Superior
Performance

Motivation and Leadership

strategy is the lens through which options are assessed, decisions made, and the logic communicated both internally and externally. Still, many decisions challenge managers. The strategy-specific approach provides direction, but it supplies neither all of the requisite data nor the clarification of an uncertain future. However, relying upon the firm's strategy lens clarifies sources of disagreement, provides a method for weighting arguments, and contributes to rational discussion.

Strategy-specific decisions are "good ones"; however they do not necessarily generate the best results. After all, some decisions generate favorable outcomes as a result of good luck. Strategy-specific decisions are "good" because they follow the rules, and the firm's strategy is the lens through which the rules are formulated.[9] This book will not improve one's luck or good fortune. Rather, strategy-specific decision making provides managers with a lens through which consistently good decisions are made and explained.

the company's strategy. With the perspective of the Cycle, issues and problems do not exist in isolation. Rather, decisions are viewed in the larger context. By assessing choices through a common strategic lens, actions across the firm are commonly guided. The organization improves the execution of its strategy and becomes a stronger competitor.

Gelle's Building Products: Strategic-Specific Decisions

For John Chudovas, the challenge is greater than the accounts receivable policy. He must establish a policy within the context of the firm's strategy and instill a common view of the strategy among his staff.

John can mandate an accounts receivable policy. But in the absence of a clear line of business strategy, the strife will surface over some other issue.

The Cycle of Success directs management actions. Decision making is easier as the firm's

Summary

This chapter reviews *the Cycle of Success*, a means through which to view the firm holistically. By seeing the firm's operations, tools, personnel, and budget allocations in terms of the requisites of executing the company's strategy, decision makers pursue a competitive theme. The firm's strategy is the lens through which problems and opportunities are assessed and decisions made. Because all employees make decisions that affect the execution of the firm's strategy, the concept of strategy-specific decision making is not limited to senior level personnel. Holistic thinking at all levels of the business allows individuals to connect their daily tasks with the effective execution of the firm's strategy.

Gelle's Building Products: Analyzing Options

The challenges facing John Chudovas highlight the importance of defining problems and assessing options in terms of the firm's strategy. John cannot prioritize arguments. The firm's strategy is unclear.

John is fully exposed. He is a ripe target for finger-pointing and second-guessing.

The Cycle of Success provides decision makers, students, and developing managers with a valuable tool. Problems and opportunities in an organization do not exist in isolation and should not be treated as stand-alone issues. They are part of a larger context involving the design and execution of the firm's strategy. Therefore, before offering advice or making a decision, readers are urged to practice strategy-specific decision making. Be certain that advice or action is aligned with the requisites of implementing the strategy.

Key Themes and Terms

Corporate-Level Strategy

A firm's corporate-level strategy refers to the intended relationship between its multiple product groups. (See pages 18–19.)

Cycle of Success

The Cycle of Success is a four-triangle holistic model of the firm that links the firm's strategy with the design of its operations, its target buyers, the skills and attributes of its workers, and the leadership and motivation practices that build a corporate culture driven by the firm's strategy. (See pages 24–32.)

Strategy-Specific Decision Making

Strategy-specific decision making is analytic progress that implements the firm's strategy. (See pages 31–32.)

Trade-offs

Trade-offs occur when increasing one variable necessarily precludes or reduces some other variable. A strategy lens prioritizes options and evaluates trade-offs. (See page 20.)

Value Proposition and Line of Business Strategy

A firm's line of business competitive strategy is defined by its value proposition. The value proposition states the weighted mix of results, process quality, price, and the cost of acquisition. (See pages 19–24.)

Discussion Questions:

1. What does it mean to use a strategic lens to evaluate options and make decisions?
2. How does a strategic lens clarify internal and external communications?
3. Do all companies have a value proposition?
4. Do all buyers have a value proposition?
5. Explain the difference between a firm's intended value proposition and the one actually delivered to buyers. What explains the differences?
6. Why is it important to evaluate the execution of a firm's strategy and not just the firm's financial performance?
7. Why is it important for a business with multiple product groups to define its corporate-level strategy before designing its individual lines of business strategies? How can a firm use its corporate-level strategy to improve the execution of its individual lines of business?
8. Discuss the importance of holistic thinking as presented in the Cycle of Success.

9. Is Sandy Koopmans a Type I Employee? Explain.

End-of-Chapter Exercises

1. For your firm, one with which you are familiar, school, or firm in a case study or simulation, build a theme-based and weighted value proposition. For a multiple products firm, refer to one product or narrow group of products.
2. Given your reply to question 1, prepare memos to two functional area managers and instruct them how to align activities, operating policies, and practices in their area of responsibility with the requisites of implementing the firm's strategy.
3. Use the theme-based and weighted value proposition developed in question 1 and write the following:
   a. A memo to the firm's advertising agency describing critical themes and the Type I Buyers.
   b. A memo to employees explaining the new compensation formula based upon the theme-based and weighted value proposition.
4. Prepare an article for the newsletter of your employer, school, or firm in a class exercise. Discuss the nature of strategic leadership and its implications for each employee's everyday behavior.
5. Propose a curriculum for newly promoted or hired managers. Use the concepts of strategy-

specific decision making to shape the management development program.
6. Refer to Rockwell's Health Club, Case 4 at the back of this book. Provide specific examples of problems trying to serve a diverse customer base. Is Rockwell's improperly straddling markets?
7. Refer to Timothy Ryan, Case 7. Discuss the nature of strategy-specific hiring and the importance of Type I Employees.
8. Use the popular press to identify a business that has multiple product groups. Describe their corporate-level strategy.
9. Prepare a memo to Nancy, Case 1. In the memo, explain the Cycle of Success and make recommendations.

Notes

1. William G. Forgang, *Competitive Strategy and Leadership: A Guide to Superior Performance* (New York: Rowman and Littlefield, 2001).

2. James Heskett, Earl Sasser, and Leonard Schlesinger, *The Service Profit Chain* (New York: Free Press, 1997), pp. 58–78.

3. Dennis McCarthy, *The Loyalty Link* (New York: Wiley and Sons, 1997), pp. 36–54.

4. Michael Porter, "What Is Strategy?" *Harvard Business Review* 74 (November–December 1996): 3.

5. Reed Nelson, *Organizational Troubleshooting* (Westport, Ct.: Quorom Books, 1997).

6. Leonard Berry, *Discovering the Soul of Service* (New York: Free Press, 1999).

7. David Maister, *True Professionalism* (New York: Free Press, 1997).

8. Forgang, *Competitive Strategy and Leadership*.

9. James March, *A Primer on Decisions: How Decisions Happen* (New York: Free Press, 1994), pp. 58–102.

Chapter 3
Strategy-Specific Decision Making

The prior chapter presented the Cycle of Success as a holistic model of a firm and guided managers to apply the firm's competitive strategy as a decision-making lens.[1] This chapter helps decision makers evaluate diverse recommendations in terms of their company's strategy and to manage by competitive theme.

Healthy and Unhealthy Debate

Strategy-specific decision making is a management tool that facilitates gathering and interpreting information, evaluating alternatives, and taking action. When executed properly, strategy-specific decision making executes a firm's strategy and results in superior performance.

But strategy-specific decision making is not a cure-all. It does not eliminate difficult decisions. Some choices involve considerable sums of money, impact the lives of many, or affect the reputation and professional status of the decision maker. Some decisions are stressful because they relate to an uncertain future; also there is often room for very legitimate differences of opinion and debate. There are several reasons why individuals make different recommendations:

- Different tolerances for risk
- Uncertainty of the future
- Competing goals and objectives

- Different knowledge bases
- Disagreements about human motivation
- Different disciplinary biases
- Different assessments of competitor behaviors

Differences of opinion based on, for example, disciplinary biases, knowledge bases, or tolerances for risk are healthy in an organization. Debate should be encouraged. For example, newspaper personnel should aggressively discuss the consequences of electronic communications technology on their industry before investing in new equipment. At a cleaning service, managers usefully discuss the merits of various pieces of equipment, the selection of solvents, and the balance between manpower and machinery. But some debates occur because there are no agreed upon criteria through which to assess information and evaluate options.

Gelle's Building Products: Unhealthy Debate

The debate over the receivables policy is unhealthy. Importantly, no one on John Chudovas's staff made an error. There are no factual mistakes or calculation errors. Each individual, having offered sound advice, grows skeptical of the recommendations and abilities of their colleagues.

(continued)

35

John needs to end the debate. But unilateral action is not sufficient. The same underlying disagreements will manifest themselves over other issues. The competitive strategy at Gelle's must be clarified and policies and practices aligned with the firm's strategy.

For example, there are many alternative ways to allocate budgets among competing uses, to design processes, and to structure policies. Managers debate budget allocations to improve labor productivity, shorten the product development cycle time, cut materials costs, increase advertising, or raise the technical capability of a product. Those making recommendations are passionate about their positions, and everyone believes they are right. In the absence of a common strategic lens, these debates are ineffective and unhealthy as individuals question the wisdom and judgment of their managers and associates.

Exercise 3.1

Provide an example of a healthy and an unhealthy debate.

1. Specify the problem and discuss why the debate is healthy.
2. Specify the problem and discuss why the debate is unhealthy.

Management and Decision Making

Making decisions is the essence of management. Some decisions are challenging, including those that are costly, lack consensus, are difficult to reverse, affect others, or rely upon imperfect information. Other decisions are easy, including those that enjoy a consensus, pose little risk, affect few, and can be reversed. Figure 3.1 shows that the differences between "easy" and "challenging" decisions fall on a continuum.

The distinctions between easy and challenging decisions are based upon the following criteria. Decisions are more challenging the greater the (a) range of issues and the required processing of information, (b) financial risk and potential reward, (c) degree of uncertainty of the outcome, (d) number of individuals affected, (e) impact, and (f) the disagreements, perspectives, objectives, and conflicting advice.

Gelle's Building Products: Strategic Lens

John Chudovas is unable to practice strategy-specific decision making because the firm lacks agreement on its competitive strategy.

Until the firm commits to a theme-based and weighted value proposition, John will be unable to resolve the receivables problem. The debate is unhealthy.

Those decisions classified as easy should receive relatively little attention: make a choice and move on. Easy decisions should be delegated to the lowest capable level of authority. Organizations that spend a lot of time studying and bemoaning easy decisions are troubled. Time and energy are wasted because employees do not have a lens through which to evaluate the difficulty or importance of problems.

Some managers concentrate on easy problems. They appear busy and delude themselves about being productive and decisive. They may be busy, but their energies are not directed toward designing and executing their firm's competitive strategy. Other managers focus on comfortable housekeeping decisions that seek efficiencies through tighter processes and procedures. For example, a budget officer assigns every employee an ID code to allocate the costs of phone calls, photocopies, and supplies. Control systems are appropriate and lead to operational efficiency, but they are not an alternative to a wisely crafted and executed competitive strategy.[2] At worst, house-

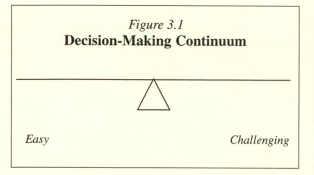

Figure 3.1
Decision-Making Continuum

Easy   *Challenging*

keeping decisions are destructive if sought-after efficiencies undermine the execution of the firm's strategy. A firm that competes on high-touch customer service weakens the execution of its strategy by reducing the size of its front-line staff in response to a budget shortfall.

Correctly classifying decisions as hard, easy, and housekeeping saves time and permits focus on important issues. However, distinguishing between strategic and nonstrategic issues is more important. Unfortunately, proper classification is not simple. A decision common to two organizations has strategic implications for one but not the other, given differences in competitive strategies. For example, a low-priced tax preparation firm determines that their year-after-year employee turnover rate is relatively unimportant. Their work is routine. Also, the continuity of the relationship between the individual who prepares the tax return and a customer is not heavily weighted in the firm's value proposition. In contrast, a CPA firm that competes on the basis of responsive and trustworthy service and seeks enduring relationships with customers views turnover differently. Believing that recurring work allows the firm to provide more effective tax planning, business consulting, and financial planning, the CPA firm seeks stability among their staff. For this CPA firm, decisions involving vesting periods, seniority-based pay, and other rewards are strategic. For the low-priced tax preparation firm, the same issues are not strategic.

Recognizing the strategic relevance of a problem is prerequisite to relying upon a strategic lens. Consider a full-service gasoline station. In addition to providing fuel, the station's skilled mechanics do repairs and routine maintenance, and a modest selection of high-mileage used cars is available for sale. The station is located close to several affluent housing developments. Buyers trust the owner and the mechanics. They believe no unnecessary repairs are made and that the charged man-hours are appropriate. Buyers appreciate that repairs are completed on time as promised. The station enjoys loyal customers who are repeat purchasers of multiple services.

Gelle's Building Products: Housekeeper's Decisions

At Gelle's, Sandy Koopmans's recommendation to tighten the accounts receivable may be good housekeeping. But if Gelle's competitive strategy is based upon convenient payment practices, Sandy's housekeeping recommendation interferes with the execution of the firm's strategy.

The supplier of the gasoline has been urging the owner to replace the station's aging pumps, emphasizing that the modern equipment offers quick pay-at-the-pump options. Several important benefits are touted: fewer employees are needed because payments are automated; gasoline is sold even when the service station is unmanned; sales data is gathered electronically to schedule deliveries, and the electronic data helps the tax accounting and restocking of inventory. Customers benefit. They fill their vehicles quickly and have access to gas at all hours of the day and night, weekends, and holidays.

The advantages of the new pumps are powerful. But the station owner knows that change does not come without costs. The net cost of the equip-

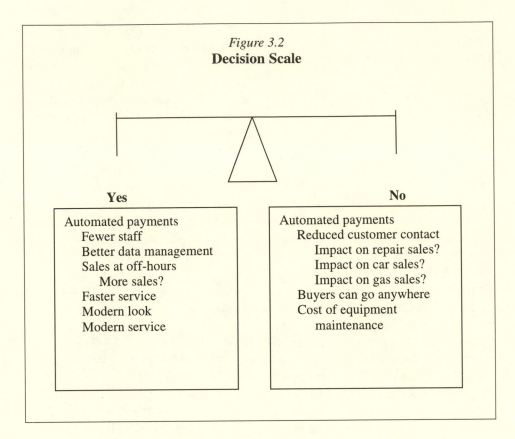

Figure 3.2
Decision Scale

Yes

Automated payments
   Fewer staff
   Better data management
   Sales at off-hours
     More sales?
   Faster service
   Modern look
   Modern service

No

Automated payments
   Reduced customer contact
     Impact on repair sales?
     Impact on car sales?
     Impact on gas sales?
   Buyers can go anywhere
   Cost of equipment
     maintenance

ment, repair, and maintenance expenses are easily identified. But the owner is worried about the impact of the new equipment on the competitive strength of the business. Several concerns exist, including the disruption of the personal relationships with customers that build trust and allow mechanics to remind drivers when routine maintenance and inspections are due. There is a trade-off, and Figure 3.2 displays a decision scale that organizes information to lead to a decision. The decision scale displays the trade-off. Only one decision can be made. Should the new pumps be purchased?

Figure 3.2 lists the arguments in favor (Yes) and against (No) the new pumps. To weigh the costs and the benefits, each of the variables is expressed in dollars. The net cost of new equipment is readily calculated. However, the revenue impact of the new equipment is much more complex.

If buyers choose the service station because of the personal relationships and associated trust, the new pumps may have a serious negative impact. The new equipment depersonalizes transactions, making gasoline service like a commodity. In turn, buyers may choose a service station based on price and location. For sellers, the price competition shrinks profit margins. However, if the personal relationships and trust are minor contributors to the seller's value proposition, less serious financial consequences occur. For instance, if buyers rely upon the service station because of its convenient location or price, the loss of personal contact is less important. The new pumps may improve sales by removing costs of acquisition (faster and twenty-four-hour service). However, if the buyer rates the quality of their repair work as the most important feature, new pumps might not mean much. In sum, the assessment of the trade-off (new pumps or no new pumps) depends upon the firm's value proposition.

Exercise 3.2

For any decision in your personal life, work, or school assignment, compile a list of the "pros" and "cons."

1. List the decision criteria and relative weights.
2. Categorize the decision as easy or challenging and strategic or nonstrategic.

Strategic Compared with Nonstrategic Decisions

Figure 3.3 is a four-quadrant matrix to classify decisions by strategic/nonstrategic and consensus/no consensus. A manager's ability to place a problem within the proper cell is a guide to action.

Cell I: Strategic/Consensus: Cell I decisions are strategic and enjoy consensus. This favorable circumstance occurs when members of an organization agree on the firm's competitive strategy, commonly assess their options, and agree upon a decision. For example, the mission statement for a church-based community soup kitchen defines its purpose to be a "haven for the poor, homeless, and elderly." As a haven rather than an emergency provider of nutrition, clients are not subject to a needs test or work-for-food obligations. Within this organization, a recommendation to limit access based on a client's need or willingness to help is

quickly rejected, and the decision falls into cell I.

An employee or volunteer who tries to limit access, who complains about the able-bodied clients who fail to help with routine chores, or who is disrespectful to patrons is engaged in unhealthy behavior. The behavior is unhealthy because it is inconsistent with the organization's mission and threatens to undermine its belief system and performance.

The soup kitchen's mission statement leads to a strategic lens, and the lens guides many decisions. In addition to determining who is eligible to eat, the lens determines the target pool of financial donors, the fund-raising message, the volunteers, the quality of the meals contributed by volunteers, the target group to whom meals are offered, the manner of serving, and the nature of the interactions between service workers and those enjoying a meal. The soup kitchen's decision making is consistent across its range of operations. A different soup kitchen that focuses on the emergency provision of food must also make decisions that raise funds, solicit volunteers, determine menus, and set operating policies. The emergency food provider applies its strategic lens and makes different decisions.

The soup kitchen examples highlight two aspects of strategy-specific decision making. The application of strategy lens:

Guides Decision Making

Coordinates Decisions across an Organization

It is easy for readers to suggest that all decisions do not need to be commonly guided. But arguments that suggest that individual problems require unique solutions are traps for decision makers. Each time a decision is contrary to a firm's strategy, the decision-making lens becomes cloudier. Consider the director of the "safe haven" soup kitchen. Periodi-

Figure 3.3
Decision Matrix

	Strategic	Nonstrategic
Consensus	Cell I	Cell III
No Consensus	Cell II	Cell IV

cally, stress and frustration lead the director to complain about the lack of help from those who eat. This language and behavior undermines the commitment to the kitchen's philosophy. Donors and volunteers lose their clarity of purpose, and the environment becomes conducive to unhealthy debate. Consistency matters! It keeps the decision-making lens clear and minimizes unhealthy debate.

Cell II: Strategic/No Consensus: Cell II decisions are troublesome. Problems are strategic; however, members of the team do not agree on a solution. For example, a manufacturer of tubes (for dispensing toothpaste, caulk, and medical ointments) is unclear about the relative importance of customized products, price, distributor discounts, delivery time, or the management of accounts.[3] Each variable is potentially important in the firm's value proposition and (all else equal) no one can oppose making improvements in any of these areas. However, different individuals place different relative weights on the variables, and the conflicts manifest themselves in the debate over the allocation of resources. In the absence of a clear decision-making lens, there is no consistent way to prioritize competing requests for funds and no way to gain consensus within the organization.

Similarly, two software engineers agree that a proposed new feature has strategic implications. One engineer vigorously urges its installation to make the product state of the art, whereas the other opposes adding the new feature now. The new feature threatens to make the product more difficult to use and to slow the product's delivery to market. At issue is the firm's strategy. Does the value proposition emphasize ease of use, time to market, or being state of the art? Neither engineer is "wrong." The firm needs a strategic lens to assess the trade-off and make a decision.

Gelle's Building Products: Benchmarking

Sandy Koopmans is quick to rely upon benchmark standards to defend her position. She refers to the industry-wide average number of days of the accounts receivable. But the industry standard may be inappropriate.

Cell II debates frequently prompt benchmarking studies. Where there is a lack of consensus, examining other organizations is intuitively appealing. If a firm experiences internal debate about a policy (compensation based on time-in-grade, payment of dues in professional and civic organizations, customer discounts, or service upgrades) it is tempting to look at other companies to settle the debate. But, while interesting to learn about other firms, acting on the basis of benchmark comparisons is hazardous. If different organizations compete on the basis of different theme-based and weighted value propositions, policies and procedures should be different.

Where cell II problems predominate, managers must turn introspective. Looking outward and expressing frustration about contentious staff is improper. Managers often create their own frustrations by failing to provide consistent strategy-based leadership. Consider a manager who explains one decision on the basis of cost, another on the basis of technical sophistication, and another because of ease of use. Each explanation sounds reasonable, but the composite of the explanations confuses employees. Where strategic leadership problems exist, effective situational leadership demands that the firm's strategy be clarified.[4] Policies, processes, and decision criteria must be aligned with the strategy. Unhealthy debates subside over time as managers practice strategy-specific decision making.

Cell III: Nonstrategic/Consensus: Cell III decisions are a positive event. In cell III, members of a decision team recognize what is nonstrategic and agree upon a choice. For example, members of a decision team agree that outsourcing the cafeteria's food service is advantageous. The outsourcing is expected to improve the quality of the food and menu selections, and reduce costs. The decision falls into cell III because the employee cafeteria is not associated with the execution of the firm's competitive strategy. Outsourcing is not an "easy" decision. After all, the work lives of many people are disrupted. The decision is costly, difficult to reverse, and based upon an uncertain future. But for the firm in question, the decision is unrelated to the execution of its strategy; there is consensus, and it resides in cell III.

Cell IV: Nonstrategic/No Consensus: Cell IV decisions create problems. Coworkers disagree over a nonstrategic issue. Reconsider the outsourcing of food service. Though nonstrategic, it prompts considerable debate. Many pro and con arguments are advanced. The primary argument in favor of outsourcing is that costs are reduced without loss of food quality or service. The arguments against outsourcing include the loss of control over dining services, the loss of "family atmosphere" in the workplace, and the termination of staff. The decision is not easy. Many are affected; the decision is costly, and it is difficult to reverse. While thoughtful study is appropriate, spending an inordinate amount of time deliberating the issue is troublesome. The issue is not strategic.

Cell IV situations arise because there is no consensus about the firm's strategy and issues are not properly classified as strategic or nonstrategic. Employees who lack consistent direction are prone to question decision makers. Managers who do not practice strategy-specific decision making create conditions where their actions are scrutinized and second-guessed. The uncertainty of the firm's strategy creates an environment conducive to cell II and IV situations and adversarial relations between employees and their managers.

Gelle's Building Products: Strategic Lens

At Gelle's, there is no basis for agreeing on a policy for managing the receivables.

Sandy Koopmans sees the question in terms of good business practices: nonstrategic. Terrence O'Shea sees the flexibility of payment as a heavily weighted component of the value proposition.

John Chudovas must decide if the receivables problem falls into cell II or cell IV.

Exercise 3.3

Provide examples of a cell I, II, III, and IV decision. Consider your firm, a firm with which you are familiar, school, or case study or simulation assignment.

A Systems Approach: Managing by Competitive Theme

A systems approach to management recognizes that a firm's operations interact in the execution of its strategy. Understanding the cause-effect linkages in an organization is an essential ingredient of strategy-specific decision making.[5] For instance, reconsider the restaurant that heavily weights the speed of service in its value proposition. It relies upon properly selected menu items, appropriate equipment, a well-trained and motivated staff, wise purchasing, and properly designed production processes. The speed of service is an outcome of prior decisions and cause-effect linkages from decisions to results.

Figure 3.4 displays the sequenced events from decisions (at the top of the diagram) to the firm's financial performance (at the bottom of the diagram).

Following Figure 3.4 from top to bottom, managerial decisions include the design of the reward system, hiring choices, and budget allocations. These choices determine the speed of service, and include staff size, capability, and motivation. In turn, the speed of service (a heavily weighted variable in the value proposition) is affected. The actual speed of services determines if the intended value proposition is realized, and the firm's financial performance is the lagged outcome of the design and execution of the strategy.

The multiple causalities (determinants of speed) suggest management challenges. Speed is affected by decisions in several different operational areas of the firm. Pay and hiring choices are human resource decisions; budgets fall in the domain of finance, and production is the responsibility of manufacturing. In a large and complex organization, each functional area has its own manager. Yet their decisions must align to execute effectively the firm's value proposition. Functional area managers must collaborate, and senior management's coordination responsibility includes assuring that parochial departmental concerns and different decision lenses do not take precedence over the common requisites of implementing the firm's strategy.

Figure 3.4 raises other questions. First, what is the relationship between a proportionate change in the execution of the value proposition (speed of service) and financial performance? This is a complex question, and the answer is unlikely to be known or constant. Proportionate increases in speed have a diminishing impact on the attractiveness of the value proposition and the firm's profitability. Also, the responsiveness of profits to speed is not sufficient information to make a decision. Is it more advantageous to improve speed or to better some other variable in the value proposition? Strategy-specific decision making does not directly answer these questions, but the decision-making methodology forces decision makers to pose the right questions, and the firm's theme-based and weighted value proposition establishes priorities.

Exercise 3.4

For your organization, one with which you are familiar, school, or case study or simulation exercise, identify one highly weighted variable in the value proposition. Trace the sequenced cause-effect linkages from managerial decisions to the realization of financial returns. Explain.

Strategy as the Decision-Making Lens

The application and utility of a strategy-specific decision-making lens is examined through the problem solving of Vera Feldman. Vera owns 25 percent of Feld-Print, a family-owned commercial printing firm. Her two brothers and a sister equally divide the remaining 75 percent. Vera consults with them regularly, though they do not participate in the day-to-day operations of the business. Vera serves as president and chief operating officer.

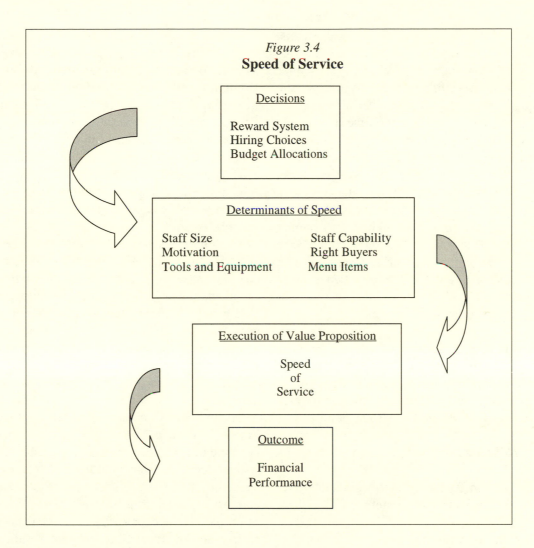

Figure 3.4
Speed of Service

Decisions

Reward System
Hiring Choices
Budget Allocations

Determinants of Speed

Staff Size   Staff Capability
Motivation   Right Buyers
Tools and Equipment   Menu Items

Execution of Value Proposition

Speed
of
Service

Outcome

Financial
Performance

Gelle's Building Products: Cause–Effect Linkages

John Chudovas is confronted with a difficult choice. In the absence of a clear strategy, John is unable to determine if there is a cause-effect linkage from the receivables policy to the execution of the strategy and to the firm's financial performance.

During fiscal years 1999–2001, Feld-Print's revenues increased from $1.8 million to $2.1 million. While the financial performance has been attractive, Vera is worried about the number of complaints and the increase in refunds. Fred Mahoff (her accountant) confirms that refunds have increased 24 percent during that period. Sensing a problem, Vera consults with her family and receives the following advice:

- Let's tighten up. Refunds should only be given when absolutely necessary.

- We're doing okay. Let's not worry about this. After all, it's better to give a refund than risk losing a long-term customer.
- Let's do everything we can to improve the quality of work and reduce those refunds.
- Our market is very competitive. Customers know they can pressure us.
- It may be necessary to put some pressure on our shop managers. If mistakes are being made, we need to know why and who is making them.
- If the mistakes are because we are too busy, let's expand. In the meanwhile, let's require a longer lead-time for our production. Make buyers submit their work earlier, and let's impose a hefty fee for any last-minute changes. Those changes adversely affect our ability to serve other customers.

Each recommendation makes sense; yet Vera has no basis to evaluate the alternatives. She lacks the information to proceed. As a strategy-specific decision maker, Vera seeks to determine into which cell the decision falls and how to respond.

Step 1: Defining the Strategic Lens

Vera's first step defines the strategic lens by reviewing the firm's mission statement:

Feld-Print Mission Statement

Feld-Print is a commercial printing firm committed to meeting the recurring needs of the regional business, educational, and government communities through the timely completion of short-run jobs. Feld-Print is dedicated to providing its staff with regionally competitive compensation, a dignified work environment, and opportunities for professional growth. It seeks to provide owners with a fair and reasonable return on their investment.

Reviewing the mission statement reminds Vera of the contentious strategic planning meetings with her family. They struggled with differences of opinion and almost settled on a bland mission statement to gain a consensus. Now, looking for a decision-making lens, Vera is pleased that the family resolved differences of opinion and established a clear path. The mission statement leads to a theme-based and weighted value proposition, and Feld-Print places considerable relative weight on timely (process quality) completion of short-run jobs (results).

The mission statement is also useful because of what is excluded. Feld-Print does not compete on price or unique printing capabilities. Feld-Print cannot charge any price at will or do sloppy work. Vera believes that buyers willingly pay a premium price for the timely and accurate completion of their orders. Any member of Vera's team who advances proposals based primarily on price or unique production jobs is engaged in unhealthy debate.

The unhealthy debate over the refunds may be Vera's fault. The firm's strategy may not have been clearly stated; Vera may have made inconsistent decisions that muddied the strategy; or Vera may have established incentives that are contrary to the execution of the strategy. She must be prepared to accept responsibility and take corrective action. In turn, employees would be at fault if they persistently resist and obstruct the execution of a clearly defined strategy.

Step 2: Viewing the Data through the Lens

Vera recognizes that refunds are a leading indicator of profitability. Refunds are lost revenue, and the increase may reflect reduced buyer satisfaction. If customer satisfaction is declining, the lagged consequences are less-frequent repurchases, adverse

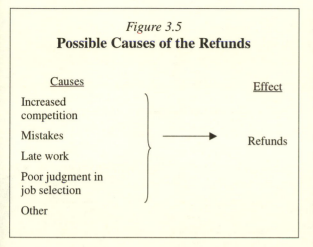

Figure 3.5
Possible Causes of the Refunds

word-of-mouth communications, and declining profitability. However, the refunds could also signal that buyers are exercising increased negotiating power in an overexpanded market. Vera wants to understand and address the problem quickly.

Vera draws Figure 3.5 to study the causes of refunds. The determinants include increased marketplace competition and problems within Feld-Print.

After reviewing the prior three months' refunds, Vera realizes that missed deadlines are the predominant cause of the refunds. In making this determination, Vera recognizes that the increase in refunds is strategy-specific. They reflect the firm's deteriorating performance in executing their value proposition. Feld-Print's commitment to timely delivery is not being met.

Step 3: Cause-Effect Analysis

Vera is a systems thinker, and she sketches cause-effect relationships that may lead to refunds (see Figure 3.6).

Reading from the left side of Figure 3.6, Vera lists decisions that could impact the time to completion of a project. These include budget allocations, equipment selections, scheduling, and hiring choices. These decisions, if incorrect in terms of the firm's strategy, could have adverse consequences, including poor maintenance, inexperienced personnel, and poor selection of jobs. Each is a possible determinant of late work, and late work results in refunds!

Vera examines the data sets and determines that equipment is not the culprit. It is contemporary and has been well maintained. There is no pattern of breakdowns, and the equipment is well suited for short production runs. Vera also concludes that the sales personnel are not the problem: They are experienced (evidenced by their average length of tenure) and well trained (shown by the number of staff training hours per employee). The downtime between jobs is brief, indicating that work schedules are not a problem.

Vera finally realizes that they have been bidding for jobs that are inappropriate for the firm's production equipment (demonstrated by the length of the production runs, the technical requirements, and the amount of work that has to be redone). Seeking to learn why inappropriate jobs are taken, Vera's studies reveal that, among other things, the commission structure does not consider the type of work or the profitability of individual jobs.

Step 4: Corrective Action

Armed with strategy-specific information, Vera embarks on a corrective path. She meets with the entire staff and reiterates the firm's competitive strategy. She shares the cause-effect diagram to display the connection between each task and the execution of the firm's strategy: Training and equipment needs are identified; and policies and practices are aligned with the requisites of executing the strategy. Importantly, Vera sees there are multiple causalities and that diverse parts of the organization interact while executing the firm's

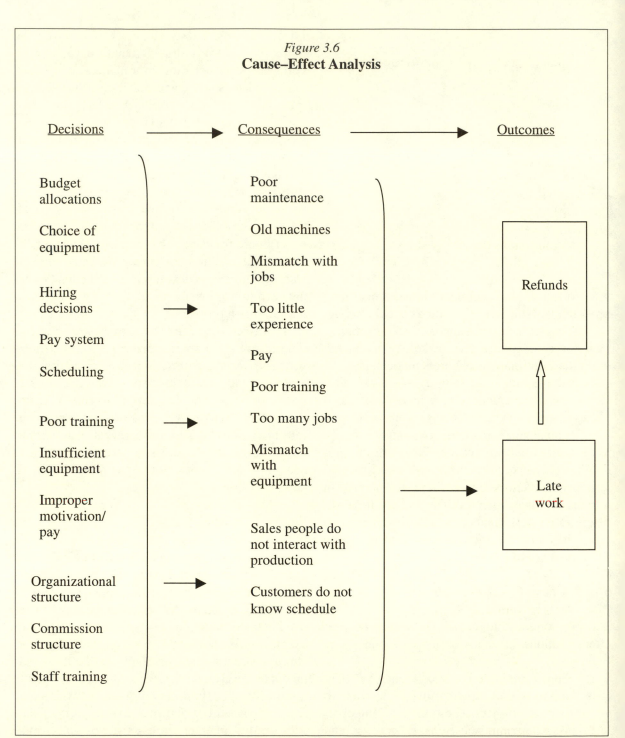

Figure 3.6
Cause–Effect Analysis

value proposition. All parts of the firm must be studied and aligned with the requisites of implementing the firm's strategy.

Step 5: Assessment

Vera seeks to reduce refunds by training her sales personnel to distinguish between good jobs and those that are inappropriate, given the firm's strategy. To provide the right incentives, Vera changes the sales staff's commission structure, which had been based on gross billing. Vera decides to base commissions on net billing: gross billing less any refund that might be claimed for that job. Vera expects to see an increase in the ratio of "good jobs" to total jobs before observing any change in the refund rate. Vera also believes the new compensation system will encourage sales personnel to coordinate with the production department to assure timely and accurate completion of work.

Reasonably, Vera wants to be able to assess the results of her actions in the future and plans to look back to see if the refunds have been reduced. However, this comparison is hazardous. Even if the refunds decline, it is improper to arbitrarily assign the causality to Vera's actions. Over time, other factors that affect refunds could change. Therefore, understanding the cause-effect relationships, Vera decides to monitor several variables, including the length of production runs, the percentage of jobs completed on time, and the cost of reworking as a percent of the gross billing. Changes in these variables provided a clear view of the effects of Vera's decisions.

Figure 3.7 summarizes Vera's decision making to determine the nature and severity of the problem. By conducting the analysis with regard to the value proposition, Vera understands the strategic nature of the problem. Next, using cause-effect analysis in the execution of the value proposition, Vera determines a set of options. By passing the

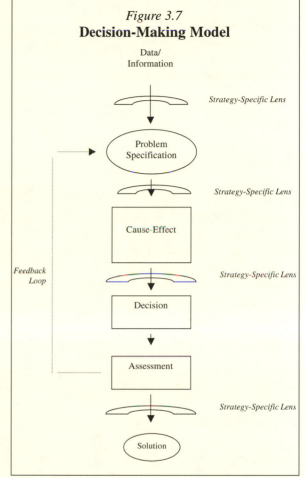

Figure 3.7
Decision-Making Model

options through the strategic lens, she makes a decision and establishes quantitative means to assess the outcomes of her decision.

Figure 3.7 indicates that the strategic lens enters the decision-making process at distinct stages of analysis. First, at the top left of the figure, data is passed through the lens to determine its strategic relevance. Second, the problem is passed through the strategic lens to understand the cause-effect linkages and to identify a set of decision options. The options are passed through the lens to make a decision, and the assessment of the outcome is based on strategy-specific criteria.

Lessons Learned: The Art of Decision Making

The examination of strategy-specific decision making yields several important lessons.

Decision Criteria

Decision makers often receive conflicting advice and recommendations. To assess the different opinions, decision makers need a lens to weight the criteria and prioritize outcomes. The decision criteria must be stated in advance of making a decision, and different lenses cannot be applied to rationalize different recommendations. A strategy-specific lens must be consistently applied and be understood by all in the organization. Strategy-specific decisions criteria result in *management by competitive theme*, strengthen the execution of the firm's strategy, and improve its competitive position.

Healthy and Unhealthy Debate

Disagreement and debate within an organization can be healthy or unhealthy. Assumptions should be questioned, conventional wisdom challenged, and uncertain futures debated. Decision makers should not stifle controversy; good ideas come from many sources, and no one individual has all the answers. But debate and disagreement that reflect a lack of consensus about the firm's competitive strategy must be avoided. Decision makers must distinguish between healthy and unhealthy debate and determine if their inconsistent actions are the cause of persistent damaging debate. Ultimately, coworkers who persist in offering non-strategy-specific advice are ineffective members of a management team.

Problems Exist within a Strategic Context

Many problems do not exist in isolation and do not lend themselves to a rifle-shot solution. Rather, problems exist in the fabric of the execution of a firm's competitive strategy. Consider a manufacturer who is considering the purchase of a just-in-time inventory management system. The company estimates the savings attributable to lower storage and financing costs. However, the issue cannot be examined apart from the firm's strategy. The just-in-time inventory proposal is more appealing if it improves the execution of the organization's strategy: the timely delivery of customized products. The same proposal is less interesting if the manufacturer competes on the basis of the ease of use of its product

> **Gelle's Building Products: Cause–Effect Linkages**
>
> John Chudovas and his staff must see the accounts receivable policy in a broad strategic context. To make an effective decision, John must understand the firm's value proposition and the cause-effect linkage from the receivables policy to the execution of the firm's strategy.

It is inappropriate for managers to deal with only one problem at a time and apart from the firm's competitive strategy. The analysis of the just-in-time inventory system must be examined in the context of the whole manufacturing processes, relationships with vendors, and buyer expectations. Dealing with one issue or problem at a time is conducive to (a) applying a different decision-making lens for each, (b) making incomplete and inconsistent decisions, and (c) confusing employees.

Role of Facts

Many organizations have a vast array of data at hand; but not all data is equally relevant. The interpretation of facts requires an analytic framework. Strategy-specific decision making provides a theme to organize data and sort the strategically relevant data from less-important facts. Organizations that take pride in a professionally designed "Fact Book" must question the relevance of the data. An endless array of data can be collected, but the strategic relevance of the information must be assessed before the numbers are gathered, interpreted, and disseminated. For example, for the low-priced tax preparation firm, staff turnover is interesting, but it is not a strategy-specific issue. The same ratio has strategy-specific relevance for the CPA firm that competes on the basis of continuous service and integrated advice.

Consistency Matters

Consistency in decision making is important for two reasons. First, each time a decision is explained in terms of the requisites of implementing the firm's strategy, it makes ensuing decisions more likely to be commonly directed. Second, cause-effect linkages in the execution of the strategy likely spill across departmental authorities. To prevent departments from pursuing conflicting objectives, commonly directed decisions are vital to the success of the organization.

Summary

This chapter extends the Cycle of Success to a strategy-based decision-making process. Managers pass options through a strategic lens to assess the alternatives and to make a decision. Working as systems thinkers, managers understand the cause-effect linkage between decisions and the execution of the firm's strategy and align all processes and practices to effectively execute the company's strategy.

These first three chapters have guided students, developing managers, and decision makers in two important ways. First, before making a recommendation or taking action, consider the firm's theme-based and weighted value proposition. Then, evaluate problems or opportunities in the context of the firm's strategy, recognizing that individual issues do not stand alone. Decisions must be made and explained in terms of implementing the organization's strategy, and the consistency of decision making matters. Consistency involves more than responding to the same situation in the same way over time and across people and departments. Consistency also includes responding to different problems with the same weighted criteria and strategic lens.

Key Themes and Terms

Healthy and Unhealthy Debate
Unhealthy debate occurs when different members of an organization apply their own decision criteria rather than use a common lens. Healthy debate happens in the context of agreement on the firm's strategy but involves considerations of uncertain futures, different disciplinary perspectives, or different tolerances for risk. (See pages 35–36.)

Managing by Competitive Theme
Managing by competitive theme involves the consistent application of the firm's strategy lens to make standard decisions across the firm and over time. (See page 39.)

Strategic and Nonstrategic Decisions
Strategic decisions are those that affect the execution of the firm's competitive strategy. These

decisions require the consistent application of a strategy lens. In contrast, non-strategy-specific debate involves issues unrelated to the execution of the firm's strategy. (See pages 39–41.)

Discussion Questions

1. Why are some debates healthy and others unhealthy?
2. Why is it important to distinguish between strategic and nonstrategic decisions?
3. What does it mean to manage by competitive theme?
4. What is the difference between "doings things right" and "doing the right thing?"
5. Why do some managers focus on "doing things right"?
6. What are the differences between "yes-men" and Type I Employees?
7. What are possible reasons employees offer different recommendations?
8. Discuss the differences between operational effectiveness and strategy-specific decision making.
9. Why is it important to respond consistently to the same problem? Also, what does it mean to respond consistently to different problems?
10. What advantages accrue to decision makers if they understand the cause-effect linkages in their firm?

End-of-Chapter Exercises

1. Refer to Case 1 at the end of this book, Nancy's Women's Shoppe, and do the following:
   a. Prepare a theme-based and weighted value proposition based upon the mission statement.
   b. List the decisions facing Nancy and classify them in cell I, II, III, or IV.
   c. Prepare a memo providing advice to Nancy.

   d. Review the advice of the accountant John Malch. Discuss the differences between strategic decisions and housekeeping decisions. Evaluate Malch's recommendations.
2. Review a memo you recently received, perhaps from your boss, senior management, or a campus official. Evaluate the memo in terms of the following:
   a. Are the decision criteria clear?
   b. Does the issue exist within a broad strategic context? Is that context clear in the memo?
   c. What facts are presented? Are they relevant for a strategy-specific decision?
3. For any organization, identify and explain decisions that fall into cell I, II, III, and IV.
4. Consider Case 2, Don Batts. What is the difference between gathering facts about an organization and collecting strategically relevant data? Send a memo to Don that directs his data collection.
5. Reflect upon a recent discussion with coworkers, roommates, or teammates in a simulation exercise.
   a. What problem did you discuss? List the different recommendations.
   b. Did individuals apply differently weighted decision criteria?
   c. Describe the debate as healthy or unhealthy.

Notes

1. William G. Forgang, *Competitive Strategy and Leadership: A Guide to Superior Performance* (New York: Rowman and Littlefield, 2001), pp. 15–33.

2. Michael Porter, "What Is Strategy?" *Harvard Business Review* 74 (November–December 1996): 33.

3. *Managing Customers for Profit: An Interactive Simulation* (Boston: Harvard Business School Press, 1998).

4. Michael Hitt, R. Edward Freeman, and Jeffrey S. Harrison, eds., *The Blackwell Handbook of Strategic Management* (Oxford: Blackwell Publishing, 2002), pp. 12–26.

5. Paul R. Niven, *The Balanced Scorecard Step-by-Step* (New York: Wiley and Sons, 2002), pp. 109–110.

4

Performance-Based Measurement Systems

This chapter extends the relationship between a firm's mission statement and its theme-based and weighted value proposition into performance measurements. Recall the photographer who needs a clear lens and accurate measure of light and distance. The measurements guide the photographer's analysis before taking a picture. In business, measurements sharpen the definition of a firm's strategy, help diagnose problems, lead to performance standards for each functional area, and allow managers to monitor the execution of the strategy.

Performance-Based Measurement Systems

The Mission Statement

The starting point is the firm's mission statement, which describes a business's scope of operations and the unique purpose that sets it apart from others.[1] For example, the mission statement for a citywide package delivery service expresses a commitment to quick and accurate deliveries. Following Figure 4.1, the service's mission statement leads to a theme-based and weighted value proposition, which heavily weights mistake-free and timely deliveries. In turn, the value proposition implies performance measurements that quantify the execution of the strategy, including the percent of deliveries completed as requested and on time.[2]

Following Figure 4.1, the deliverer cannot mandate accuracy and timeliness. Rather, it must make decisions that allow its personnel to execute the strategy and to meet buyer expectations. Decisions that are *downstream* from the value proposition include the selection and training of personnel, the size of the staff, and the equipment provided to workers. *Upstream* from the performance measurements are those decisions that market and deliver the good or service to buyers. For the package deliverer, upstream decisions include its outbound logistical systems and marketing initiatives. A firm's financial outcome (see Figure 4.1) is the lagged result of the design and execution of the firm's strategy. The feedback loop suggests that a firm's financial performance in one period affects its ability to execute the strategy in the following time period.

Greene's Grocery provides a more detailed example, beginning with the firm's mission statement:

Greene's Grocery: Mission Statement

Greene's Grocery is a full-service grocery store committed to serving the Northeast, offering shoppers the widest variety of products and freshest meats, seafood, and produce. Greene's promises: to serve its customers with the utmost courtesy, to attract and retain superior personnel, to be an outstanding corporate citizen, and to provide stakeholders with satisfactory returns.

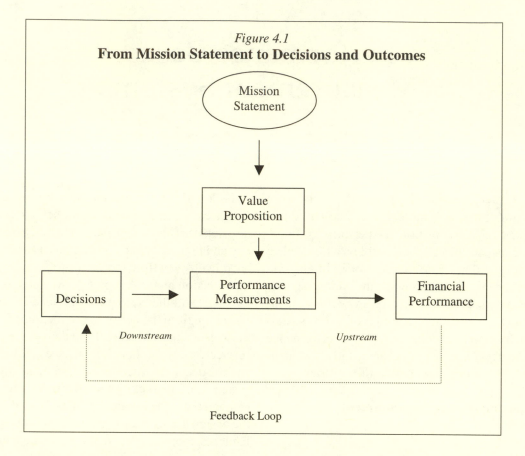

Figure 4.1
From Mission Statement to Decisions and Outcomes

Greene's mission statement is effective. It passes four critical tests: (a) trade-offs are clear, (b) it is buyer-focused, (c) it is expressed in relative and not absolute terms, and (d) it is operational without ambiguity.

The Trade-offs Are Clear

A firm's mission and purpose define its priorities to assess trade-offs. Greene's mission statement ranks priorities. The firm intends to offer the widest selection, the freshest meat and produce, and utmost courtesy. These are not compromised in favor of other objectives, and Greene's will not be mistaken as a convenience store or warehouse grocery store. A recommendation to reduce the number of stock-keeping units to increase the inventory turnover ratio and improve the firm's cash position is examined suspiciously because it undermines the execution of the firm's strategy.

Greene's mission statement does not include a reference to the prices of its products because the firm is aware of the trade-offs. It cannot be the selection, freshness, and courtesy leader and be the low-price seller at the same time. The cost of executing the value proposition prohibits Greene's from competing on price while earning superior returns. However, Greene's is not indifferent to its prices relative to rivals. Greene's understands that the price premium willingly paid by its Type I Buyers depends upon many factors, including the importance they assign to Greene's theme-based and weighted value proposition relative to the value propositions of rivals.

It Is Buyer-Focused

Greene's passes this test—the mission statement makes clear what the firm offers to its buyers. Many firms fail to include a clear buyer focus in their mission statement and choose mistakenly to emphasize their inputs.

The mission statement at Holland and Associates (see below) asserts that their personnel are certified and abide by the industry's ethical and professional standards. It also expresses a commitment to its employees and owners. The mission statement is inwardly focused. It specifies the firm's inputs and commitments to its employees rather than the benefits offered to purchasers.

Holland and Associates: Mission Statement

Holland and Associates is dedicated to providing affordable and high-quality architectural services in New England. With a commitment to the industry's ethical and professional standards, Holland and Associates employs certified professionals in a collegial environment. Holland is a socially responsible employer. It provides its employees a stable work environment and a balanced lifestyle while providing sound economic returns to its owners.

Holland's outward look to clients is limited and vague. It offers "affordable and high-quality architectural services." The claim sounds appealing but fails to recognize trade-offs. Frequently, high-quality goods and services (defined, for example, by

technical precision or durability) are costly to produce, thereby making it unlikely that a firm can be a product's quality and price leader at the same time. Such inconsistencies creep into mission statements if a firm is overly eager to gain buyer acceptance and wants to "be all things to all people." Where such inconsistencies persist, employees become confused because the decision-making lens is cloudy. Their expectations are not met. Low repurchase and referral rates depress the seller's profits.

Relative, Not Absolute Terms

Greene's mission statement expresses how it plans to outperform rivals. In contrast, Holland and Associates fails this test. It refers to operating with integrity and in compliance with industry standards, which are essential principles. But neither is a basis for superior performance. The claims are minimum standards for operating within any industry and do not yield a relative advantage over rivals.

Gelle's Building Products: Mission Statement

The case does not include the firm's mission statement. However, the ambiguity of the firm's competitive strategy can be explained by either: (a) a vaguely worded mission statement, or (b) by members of the organization failing to associate their daily behaviors with the firm's competitive strategy.

It Is Operational

Many firms fail this test, choosing vague and imprecise words in their mission statements. Holland and Associates, for example, refers to "quality" services. But what does the "quality" claim mean? Are the designs contemporary? Are they aesthetic, functional, or require minimal maintenance? Do they meet the highest standards of safety and access? Are the buildings designed for a very long, useful life? Are the structures the most energy efficient? The reference to quality leaves these questions unanswered, creating opportunities for unhealthy debate. Different members of the firm can assign different operational definitions to the term and apply their own decision-making criteria.

Greene's mission statement satisfies the four assessment criteria. The trade-offs are clear: It is buyer-focused. It expresses a source of relative advantage, and it provides operational guidance. Referring to Figure 4.1, the next step translates the mission into a theme-based and weighted value proposition (see Figure 4.2).

Exercise 4.1

Evaluate the mission statement for your firm or one with which you are familiar. Or, write a mission statement for the firm in your simulation exercise. Apply the four assessment criteria.

A similar exercise is provided in the Instructor's and Student's Simulation Guide, questions 3 and 4.

From Mission Statement to Value Proposition

Greene's mission statement communicates its priorities to employees and customers. The firm's competitive strategy emphasizes selection, freshness, and courtesy, and Figure 4.2 shows the translation of the mission statement into a theme-based and weighted value proposition.

Preparing such a value proposition is difficult for some organizations. Some contend the process is cumbersome and restricts their flexibility. Others argue that buyers make purchases for many different reasons and that a theme-based and

weighted value proposition cannot account for the different ways a firm creates value for buyers. Also, there may be debate among employees about the relative importance of the components of value. For example, selection is an important theme at Greene's. But is the relative weight 45 percent, higher, or lower? The question is not trivial. It affects organizational priorities and the allocation of resources among competing uses. A clearly articulated mission statement minimizes the numeric range of disagreement about the relative weight. Despite limitations, a theme-based and weighted value proposition is important and yields many benefits. Reaching a consensus on the firm's value proposition establishes priorities and assures that employees have a common strategic focus. The strategy becomes the lens that guides decision makers and coordinates activities across an organization.

Exercise 4.2

Refer to exercise 4.1 and the first draft of the mission statement for your firm. Prepare a theme-based and weighted value proposition.

A similar exercise is provided in the Instructor's and Student's Simulation Guide, questions 3 and 4.

From Value Proposition to Performance Measures and Target Values

The firm's value proposition specifies what it intends to offer to prospective buyers, including the features of the product, customer service, price, and the cost of using the good or service over time. But are the intentions realized? A firm's desire to extend a particular value proposition to buyers does not assure it occurs, and issuing orders is not sufficient.

Figure 4.2
Green's Theme-Based and Weighted Value Proposition

	% Total	Subtotal
Results	45%	
Selection		50%
Number of items		
Seasonal variations		
Unusual products		
Fresh		50%
Quick to market		
Displays		
Temperature		
Cleanliness		
Rotation/washing		
		100%
Process quality	25%	
Courtesy		70%
Clean		
Quick checkout		
Wide aisles		
Maintained carts		
Location		30%
High traffic areas		
Easy access		
Sufficient parking		
		100%
Price	20%	
Regular prices		90%
Discounts		10%
Coupons		
Frequent shopper		
		100%
Cost of acquisition	10%	
Hours of operation		65%
Limited payment methods		35%
	100%	100%

Consider, for example, a financial services firm whose mission statement and value proposition place heavy weight on close contact and trusted relationships between account executives (AE) and their clients. The intended relationship involves several components, including the AE's learning a client's personal circumstances, aspirations, and risk tolerances. Frequent review sessions and periodic phone conversations are part of the execution of the firm's competitive strategy. Once the desired AE–client relationship is defined, the ensuing question is simple to pose. Do such relationships actually occur?

This pragmatic question encourages the firm to assess the effectiveness of the execution of a firm's competitive strategy, and Figure 4.3 extends Greene's value proposition to *performance measurements* that allow Greene's to monitor the execution of its value proposition. At Greene's, the breadth of selection is measured by the number of stock-keeping units and the number of seasonal specialty items per month. Courtesy is measured by the average time waiting in the check-out line, the percentage of bags carried to the customer's vehicle, and the frequency of cleaning the store. Freshness is measured by the time to shelf for meat and produce and the duration of time on the shelf. Greene's monitors its prices and the frequency of use of discount coupons. Greene's also recognizes that its hours of operations impose a cost of acquisition, and the firm keeps abreast of buyer attitudes.

The performance measures in Figure 4.3 specifically refer to measurements of the execution of the firm's value proposition. These measures are carefully distinguished from *outcome measures* (profit, market share, and equity valuation). Outcome measures are the lagged consequence of the design and execution of the firm's strategy.

Following the specification of performance measures, it is necessary to establish target values to guide decisions to achieve a relative advantage over rivals. For Greene's, a large number of stock-keeping units is not sufficient to gain a competitive advantage. Its number of units must exceed that of rivals by an amount sufficient to attract and retain customers. However, four complications immediately arise. Target values for the performance measures must be: (a) achievable and motivating, (b) forward-looking and based on competitor intelligence, (c) important to buyers and generate a competitive advantage, and (d) achieve superior returns.

First, the target values must be achievable and motivating. Otherwise the firm is pursuing a strategy mismatched with its resources and abilities. Second, target values require competitor intelligence, and the intelligence must be forward-looking. At Greene's there is a lag between setting a target number of stock-keeping units and the units appearing on the shelf. Merchandise must be selected, ordered, received, and shelved. Over that time, rivals are not stagnant. Therefore, Greene's target number of units is based upon a forecast of the number of units offered by rivals. Third, the number of stock-keeping units must earn the allegiance of a sufficient number of buyers. Finally, Greene's must deliver its value proposition at a cost and charge prices that yield superior returns.

Figure 4.3 highlights important ideas.

- Performance measurements refer specifically to the execution of the firm's value proposition.
- Performance measurements are defined precisely and eliminate ambiguity.
- Competitor intelligence is an essential ingredient to outwit and outmaneuver rivals.[3]
- A firm's strategy must be sufficiently important to attract and retain buyers.
- The strategy must be executed at a cost (and price) that yields superior financial performance.

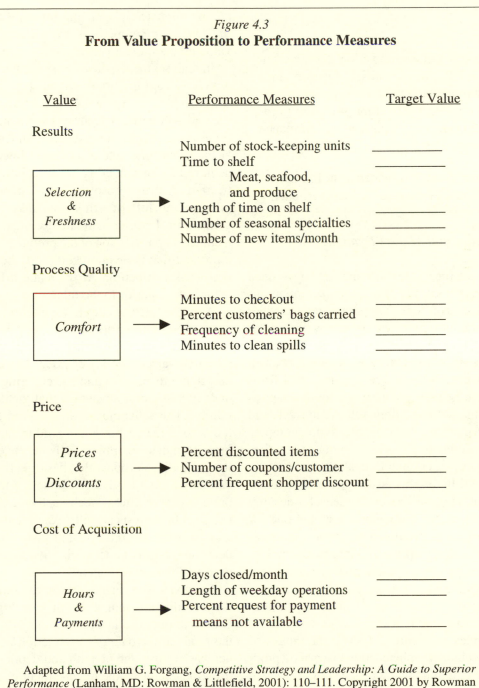

Figure 4.3
From Value Proposition to Performance Measures

Value	Performance Measures	Target Value
Results		
Selection & Freshness	Number of stock-keeping units	_____
	Time to shelf	_____
	Meat, seafood, and produce	
	Length of time on shelf	_____
	Number of seasonal specialties	_____
	Number of new items/month	_____
Process Quality		
Comfort	Minutes to checkout	_____
	Percent customers' bags carried	_____
	Frequency of cleaning	_____
	Minutes to clean spills	_____
Price		
Prices & Discounts	Percent discounted items	_____
	Number of coupons/customer	_____
	Percent frequent shopper discount	_____
Cost of Acquisition		
Hours & Payments	Days closed/month	_____
	Length of weekday operations	_____
	Percent request for payment means not available	_____

Adapted from William G. Forgang, *Competitive Strategy and Leadership: A Guide to Superior Performance* (Lanham, MD: Rowman & Littlefield, 2001): 110–111. Copyright 2001 by Rowman & Littlefield. Used by permission.

Target Values and Market Dynamics

Target values for the performance measures must be adjusted periodically because market conditions are not static. Over time, competitors upgrade their products and introduce new ones, new firms enter the market, technology alters trade-offs in sellers' value propositions, and buyer expectations change. Competitive advantages are dynamic, and firms must carefully monitor their ability to adapt to changing market conditions relative to rivals and buyer expectations. A firm's ability to anticipate and react to changing market conditions is an important source of competitive advantage.

Figure 4.4 highlights issues of market dynamics by displaying two buyer segments for desktop computers: one for the general user and one for the technical user. Both sets of buyers are sensitive to the product's price and technical sophistication. General users want products with less sophistication and lower price than those for the technical user. The technical users pay higher prices for more sophisticated products.

The circles in Figure 4.4 show the ranges of price and technical sophistication that make a product salable within its segment. The asterisks (*) in each segment represent the price and technical sophistication coordinates of products offered by competitors. The dispersion among the asterisks indicates that competitors are pursuing different value propositions in each market segment. [4]

In both segments, the asterisks generally fall in a pattern from the upper left of the circle to the lower right (see Figure 4.4). This pattern reflects the trade-off between technical sophistication and price. No firm is the sophistication and price leader at the same time, and a relatively lower price is achieved by surrendering some technical sophistication. A firm whose product resides horizontally to the left of other asterisks is a weak competitor. Its price is relatively high, given the technical sophistication of the products. Similarly, a product that is positioned directly below rivals is a weak competitor. At the same price, one is technically inferior to the other.

A product that resides horizontally to the right of the others has a price advantage, given its technical sophistication. But this firm must examine if its costs warrant the lower price. Is the firm underpricing its product and surrendering profits or does it hold a cost advantage that yields superior returns? This seller must examine its costs per unit, the ratio of the cost of goods sold to sales, and its gross margin to determine if it is surrendering profits. Similarly, a product that lies directly above rivals has a competitive advantage. At the given price, one firm offers a technically superior product. This firm must carefully examine its competitors, buyer expectations, and profit margins to determine if it is underpricing its product or exceeding buyer requirements.

The market segments are more complex than the two-dimensional diagram (see Figure 4.4). Other buying criteria exist and include access to the product, the date of introduction of the product, ease of use, the breadth and depth of the distribution channels, the management of individual accounts, the durability of the product, the product's resale value, and the technical support.

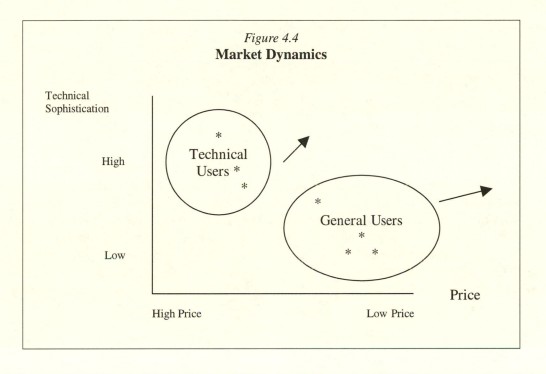

Figure 4.4
Market Dynamics

These criteria create additional opportunities to gain a competitive advantage. For example, a product in the general user's segment that lies to the left of rivals (higher price for given technical sophistication) is preferred because it is easier to use or is more accessible. A firm's competitiveness is a result of the composite of all of the factors relative to the target buyer's expectations and weighted buying criteria.

Trade-offs and Strategy

The market segment circles cover areas and are not single points.[5] The area of each circle (see Figure 4.4) indicates that different combinations of price and technical sophistication satisfy different buyer requirements. However, three points are stressed. First, the area of each circle corresponds with opportunities for competitors to pursue different value propositions. Second, at any time,

greater technical sophistication is associated with high development and production costs and necessitates higher prices. Finally, the different combinations of sophistication and price within each circle are not equally attractive. Some price and sophistication coordinates are more attractive than other combinations, given the weighted criteria that define buyer preferences.

The market segment circles allow different sellers to pursue different value propositions, and the asterisks show the product positions of different firms. For example, one seller is the technical sophistication leader (in its segment) while charging a relatively higher price. A rival purposefully lags the technical sophistication of its product and translates lower product development and materials costs into a relatively lower price. A third rival seeks a midpoint between the other two: being more technically sophisticated than one rival and lower priced than the other. Also, because other buying criteria exist, other rivals pursue strategies that meet broad price and sophistication criteria while emphasizing access to their product, product durability, or ease of use.

The spacing between the asterisks is important to consider. The trade-off between technical sophistication and price allows different firms to pursue different competitive strategies. But how much sophistication are buyers willing to surrender in favor of a lower price? Correspondingly, for any sacrifice of sophistication, how much lower must be the price to gain a competitive advantage? The answers depend upon a variety of factors, including the relative importance of sophistication and price to buyers and the price and sophistication coordinates of rival products.

Market Changes

In the desktop computer market and many other markets, buyer expectations change over time. For example, purchasers of desktop computers periodically upgrade their processing requirements while expecting lower prices. The arrows in Figure 4.4 indicate that both general users and technical users seek greater product sophistication and lower prices over time. However, the slopes of the arrows indicate that the general users seek a more rapid rate of decline in the price whereas the technical users upgrade technical requirements faster. The rate of change in buyer expectations in each segment is unknown and may change over time. But a firm's ability to anticipate the market shifts and reposition its products is a source of competitive advantage.

Because buyer expectations change over time, a firm's positioning of its products within the "selling circle" is not a one-time decision. The shift of buyer expectations requires the periodic repositioning of products. New target values for the performance measures must be set and achieved. However,

firms are not equally able to upgrade their value proposition. Many factors influence a seller's ability to adapt to changing buyer expectations. For example, a firm with a heavy debt burden, poor cash flow, historically low R & D, or old equipment is challenged to upgrade its products relative to rivals and relative to buyer expectations.

The rate of change of buyer requirements creates problems because it takes time for the firm to upgrade products. Therefore, one important issue is as follows: Can the seller upgrade its products fast enough to keep pace with buyer expectations and remain profitable? If the time and the expense of periodic upgrades are too great, a seller has an option to migrate its products from one market segment to another. Consider the desktop computer maker who offers products in both the technical and general user segments. The manufacturer has the option to upgrade both products over time or to: (a) migrate their more technical product to the general segment to meet rising expectations while (b) introducing a new product in the technical segment and (c) eliminating the old general user's product. Though timing the migration is difficult, a seller may be able to save considerable product development expenses by developing one new product rather than upgrading two products.

Competitor Shifts

Individual sellers must expect rivals to upgrade their own value proposition over time. For example, rivals may increase the technical sophistication of their product, deliver products or services more rapidly, or make products easier to use. Hence, a firm's competitive advantage in any period is not automatically extended over time. The challenges are to anticipate both changing buyer requirements and competitor upgrades to sustain a relative advantage over time. A firm's decision making must, therefore, recognize trade-offs between time periods. For instance, a decision in one year to minimize a product upgrade, to reduce training, or to defer investing in distribution channels in order to raise current profits or increase dividends has multiperiod effects. A firm that chooses to minimize product upgrades in one period to achieve some other objective finds it difficult to catch up to more sophisticated products in the future.

Changes in the Trade-offs

At any time, the available technology dictates the trade-offs in a firm's value proposition. For example, given existing materials and engine technologies, vehicle manufacturers are faced with a trade-off between miles per gallon and safety. Greater safety increases vehicular weight and reduces fuel efficiency. However, over time, materials, product design, and new technologies permit increased safety and fuel efficiency at the same time. The trade-off does not go away. Rather, technological changes alter the possible combinations of safety and efficiency.

Some changes in the trade-offs are the result of events external to the firm. For example, a steel company develops a new lightweight metal that alters the trade-off between safety and fuel efficiency for all vehicle manufacturers. A vehicle manufacturer's ability to integrate the new technology more rapidly than rivals gains a competitive advantage. Other changes in trade-offs are, however, the result of carefully planned internal decisions. For example, a vehicle manufacturer's research leads to a new engine that alters the trade-off between fuel efficiency and acceleration. Another firm invests in R & D to shorten its product development cycle time and alters the trade-off between time to market and the magnitude of product upgrade. Both firms have an opportunity to use the change in the trade-off to offer a relatively more attractive value proposition to gain a competitive advantage.

Performance Measures and Internal Communications

Performance measurements (see Figure 4.3) are strategy-specific and allow the firm to monitor the execution of its strategy. Also, the measurements are important communication devices and help employees understand the firm's strategy and their contributions to its execution. Greene's workers who restock shelves, meat trays, and produce bins understand the competitive importance of their duties. In turn, Greene's compensation system is based upon time-to-shelf requirements, and the criteria to select new employees include the assessment of applicants' abilities to meet target values.

The communication of performance measures and targets is also external to the firm. The themes and weights in the value proposition determine the marketing messages and express themes that respond to the expectations of the targeted buyers. By sending strategy-based messages to targeted buyers, Greene's attracts and retains a high percentage of Type I Buyers. Importantly, Greene's seeks reinforcing cycles of employees who are comfortable executing the firm's strategy, who are loyal, who refer new employees, and who satisfy customers who make repeat purchases and spread favorable word-of-mouth promotion.

Cause and Effect Linkages

Figure 4.5 displays the logic of strategy-specific decision making. Greene's Grocery is the example. Reading from the middle of the figure, the starting point is the three ovals: selection, freshness, and courtesy. These measures are the most heavily weighted variables in the value proposition. Achieving target values for these measures is not a matter of issuing orders. Rather, the target values are achieved as a result of management downstream decisions, including hiring, staffing, and the selection of equipment.

Gelle's Building Products: Marketing Messages

If Gelle's competes on the basis of easy credit terms, is this a comfortable message to send to buyers?

Does Gelle's risk attracting customers who, over time, continuously extend the time to payment? Is Gelle's building a foundation for its own destruction based on a liquidity crisis?

Figure 4.5 indicates sequential events between management's decisions and the execution of the value proposition. Reading from the bottom of the figure, management decisions that execute the value proposition include hiring and selecting equipment. *Interim performance measures* quantify the stepwise occurrences between decisions and the execution of the value proposition. For example, Greene's must receive appropriate merchandise in a timely manner and fully staff their work crews to execute effectively its value proposition. The percentage of seafood, meat, and produce that meets Greene's standards (based upon its value proposition) is an interim performance measure, and the measure is a leading indicator of the firm's ability to achieve its freshness target.

Upstream analysis begins from the execution of the value proposition and tracks the events that lead to the firm's financial performance. From the center of Figure 4.5, the heavily weighted variables in Greene's value proposition are selection, freshness, and courtesy. Reading toward the top of the exhibit, the value proposition guides the firm's marketing initiatives. Promotion and place decisions target and serve the firm's Type I Buyers. In turn, the execu-

tion of the strategy and the promotion and place decisions lead to *interim outcome measures*, including the level of buyer satisfaction, the repeat purchase rate, the average size purchase, and favorable word-of-mouth promotion. These interim outcome measurements precede the financial performance of the firm. The firm's profit, equity valuation, and market share are outcome measures and are the lagged consequences of the design and execution of the firm's strategy. The firm's financial performance is also a *feedback measure*, and it supports the execution of its strategy in the following period.

Strategy-Specific Decision Making

Figure 4.5 applies a strategic lens to make decisions that effectively execute a firm's strategy. Strategy-specific decision making allows managers to execute their firm's strategy by aligning operations with the strategy. Strategic leaders are more than visionaries.[6] They understand the activities within a firm that execute the strategy, and the competitive vision is supplemented with a compulsiveness that applies the strategy lens to shape all policies and behaviors within the firm.

Integrated and Consistent Decision Making

Each functional area contributes to the execution of the firm's strategy, and operating areas must be commonly directed, even at the expense of their individual department's interests. Senior-level managers must exercise their coordination responsibilities and assure that each functional area is commonly guided to execute the firm's strategy. As seen in Figure 4.5, many decisions contribute to the execution of the firm's strategy, and these decisions are made in different functional areas of an organization. Target values for the performance measures are met only if decisions across the firm and over time are consistently directed.

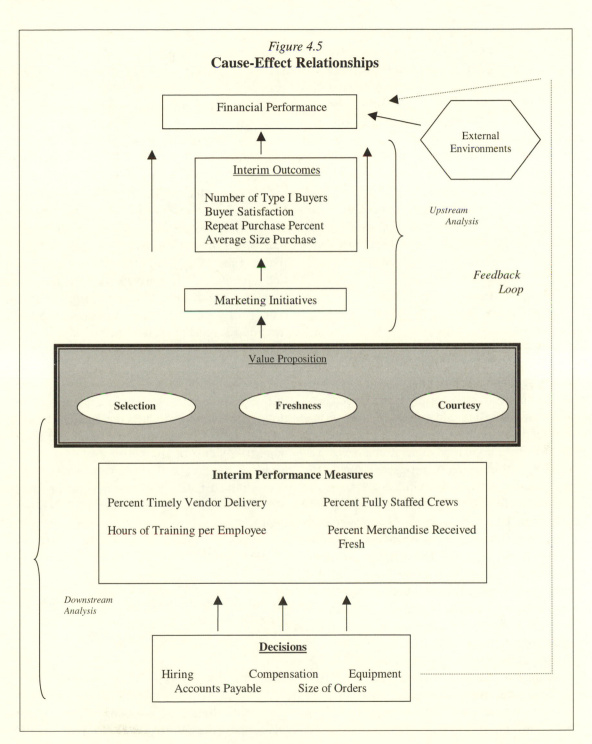

Figure 4.5
Cause-Effect Relationships

Complete Decision Making

Consistent decision making is important, but deci-sions must also be complete. The effective execu-tion of a firm's strategy requires a set of choices, and each piece of the puzzle must be in place. For Greene's, meeting the time-to-shelf targets depends upon several elements, including the selection of vendors, the staffing of crews, and the provision of the right tools and equipment. Omitting any ele-ments of the decision mix undermines the execu-tion of the strategy. If Greene's does not make com-plete decisions, it becomes vulnerable to rivals who effectively execute their value propositions.

*Financial Results Lag Strategy Design
and Execution*

The flow of the analysis in Figure 4.5 is from deci-sions to financial performance and back to deci-sions through the feedback loop. The analysis sug-gests that the firm's profitability is the lagged con-sequence of the design and execution of the firm's strategy and that cycles of success and decline oc-cur. However, a company's operational effective-ness, measured in terms of productivity and effi-ciency, cannot be ignored.[7] While not a substitute for strategy, a firm's operational effectiveness im-pacts its financial performance. Two ideas are raised.

First, using Greene's Grocery as the example, their operational effectiveness includes establish-ing target values for its performance measures that do not exceed levels needed to achieve a competi-tive advantage. For example, Greene's can have more stock-keeping units than needed to gain a competitive advantage. Because buyers will not pay incrementally higher prices for a selection that exceeds their requirements, the failure to achieve operational effectiveness reduces profits.

Second, Greene's must minimize expenses that do not contribute to its competitive advantage. It

may be unwise for Greene's to remain open twenty-four hours per day, assuming their Type I Buyers are unlikely to be shopping late at night or very early in the morning.

Students and developing managers who are en-gaged in a simulation must be accountable for the operational effectiveness of their firm in addition to the design and execution of strategy. First, the incremental costs of gaining a competitive advan-tage must be studied. For example, a producer of-fers a product whose performance qualities exceed that of rivals as well as buyer expectations. This means that the performance qualities are ineffec-tive and therefore reduce the firm's profits. Sec-ond, operational effectiveness is assessed relative to market conditions. The appropriate marketing outlay for a firm depends upon the competitive-ness of its market. Where products are scarce, lower marketing budgets are proper to bolster prof-its. Finally, efforts to achieve operational effec-tiveness require firms to calculate the internal rate of return on any investment in capacity, automa-tion, or investments in human resources to assure that the return covers the cost of capital and the opportunity cost of alternative uses of the funds.[8] Similarly, operational effectiveness requires the assessment of the relative costs of producing through overtime, expanding capacity, or improv-ing training.

Exercise 4.4

Refer to the value proposition in Exercise 4.3. Trace the variables upstream to outcomes and downstream to cause-effect relationships. Use Figure 4.4 as the model. Explain.

Elasticity: From Decisions to Outcomes

The cause-effect diagram, see Figure 4.5, leaves unanswered the question of the degree of sensitivity. Financial performance is a lagged consequence of the execution of the firm's strategy. But what is the proportionate change (all else equal) in profitability relative to a proportionate change in one performance measure? At issue is the ratio displayed below. How sensitive is profitability to a change in the time to shelf?

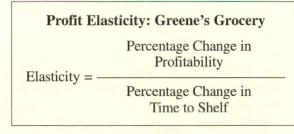

Profit Elasticity: Greene's Grocery

$$\text{Elasticity} = \frac{\text{Percentage Change in Profitability}}{\text{Percentage Change in Time to Shelf}}$$

Decision makers are unlikely to know this ratio, and the ratio is not a constant over different ranges of change in the time to shelf. Successive reductions in the time to shelf have diminishing effects on the firm's profitability. At some point, incremental reductions have smaller impacts on buyer satisfaction, and successive reductions in the time to shelf are increasingly costly to achieve. Managers are challenged to balance at the margin the incremental outlays against the financial gains.

The calculation of the elasticity measure in the above equation depends upon the sequence of events between changing time to shelf and profits. For example, what has to be done to reduce this time ? What are the costs? Before estimating the costs, how is it to be achieved? Reduced time can be achieved in several different ways, including the selection of vendors, more rapid payment of invoices and interest costs, improved equipment, or larger staff. Each of the options must be examined and the most favorable option identified.

The next equation raises another important question of sensitivity. The time to shelf is one of the variables in the value proposition, and it is affected by several causes, including the size of the staff, the tools and equipment provided, and the training of the personnel. Managers must understand the sensitivity of this time for each of the determinants and the cost of achieving time-to-shelf goals in different ways. After choosing the most efficient way to reduce the time, the firm is able to estimate the ratio of costs to time to shelf.

Performance Elasticity: Greene's Grocery

$$\text{Elasticity} = \frac{\text{Percentage Change in Costs of Stocking Crew}}{\text{Percentage Change in Time to Shelf}}$$

Furthermore, it is insufficient to know only the ratio between the proportionate change in costs and time to shelf. A firm's financial performance is affected by many variables. Decision makers must choose among reducing this time, accelerating the time to checkout of the store, and the breadth of inventory. Each favorably affects buyer satisfaction. But which leads to the greatest proportionate improvement in profit?

Managers are unlikely to know the degrees of sensitivity in the cause-effect connections. The uncertainties are the source of considerable debate and disagreement within an organization, and these debates have considerable impact on the allocation of scarce financial and personnel resources. But these debates are healthy if founded on a common understanding of the firm's value proposition.

Knowledge Management

Performance measurements provide managers with data to assess the execution of the strategy, and the upstream and downstream analyses (see page 63) formally establish and measure the cause-effect linkages from decisions to the financial outcome. However, the performance measurement system is ineffective unless the data are available. The firm's information system must generate timely data.

Managers are frequently forced to make decisions on anecdotal evidence.[9] But incomplete data or data without the appropriate strategic context are dangerous and lead to improper analysis and recommendations. From the perspective of strategy-specific decision making, the design of an information management system is not an issue of technology. Rather, the driver of the information management system and systematic gathering of data is strategy-specific. Information management and the design of reports must provide decision makers with the data to monitor the execution of the firm's strategy.

Summary

This chapter extends the concepts of strategy-specific decision making to a performance measurement system. The identification of the cause-effect linkages in the execution of the firm's strategy suggests a tracking system, allowing the firm to monitor the execution of its strategy. Importantly, the performance measurements monitoring system is an early-warning system. Managers must see the ineffective implementation of the firm's strategy *before* financial performance deteriorates. A tracking system also allows managers to translate the execution of the strategy into performance targets for individual employees. Decisions can be explained in terms of the requisites of executing the strategy, reducing managerial stress, reducing second-guessing, and improving the morale of an organization.

Those responsible for making decisions or recommendations and students engaged in case studies or a simulation are guided by a strategic lens. Choices are explained by the requisites of implementing the firm's strategy. The communication to coworkers or an instructor must emphasize the strategy-specific nature of the recommendations.

Key Themes and Terms

Assessing the Firm's Strategy

A firm's line of business strategy is defined by the weighted mix of variables in the value proposition, and its competitive strategy is assessed in terms of: (a) its ability to execute the strategy, (b) the compatibility of the strategy with the firm's external environments, and (c) the relative importance of the value proposition to buyers. (See pages 52–54.)

Downstream Analysis

Downstream analysis links individual decisions to the execution of the firm's value proposition. (See pages 61–62.)

Feedback Measurements

Feedback measures quantify the financial and infrastructure assets that a firm brings forward from one year to support the execution of its strategy in the following period. (See page 62.)

Financial Performance Measurements

A firm's financial performance is the lagged consequence of the design and execution of the firm's competitive strategy. (See page 56.)

Outcome Measurements

Outcome measures quantify the financial and market share performance of the firm. Outcome measurements are the lagged consequence of the design and execution of the firm's strategy. (See page 56.)

Performance Measurements

Performance measurements quantify the execution of the firm's value proposition. (See pages 52–54.)

Interim Outcome Measurements

Interim outcome measurements quantify the events between decisions and the execution of the firm's value proposition. (See page 62.)

Interim Performance Measurements

Interim performance measurements quantify the sequenced events that occur between management decisions and the execution of the firm's value proposition. (See page 62.)

Upstream Analysis

Upstream analysis guides strategy-specific marketing decisions and traces the sequence of events from the execution of the firm's value proposition to the realization of financial returns. (See page 62.)

Discussion Questions

1. What does it mean to make integrated and consistent decisions?
2. What does it mean to make complete decisions?
3. What are unintended consequences and how can they be anticipated and averted?
4. Identify and discuss factors that make some strategies more effective than others?
5. What are "activities" in a firm?
6. What difficulties arise when setting target values for performance measurements?
7. How do rivals affect the outcome of a firm's strategic design and execution?
8. What causes trade-offs in a firm's value proposition to change over time? How can a firm use these changes to their advantage?

9. How can a firm alter trade-offs in its value proposition? Is this a source of competitive advantage?
10. Discuss changes in buyer expectations, providing real-world examples.
11. Discuss how to anticipate the improvement in rival sellers' value propositions.

End-of-Chapter Exercises

1. Refer to the Don Batts case, Case 2. Prepare a memo to Don that includes the following:
   a. A mission statement.
   b. A theme-based and weighted value proposition based upon the mission statement.
   c. A set of performance measures that reflects the implementation of the mission statement.
   d. An operations manual for functional area managers.
2. Evaluate the Feld-Print mission statement (see page 44) based upon the criteria presented on pages 51–54.
3. Refer to Nancy's Women's Shoppe, Case 1. Using specific examples, discuss the difficulties of choosing performance measurements. How does the uncertainty of the firm's competitive strategy undermine monitoring its execution?
4. Describe the competitive strategy for your firm, school, or firm with which you are familiar.
   a. How does it differ from rivals?
   b. What are the implied differences in the definition of Type I Buyers?
5. Write a mission statement for Rockwell's Health Club, Case 4.
6. How does competitor intelligence affect decision making at Rockwell's?
7. Discuss the confusion at Rockwell's in defining the Type I Buyer. How many different definitions are presented? How does the lack of consensus affect decision making?

Notes

1. John A. Pearce and Richard Robinson Jr., *Strategic Management,* 4th ed. (Homewood, Ill.: Irwin Press, 1991), p. 13.

2. Robert S. Kaplan and David P. Norton, *The Balanced Corporate Scorecard* (Cambridge, Mass.: Harvard University Press, 1996), pp. 20–45.

3. Liam Fahey, *Outwitting, Outmaneuvering, and Outperforming Competitors* (New York: Wiley and Sons, 1999), pp. 5–7.

4. Charles W.L. Hill and Gareth R. Jones, *Strategic Management Theory: An Integrated Approach*, 5th ed. (Boston: Houghton Mifflin, 1999), pp. 95–100.

5. This section borrows several themes and presentation formats from the Capstone Management Simulation (www.capsim.com).

6. Larry Bossidy and Ram Charan, *Execution: The Discipline of Getting Things Done* (New York: Crown Business, 2002), pp. 12–27.

7. Michael Porter, "What Is Strategy?" *Harvard Business Review* 74 (November–December 1996): 7.

8. J. Fred Weston and Eugene F. Brigham, *Managerial Finance*, 7th ed. (Hillsdale, Ill.: Dryden Press, 1981), pp. 396–434.

9. Edward Russo and Paul J.H. Schoemaker, *Decision Traps: 10 Barriers to Brilliant Decision-Making and How to Overcome Them* (New York: Fireside Press, 1999), pp. 95–115.

5

Implementing the Strategy

Downstream and Upstream Analysis

The first four chapters established the concept of strategy-specific decision making and built a performance measurement system to guide and monitor the execution of a firm's strategy. This chapter presents a strategy-specific road map from decisions that execute the firm's competitive strategy, to the firm's financial returns, and to the firm's ability to execute its strategy in the following period.

Upstream and Downstream Analysis

A firm's competitive strategy is defined by its theme-based and weighted value proposition, but the execution of the strategy is not directly controlled by management.[1] For example, a trucking firm competes on the basis of guaranteed overnight delivery. The effective execution of the strategy requires more than issuing orders to their drivers. The drivers' abilities to meet promised schedules are the result of management decisions. *Downstream analysis* traces the execution of the firm's strategy to actions under the control of management, including choices from among alternative logistical systems, equipment, maintenance schedules, training programs, personnel, and compensation plans.

Downstream Analysis

Downstream analysis applies a strategy lens to assess options and make decisions that execute the

firm's strategy. For example, the trucking firm must select a fleet maintenance routine. Each option offers important benefits. One maintenance program minimizes monthly costs; another increases the life expectancy of a truck; another leads to a higher resale value for a truck; another offers ease of use and convenience; and another increases the daily reliability of a fleet of trucks. The choice is complicated by trade-offs. The maintenance routine that increases fleet reliability raises monthly costs. The routine that limits maintenance to quick and easy-to-accomplish tasks risks breakdowns and lowers the reliability of the fleet.

Gelle's Building Products: Evaluating Recommendations

Members of John Chudovas's staff offered conflicting advice about the management of the accounts receivable. Each recommendation is sensible. No one is guilty of a calculation error or a factual mistake. John Chudovas needs a strategy lens to evaluate the alternatives.

The trucking firm needs a strategy lens to prioritize the selection criteria and to clarify the trade-off. Given the firm's value proposition's emphasis on guaranteed overnight delivery, management chooses the maintenance routine that minimizes breakdowns. Given the strategy lens, reducing breakdowns takes precedence over, for example, lower costs. Fewer breakdowns lead to fewer service interruptions. Deliveries are completed on time, and the decision allows the firm to execute effectively its competitive strategy.

The trucking firm's choice of a maintenance routine is a strategic decision because it affects the execution of its value proposition. The firm's decision is, however, not singularly focused on reliability. Cost and benefit are evaluated. After all, incremental outlays for maintenance ultimately yield diminishing returns in reliability, and the successively smaller gains in reliability are increasingly less important to buyers. At some point the costs to further increase reliability cannot be passed forward to customers through higher prices. Incremental gains in reliability also impose trade-offs. Systems that enhance reliability raise costs (and prices) and limit the firm's ability to respond to emergency needs of customers. The decision maker considers many factors; however, the strategy lens prioritizes decision criteria, fosters healthy debate, and clarifies trade-offs.

Upstream Analysis

Upstream analysis applies the same strategy-specific decision-making lens to guide the firm's selling initiatives. The strategy lens evaluates alternative promotion, advertising, location, inventory systems, and outbound logistics options. For the trucking firm, the marketing message could emphasize price, delivery time, damage-free service, or the electronic tracking of shipments. Promotional pieces can be placed in different media outlets; the firm can rely upon different mixes of inside and outside sales personnel, print advertising, electronic advertising, and trade show displays. Given its competitive strategy, the trucking firm emphasizes the delivery guarantee, and marketing initiatives are directed toward prospective buyers with overnight delivery needs.

Firms that consistently apply a strategy-specific decision lens both downstream and upstream realize several benefits:

- Internal discussion is focused; only strategy-specific argument is relevant.
- Healthful debate is facilitated and unhealthy debate discouraged.
- Functional area operations are directed by a single strategic lens.
- Managerial stress levels and second-guessing are reduced, morale improves, and internal and external communications present clear and consistent themes.
- The firm effectively executes its strategy and strengthens its competitive position in the marketplace.

From Decisions to Outcomes

Figure 5.1 provides an overview of downstream and upstream analysis. Because the diagram is complex, the review is divided into nine steps:

Downstream Analysis

Downstream analysis traces the cause-effect relationship from decisions to the execution of the firm's value proposition.

Step 1: From Mission Statement to Performance Measurement

The starting point is the firm's mission statement, and then its subsequent translation into a theme-based and weighted value proposition and into appropriately selected performance measurements. For Greene's Grocery the mission statement (see page 51) leads directly to the value proposition and performance measures. The performance measures quantify the execution of the firm's value

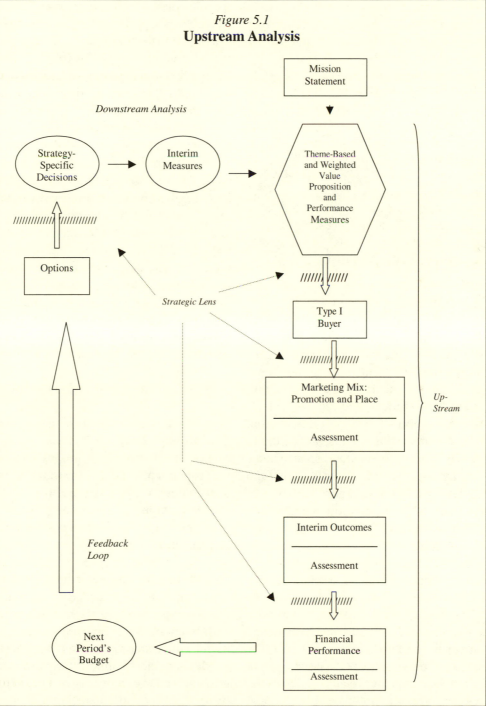

Figure 5.1
Upstream Analysis

proposition (see page 57) and include the time to shelf for meat, fish, and produce, the number of stock-keeping units, and the average number of minutes in the checkout line.

Gelle's Building Products: Unhealthy Debate

At Gelle's the unhealthy debate occurs over the accounts receivable policy. The different recommendations indicate a lack of agreement about the firm's strategy.

Unhealthy debate could also occur at Greene's. After all, there are many different freshness and courtesy standards. A clear strategic lens prevents unhealthy debate.

Step 2: From Options to Decisions

Reading from the left side of Figure 5.1, managers face multiple options for responding to a problem or opportunity. For example, the procurement manager at Greene's Grocery must choose among competing produce vendors, and each vendor offers a different combination of price, selection, freshness, access to specialty items, and certainty of delivery. The procurement manager evaluates each vendor by applying the strategic lens. The lens filters out those who surrender selection or freshness in favor of price and those whose logistics slow their deliveries. The procurement manager chooses vendors who contribute to meeting the requirements of their competitive strategy.

For Greene's Grocery the choice of vendors is strategic and falls into cell I (strategic/consensus; see pages 71–73). The decision is strategic because it affects the execution of the value proposition, and there is consensus. But the decision is not easy. The decision requires the procurement manager to gather data on each of the competing vendors and to assess their historic performance on the basis of strategy-

specific criteria. Risk and uncertainty are not eliminated. Historic performance cannot automatically be extended into the future, nor is Greene's assured that a vendor's promises will be fulfilled. The debate is healthy. Though there are valid differences of opinion, those engaged in the decision process apply a common strategic lens.

The selection of vendors at Greene's meets several important criteria.[2] The decision is properly *framed*. There is a clear understanding of what is to be decided (select vendors), and the strategy lens weights the criteria to evaluate the alternatives. The decision is based upon *gathered data*, and the collection of information is deliberate and focused. The strategy lens and decision criteria direct the data collection and prioritize the information. The decision process is *systematic*, and the analysis leads to a conclusion. Finally, Greene's enjoys a *feedback mechanism*; it is able to assess vendor performance based upon predetermined timeliness and freshness criteria.

Step 3: From Decisions to Interim Measurements

Downstream analysis links management decisions through sequential cause-effect events to the execution of the firm's value proposition. At Greene's the selection of vendors is a strategic decision that contributes to meeting breadth of selection and freshness targets in the value proposition. However, before Greene's Grocery meets its freshness and selection requirements, it receives appropriate meat, seafood, and produce shipments as scheduled. Therefore, the percentage of deliveries received on time, the percentage of products received that are appropriate for Greene's, and the number of different stock-keeping units ordered are *interim performance measures* (see Figure 5.1).

Meeting the freshness target, a performance measure, requires more than proper and timely deliveries.[3] Fully staffed stocking crews, motivated

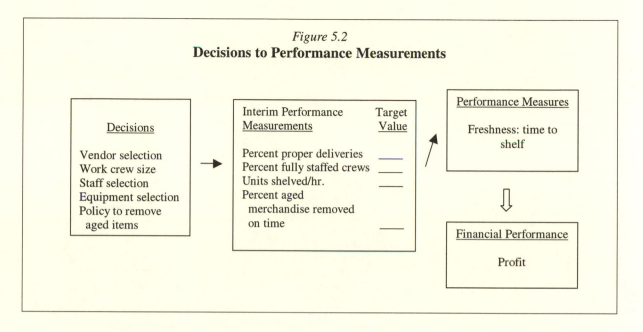

Figure 5.2
Decisions to Performance Measurements

workers, appropriate tools, and the removal of aged products from the shelf also contribute. Therefore, interim performance measurers include the percentage of stocking crews that are fully staffed, the number of units shelved per worker per hour, and the duration of time that items remain on the shelf (see Figure 5.2).

Figure 5.2 raises three important issues: (a) the importance of coordinated and complete decisions across a firm, (b) the role of performance measures as leading indicators of a company's financial performance, and (c) a firm's financial performance is the lagged outcome of the design and execution of the firm's strategy.

Complete and Coordinated

Greene's ability to meet its self-imposed time to shelf target is determined by the decisions made in procurement, human resources, logistics, and finance. For Greene's to execute effectively its value proposition, decisions across the firm must be commonly guided by the firm's strategy, and all of the operations that contribute to the execution of the strategy must fulfill their responsibilities. To make complete and coordinated decisions, managers must understand the cause-effect linkages between their actions and the execution of the firm's strategy. Management control systems must align each functional area's activities with the strategy.[4]

Exercise 5.1

For your employer, a firm with which you are familiar, school, or firm in a case study or simulation, provide the following:

a. Identify one heavily weighted component in the value proposition.
b. List the decisions and departments that contribute to the execution of the strategy, and identify who is responsible for each decision.

A similar exercise is provided in the Instructor's and Student's Simulation Guide, question 5.

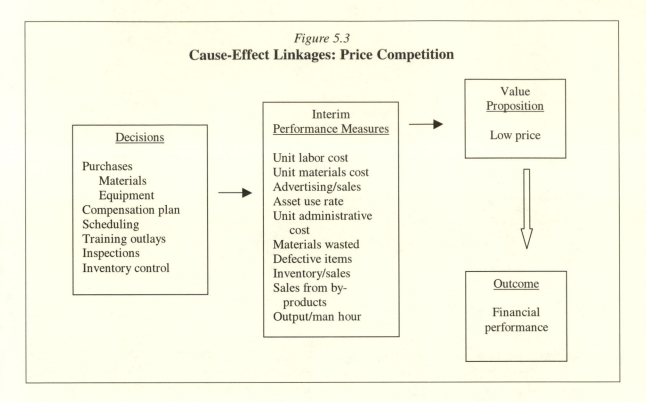

Figure 5.3
Cause-Effect Linkages: Price Competition

Leading Indicators

Interim performance measures monitor the cause-effect connections between decisions and execution of the firm's value proposition and are leading indicators.[5] For example, Greene's Grocery determines that the target value for the waiting time in the checkout line (a performance measure) is two and one half minutes, with a standard deviation of forty five seconds. To realize this performance measure target, 95 percent of the checkout crews must be fully staffed; cash register scanning devices must read 99 percent of the uniform product codes, and cash register personnel must scan an average of twenty-five items per minute with a standard deviation of five items per minute.

The target interim performance measures guide functional area decision making; they define and quantify the dependencies between departments; they allow area managers to assess performance in terms of the contribution to executing the competitive strategy; and they provide a quantitative basis to reward success. By monitoring the measurements, Greene's traces the execution of its competitive strategy and observes problems before financial results deteriorate.

To highlight the nature of interim performance measures, Figure 5.3 refers to a firm that emphasizes low price in its value proposition. The exhibit identifies decisions that execute the strategy through cause-effect linkages. The decisions involve actions that are under the direct control of management and include their purchase of materials and equipment, selection of a compensation plan, and training regimen. The decisions affect the measures (including unit labor and materials

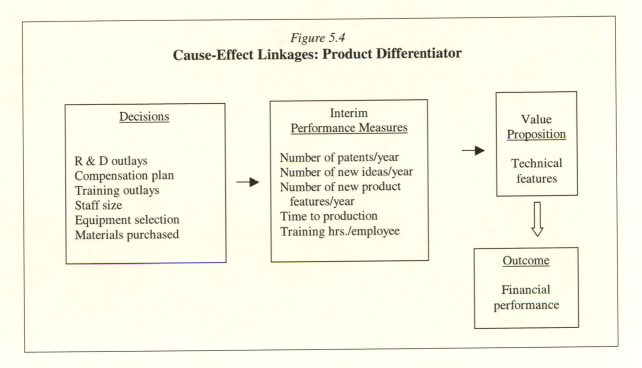

Figure 5.4
Cause-Effect Linkages: Product Differentiator

costs) and are the foundation of the company's ability to offer a relatively lower price. This firm's financial performance is the lagged result of the design and execution of its strategy.

The same ideas are presented in Figure 5.3 with respect to a firm that competes on the basis of the technical features of its products.

For the firm in Figure 5.4, strategy-specific decisions include R & D spending and training outlays. Interim performance measures include the number of patents per year and the number of new features and upgrades per year. These measures lead the execution of the firm's value proposition. The financial performance is a lagged result of the design and execution of the firm's strategy.

Lagged Outcomes

A firm's market share and equity value are lagged outcomes of the design and execution of its competitive strategy. Greene's Grocery's financial performance depends upon three critical factors. First, buyers must value the freshness, selection, and courtesy (relative to the value propositions offered by rivals) and pay a premium price that covers the incremental costs of implementing the competitive strategy. Second, operating budgets must allow selection, freshness, and courtesy performance targets to be met. Finally, targets should not exceed buyer requirements and willingness to pay, and nonstrategic outlays must be minimized.

The following points summarize the importance of interim performance measurements:

• Interim performance measurements are close to each worker's daily responsibilities, and individual employees associate their daily tasks with them. Functional area managers design operations, establish performance targets, motivate employees, explain decisions, justify requests for staff, equipment, or personnel, and reward success to achieve target values.

• Interim performance measurements are a communications tool. The measurements remind employees of the firm's competitive strategy, explain the logic of managerial decisions, and direct individual choices.

• Interim performance measurements track the sequence of events from decision to execution of the firm's strategy, quantify the dependencies, and integrate functional operations around the strategy.

• Interim performance measurements limit unhealthy debate. At Greene's Grocery, the strategy dictates a relatively large number of stock-keeping units, large bagging and checkout crews, and the prompt removal of aged products from the shelves. Arguments that apply benchmark industry standards to cut costs, reduce waste, or reduce the number of different products to raise the inventory turnover ratio are unhealthy. These sensible-sounding recommendations undermine the effective execution of the firm's strategy.

• Interim performance measurements provide an early warning of developing problems. For example, slower deliveries occur before any decline in the freshness of items on the shelf is realized. The firm has an opportunity to correct problems before financial performance is adversely affected.

• Interim performance measurements diagnose operational problems and direct corrective action. For example, if freshness standards at Greene's are not being met, these measurements help identify if there is a vendor problem, a staffing problem, or a productivity problem.

Step 4: Executing the Firm's Competitive Strategy

Reading from the left side of Figure 5.1 (see page 71), downstream decisions lead to the ex-ecution of the firm's strategy. Interim performance measurements reflect the stepwise events leading to the execution of the firm's value proposition. Performance measurements quantify the firm's delivery of its value proposition. At Greene's Grocery, measurements include the number of stock-keeping units and the time customers spend in the checkout line. The percentage of shipments received on time is an interim performance measure.

Downstream analysis raises four issues: (a) the intended compared with the actual value proposition, (b) performance assessment, (c) the role of competitor intelligence, and (d) the intended value proposition and competitive advantage.

The Intended Value Proposition Compared with the Actual Value Proposition

The value proposition for Greene's Grocery (see page 57) is the weighted mix of benefits and costs the firm intends to offer to buyers. But aspirations are not sufficient. The mix actually extended to buyers differs from the firm's intentions if downstream decisions are inconsistent or incomplete. For example, Greene's Grocery does not extend to buyers its intended value proposition unless procurement, human resources, and finance effectively execute the intended value proposition through strategy-specific decisions. If Greene's Grocery selects vendors on the basis of price or understaffs its crews, it will not be the industry leader in selection or freshness. One important implication is that strategic planning and leadership involve more than vision. The important complement to vision is the ability to align and manage the details that execute the strategy.[6]

Because the value proposition extended to buyers may differ from the firm's intentions, managers must ask the following: Are we actually doing the things we state in the value proposition that are important to compete against rivals? Answering the question is complex. Often, organizations incorrectly develop their own myths and conventional wisdom, convincing themselves that they are executing their strategy. In many organizations, if something is said with frequency, it is believed to be true. For example, consider a small college whose value proposition heavily weights student-faculty interaction. The average class size creates the opportunity. Do the desired interactions actually occur? The students know. But in the absence of data, the college's administration is able to delude itself. The student's experience may differ from the school's intentions. To avoid misjudgments, the execution of the value proposition must be measured.

Performance Assessment

Performance assessments examine the execution of the strategy. Did the firm do what it set out to do in order to attract and retain buyers? This assessment markedly differs from evaluating the firm's financial performance. Doubtlessly, financial performance is important to stakeholders and to the firm's future ability to execute its strategy. But financial returns are often deceptive. A firm, for example, may enjoy financial success despite poor execution of its competitive strategy because its marketplace is unusually favorable. With rapid growth in demand and an overall shortage of products, even a poorly designed or executed value proposition leads to profitable sales. But the firm that ineffectively implements its competitive strategy is quick to struggle when the marketplace turns less attractive.

The assessment of the execution of the value proposition occurs at two stages. First, the firm compares its performance measurement against target values. For Greene's, one important comparison is the average wait in the checkout line relative to its target value. This comparison reflects the effectiveness of the execution of its strategy. The second assessment is diagnostic. It compares the actual interim performance measurements with their respective target values. For Greene's, one comparison is the actual percentage of fully staffed checkout crews with the target value. If Greene's fails to meet its freshness targets, the assessment of the measurements identifies the source of the operational shortfall.

The Role of Competitor Intelligence

Performance assessments are a vital source of management information. However, the assessments require that target values for the measurements conform to a marketplace advantage relative to its rivals. Being good at some element of value creation is not sufficient. Competitive advantage results from being better or different.[7] For Greene's Grocery, a large selection is not a source of relative advantage unless it exceeds that of its rivals; hence, effective target values depend upon competitor intelligence. Greene's must know the number of units offered by competitors to set a target that is larger. Importantly, the difference in the number of units must be large enough to attract and retain buyers. But the number of stock-keeping units cannot be undisciplined. At some point, Greene's breadth of selection can exceed buyer requirements, and the costs associated with the additional inventory cannot be recovered through higher prices.

Competitor intelligence is inherently forward-looking. Firms must recognize that their own decisions have lagged consequences. For example, a manufacturer decides to upgrade its product's capabilities, expecting to earn a competitive advantage over rivals. The decision to upgrade involves setting specific targets for the product's durability, technical precision, and size. However, the manufacturer needs time to design, develop,

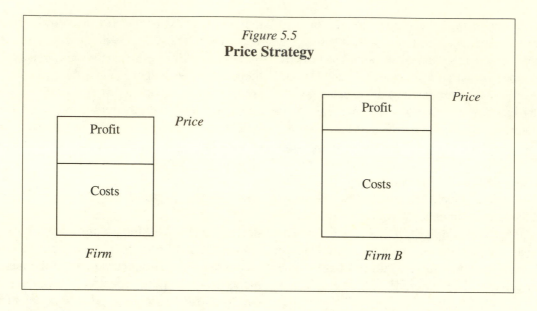

Figure 5.5
Price Strategy

produce, and market their upgraded product. This cycle time is an opportunity for rivals to upgrade their own products. To gain a competitive advantage, a firm must anticipate the capabilities and prices of rivals' products at the time in the future their own upgrade is complete.

The Intended Value Proposition and Competitive Advantage

A firm's intended value proposition and performance targets seek a relative advantage over rivals. The purpose of the intended advantage is sustained and superior financial returns. For example, firm A (see Figure 5.5) competes against firm B by selling its product at a relatively lower price. In this example, firm A's price advantage translates to superior returns because its costs are lower. Though not seen in the diagram, A's interim performance measurements (unit labor, materials, and administrative costs and productivity) allow it to gain a relative price advantage and realize superior returns.

Similarly, firm C (see Figure 5.6) successfully

competes on the basis of a product characteristic or service advantage. Firm C's costs are higher than firm D's, a result of the differentiation. But C's product difference is important to buyers, warrants a higher price, and yields superior profitability.

Firm A (see Figure 5.5), the successful price competitor, and Firm C (see Figure 5.6), the successful product differentiator, monitor different interim performance measurements. The price competitor focuses on costs and productivity measurements. The product differentiator examines its research and development outlays, products under development, and new feature introductions per year.

Exercise 5.2

Refer to Exercise 4.2 (see page 54). Use the value proposition to establish performance measures and interim performance measures. Explain.

A similar exercise is provided in the Instructor's and Student's Simulation Guide, question 5.

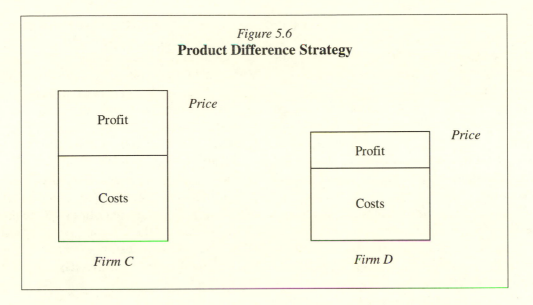

Figure 5.6
Product Difference Strategy

Upstream Analysis

Upstream analysis traces the cause-effect relationships from the execution of the firm's competitive strategy through its marketing mix decisions to the realization of financial outcomes. Upstream analysis is reviewed in steps 5–9.

Step 5: From Value Proposition to the Type I Buyer

The strategy-specific decision-making lens that guides functional area managers to implement the strategy is applied upstream to direct marketing initiatives. From the value proposition and performance measurements, the first step upstream translates the value proposition into a definition of the firm's Type I Buyers, those whose value proposition closely aligns with that offered by the seller. For Greene's, the Type I Buyer may be defined by income, wealth, education, age, ethnicity, and lifestyle.

The specification of the firm's Type I Buyers allows the firm to estimate its quality buyer ratio (QBR).[7]

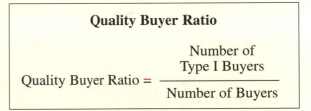

Quality Buyer Ratio

$$\text{Quality Buyer Ratio} = \frac{\text{Number of Type I Buyers}}{\text{Number of Buyers}}$$

Estimating this ratio provides five important benefits: (a) it strengthens the firm's commitment to its strategy, (b) yields buyer allegiance, (c) allows employees to work within existing systems, (d) directs marketing, and (e) builds customer equity.

Commitment to Strategy

To estimate its QBR, a firm must define its strategy and target buyer group. An organization's periodic debate of its strategy and Type I Buyers is useful and healthy. The debate evaluates the company's strengths, weaknesses, opportunities, and threats (see pages 6–7). It also strengthens the commitment to the strategy or leads to strategic change. Further, a periodic review of the QBR allows the business to screen its client base.[8] The process evaluates each buyer relative to the firm's intended value proposition and determines the appropriateness of each buyer and the profitability of individual engagements, accounts, or projects. This customer review process allows a company to manage its client base and to "fire" non–Type I Buyers.[9]

Consider a manufacturer of tubing products that are used to hold and dispense toothpaste, glue, caulk, and medicinal ointments.[10] The firm produces standardized products and competes on the basis of price. The company's manufacturing equipment is not flexible, thereby making it costly to produce unusual sizes or shapes. However, several customers regularly request specialty items. This manufacturer is reluctant to turn away any customer, and its cost accounting system is unable to determine the profitability of any single order. This firm risks accepting orders and clients who force the manufacturer to work outside of established systems and procedures. The firm's lack of focus and straddling of markets (see page 12) adversely impact its financial performance.

Buyer Allegiance

Firms who enjoy a relatively high QBR experience frequent repeat purchases, customer referrals, and a high percentage of the buyers' wallets. A high percentage of Type I Buyers and a high rate of repeat purchases have favorable cost implications. The cost of retaining buyers is lower than the cost of attracting new buyers.[11] All else equal, referrals lower a firm's marketing costs. A high percentage of the buyers' wallets allows sellers to realize economies in marketing, account management, and distribution.

Work within Established Systems

A high percentage of Type I Buyers allows the firm to work within the constraints of its existing tools,

equipment, and systems. Given the fit between its activities and buyer expectations (see pages 11–13), the firm minimizes inefficiencies associated with performing unfamiliar tasks. Working outside of established systems or knowledge bases is expensive. Consider a CPA who usually provides tax and consulting services for medical practices. However, the accountant's new client is engaged in construction-equipment leasing. It takes time for the accountant to learn the nuances of the new industry, and the learning time cannot be billed to the client. The inefficiencies limit the accountant's ability to serve other clients. Also, despite the accountant's best efforts, the work is likely to be less effective than that performed by an equipment-leasing specialist.

Directed Marketing

A firm directs its marketing initiatives given the definition of the Type I Buyer. Consider a poorly focused accounting firm. To encourage the recruitment of new clients, the partners offer an incentive based on "origination credits." Employees who recruit a new client are paid a bonus. Despite the attractive financial incentive, employees lack direction and struggle to help the firm and themselves. Their marketing efforts are unfocused and deteriorate to random networking and participation in community civic organizations. At a more focused firm, new client recruiting is directed toward particular industry or professional groups and firms with comparable gross sales, income, price sensitivity, ownership structure, or special needs. Employees respond to the incentive and develop new business guided by the firm's competitive strategy.

Building Customer Equity

A high quality buyer ratio builds customer equity: the present value of the lifetime earnings from a client.[12] The concept of customer equity encourages two modes of thought. First, it urges managers to shift attention from attracting customers and the profitability of an individual transaction to a longer-term perspective of customer retention and lifetime customer profitability. Second, it shifts management's focus from its products to its relationships with customers and how the seller creates value for the buyer.

The target value for a firm's QBR depends upon its age and history. Older firms who have enjoyed a more focused history are positioned to enjoy a high ratio, whereas young and less-focused firms may respond to the pressures of getting customers. But regardless of the firm's QBR, it is important to periodically review its client base, cull inappropriate buyers, focus marketing efforts, and improve the ratio over time.

For some firms, the quality buyer ratio is properly supplemented by a quality vendor or quality distributor ratio. The logic is unchanged. The appropriateness of vendors and distributors is affected by their positioning in the market to complete the linkage from the producer's value proposition to Type I Buyers.

Step 6: From Type I Buyer to Selling Initiatives

Upstream from the definition of the firm's Type I Buyer, a strategy lens guides selling initiatives. Greene's Grocery, for example, selects its advertising message and media to communicate clearly and efficiently with its Type I Buyers. For other firms, marketing considerations include the selection of vendors, the mix between inside and outside sales personnel, the mix between distributors and account management, inventory management systems, and outbound logistics. Marketing decisions include the allotment of funds and personnel among competing uses, and the resource allocations are strategy-specific. For instance, a manufacturer who competes on the basis of technical precision exhibits products at trade shows, whereas a low-price competitor relies upon distribution channels.

Selling initiatives may also be part of a firm's value proposition. For example, a manufacturer has a product whose technical capabilities and price are equivalent to rivals; however, the firm's value proposition heavily weights ease of access to the product (process quality). Vendor selection, logistical systems, and account management are upstream and downstream strategy-specific decisions at the same time. Similarly, a company that competes on the basis of image and style uses advertising and promotion to establish its competitive advantage through building product awareness. Upstream and downstream decisions merge.

Step 7: From Marketing Initiatives to Interim Outcomes

Following marketing initiatives, upstream analysis links the firm's decisions in sequence to interim outcome measures and to outcome measures of financial performance. Interim outcome measures include the number of buyers, growth in the number of buyers, the rate of repurchase, the number of buyer referrals, and the percentage of the buyer's wallet realized. Buyer loyalty is a particularly important determinant of profitability and focuses on building the lifetime value of a customer rather than making individual sales.[13] The interim outcome measurements are a lagged consequence of the execution of the firm's value proposition and promotion and place decisions and precede the realization of financial returns. Outcome measurements, including profit, market share, and equity valuation, are lagged consequences of the design and execution of the firm's strategy.

Step 8: From Interim Outcomes to Financial Performance

The firm's financial performance is the lagged consequence of the design and execution of its strategy and is classified as an outcome measurement. A firm's financial performance is assessed by comparing profits, rate of return on invested capital, equity valuation, and the price-to-earning ratio relative to target values. Target values must be reasonable as dictated by the organization's strategy and the competitive conditions in the marketplace.

The focus on the execution of the firm's value proposition does not minimize the importance of financial strategies. Effective financial management contributes to the execution of the strategy and improves the firm's profitability. For example, a firm that competes on the basis of price monitors its sales per employee, asset utilization, unit labor, materials, administration, marketing, and shipping costs. Similarly, the management of accounts payable is an important downstream decision for a firm competing on the basis of premium value products with unique input requirements that have short production schedules. A firm's outcomes measurements (profit, equity value) are also affected by its financial management practices. For example, a firm that seeks to maximize stockholder wealth carefully manages its asset use rate, interest expense, inventory level, dividend policy, and debt-to-equity ratio and takes full advantage of financial leverage opportunities.

Feedback Loop

Step 9: Feedback

Figure 5.1 (see page 71) emphasizes the circular nature of downstream and upstream decision making. The feedback loop indicates that a firm's success in one year provides infrastructure and budget support to execute its strategy the following year. For example, financial success at Greene's Grocery allows it to restock a broad inventory, including selected slow-turnover items. Financially successful firms also bring forward to the next year a vibrant infrastructure, including satisfied buyers, products or services under development, a high bond rating, quality initiatives that reduce cycle time or minimize material use, commonly directed employees, procedures, equipment, and policies aligned with the strategy.

Feedback measurements often indicate cycles of success or decline. For instance, a firm's current-period profits may meet expectation, but the firm's bond rating, products under development, or customer retention may point to future problems that may be difficult to reverse. Feedback measures are examined relative to rivals and to changing buyer needs and must be strong enough to allow a company to upgrade its products and sustain an advantage over rivals.

Summary of Measurements

Downstream and upstream analysis creates the following categories of measures of organizational performance (see Figure 5.7 and pages 69–71).

The proper classification of performance measures is important. The classifications correspond to the measurement's placement in the sequence of cause-effect events from decisions to the realization of the firm's financial performance.

Strategy-specific decision making and performance monitoring systems yield many benefits, including the following:

- Internal discussion is focused; only strategy-specific arguments and data are relevant.
- Healthful debate is facilitated and unhealthy debate discouraged.
- Functional area operations are integrated

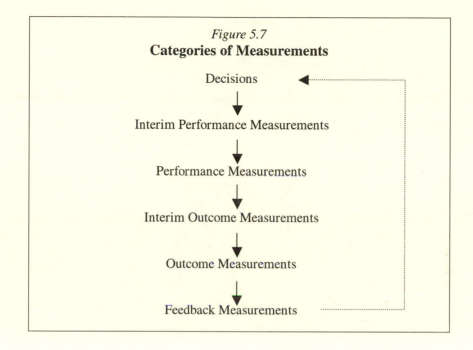

Figure 5.7
Categories of Measurements

Decisions

Interim Performance Measurements

Performance Measurements

Interim Outcome Measurements

Outcome Measurements

Feedback Measurements

around the requisites of implementing a common competitive strategy.

- A firm's strategy is more effectively implemented, thereby leading to a stronger competitive position and favorable financial returns.
- Interim outcome measures allow a company to monitor the expected sequence of events from the execution of the firm's strategy to its financial performance. Problems are detected in advance of any adverse effects on the firm's financial performance.

Exercise 5.3

Refer to exercise 4.1 (see page 54). Complete the following based upon the value proposition:

1. Define the Type I Buyer.
2. List interim outcome and outcome measurements.

Strategy-Specific Decision Making

Figure 5.8 extends downstream and upstream analysis by showing that decision makers are—at any point in time—challenged by multiple problems and opportunities and multiple options that interact. The value proposition emerges from the blended mix of decisions.

Figure 5.8 raises four important issues: (a) multiple issues and options, (b) clear and muddied strategies, (c) issues that do not exist in isolation, and (d) the anticipation of the unintended consequences.

Multiple Issues and Options

Reading from the left side of Figure 5.8, at any time there are multiple problems, issues, and opportunities challenging managers, and each presents multiple options. For example, a marketing manager must make several decisions: how to respond to a disgruntled account, which sales repre-

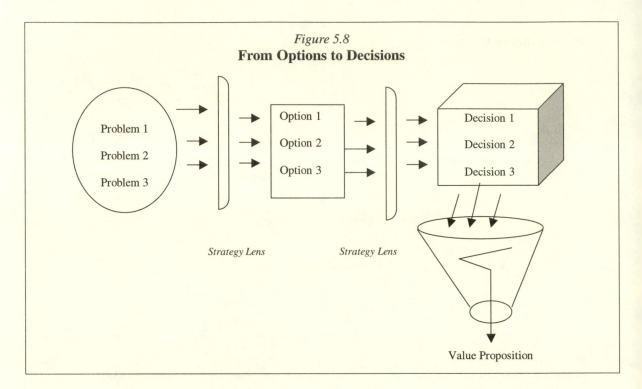

Figure 5.8
From Options to Decisions

sentative to promote to regional manager, how to train personnel to use a new computer system, and how to price a new product. At the same time, a production manager examines alternative suggestions to correct a design problem, schedules production runs, manages raw materials and finished goods inventory levels, and evaluates employees.

Gelle's Building Products: Evaluating Options

John Chudovas is faced with different recommendations regarding the firm's accounts receivable policy. One recommendation is to tighten collections practices. An alternative position is that the existing flexibility is an important part of the firm's competitive strategy. A third argument is that improving delivery times is more important than payment flexibility.

For each problem, several reasonable options exist, and different options may have strong advocates within a firm. For example, a law firm can choose only one of many qualified job applicants. Recommendations differ because selection criteria (academic record, specialization, experience, appearance, writing skills, and expected ability to work with clients) are differently weighted. Similarly, a manufacturer must select equipment. It studies several highly regarded machines, and recommendations differ because ease of use, technical proficiency, price, flexibility, maintenance costs, and implied demands on labor are differently weighted. In both examples each selection criterion makes sense. However, strategy-specific decision makers prioritize the criteria by applying the firm's competitive strategy as the decision-making lens and choose wisely.

Gelle's Building Products: Coordinated Decisions

Rebecca Green recommended that the firm improve customer service by reducing the duration of time from placement of an order to receipt of the merchandise.

If this recommendation is adopted, the firm must make many changes. Manufacturing must shift operations from long production runs to a more flexible process. Equipment, procurement, and outbound logistics must adapt.

Figure 5.8 suggests even more complex problems, evidenced by decisions 1, 2, and 3 blending together in the funnel. For example, a manufacturing firm's choice of material inputs, training programs, product designs, maintenance routines, and compensation plans interacts with its selection of equipment. A poorly executed competitive strategy emerges from the funnel if functional area managers make inconsistent choices. For instance, a full-service law firm competes on technical competency. Its recruiting and compensation practices are appropriate, but its information management system is insufficient to implement the competitive strategy. Tax information is unavailable to estate planners, and property transactions are not reported across the firm. The effective execution of the strategy requires complete and strategy-specific decisions across the firm.

Gelle's Building Products: Empowerment

John Chudovas has built a reputation of letting members of his staff make their own decisions. But empowering his staff to make decisions may be a problem, given the lack of agreement about the firm's strategy among his staff. Though no information is provided, the firm's slow growth could be a result of inconsistent decisions.

Strategy-specific decisions must also be consistent over time. Decisions do not immediately pass through the funnel; rather, effects linger and continue to influence the clarity of the firm's strategy. For example, a professional services firm cancels a staff training program in response to an unexpected decline in sales. Whether a wise decision or not, the effects of the lack of skill building linger. Similarly, a firm reduces R & D spending; later, the firm finds it difficult to catch up to rivals' products. Finally, consider a firm whose compensation practices vary over time. Switching from a merit pay system to one that emphasizes seniority and to another that minimizes pay disparities confuses employees. They lose sight of the connection between their responsibilities, their compensation, and the execution of the firm's strategy. The inconsistency weakens the execution of its strategy, undermines the morale of employees, and leads to the chronic second-guessing of management.

Is the Strategy Clear or Muddied?

The value proposition that emerges from the bottom of the funnel is the blended mix of decisions over time and can be clear or muddy to employees and to buyers. A clear mixture coincides with a well-defined and effectively implemented strategy: the value proposition actually extended to buyers is the one intended by the seller. In contrast, a muddied mixture (strategy) results from decisions that are not commonly directed by the firm's competitive strategy. A muddied mixture leads to unhealthy debate because coworkers do not agree upon weighted decision-making criteria.

A muddied strategy is difficult to overcome. A continuous stream of strategy-specific decisions and clear communications over time is necessary to overcome prior misjudgments and cleanse the mixture. Firms that have not consistently practiced strategy-specific decision making need time to reverse their fortunes. Managers do not gain credibility and clear the decision-making lens with one decision, no matter how emphatically they affirm a commitment to a course of action. There are no quick fixes to low morale, poor strategy execution, and ineffective marketplace positioning.

Issues Do Not Exist in Isolation

Figure 5.8 also indicates that individual choices do not exist in isolation. Each decision contributes to the mixture in the funnel and affects the value proposition that emerges. For example, a manufacturer's hiring choices interact with existing tools and equipment, compensation practices, and training regimens. The hiring choices must be assessed in terms of the compatibility with other decisions. The same is true of a car manufacturer's decision to upgrade the size and performance of a particular vehicle. This decision interacts with other choices and affects the mixture in the funnel. Is the decision compatible with other choices? This question is complex and requires consideration of, for example, the compatibility of the upgrade with the firm's tools and equipment, materials and labor's training, and skill set.

Gelle's Building Products: Consistent Decisions

Assuming Gelle's competes on the basis of an easy payment policy, many operating decisions must complement this strategy. Extending favorable credit terms drains cash. Therefore, all cash management practices must be designed to accommodate the firm's collections policy. Gelle's tries to minimize debt and prefers equity financing.

Continuous Flow of Decisions

The mixture that emerges from the bottom of the funnel (see Figure 5.8) is a continuous flow. Current choices mix with prior choices and affect the execution of the value proposition. Inconsistent decisions muddy the mixture; their influences persist, and they are difficult and time consuming to overcome. Strategy-specific decisions clear a muddied mixture over time, and a continuous stream of strategy-specific decisions improves the execution of the strategy, the firm's competitiveness, and financial performance.

Consistency

Because individual decisions interact, decisions must be consistent to execute effectively the firm's strategy. For example, the technical proficiency of a product is determined by a set of choices, including product design, the selection of material inputs, and labor force skills. Consistent decision making is a difficult management problem. The same weighted criteria must be applied over time, by different people, and in different parts of the organization.

Gelle's Building Products: Complete Decisions

John Chudovas must be careful. The impending decision on the firm's accounts receivable policy is not a "stand-alone" action. The decision sends a message. Other issues will be affected by the decisions on the accounts receivable policy.

Completeness

Decisions must also be complete. Consider a firm who competes on price. Figure 5.9 indicates that production costs result from the interaction be-

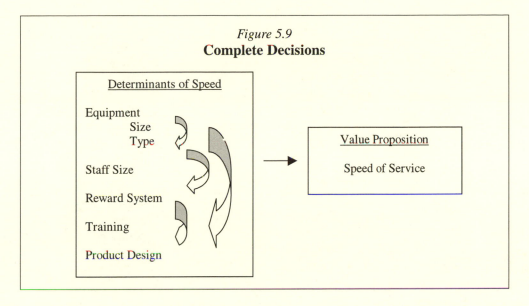

Figure 5.9
Complete Decisions

tween the firm's equipment, staff size, reward system, motivation, and product design. The individual linkages between these issues and costs and price are sensible. However, it is difficult to identify and to make a complete set of decisions. For example, the firm makes strategy-specific choices in product design, expends wisely on quality initiatives to lower labor and materials costs, and carefully manages labor costs. However, this firm fails to automate their plant to reduce labor costs. By not automating, the firm loses competitive strength relative to rivals who are able to make complete decisions.

Making a complete set of decisions is difficult for several reasons. First, managers must understand the full set of dependencies. This is not a simple task. It requires understanding the intricacies of the cause-effect relationships within their firm (see page 42). This challenge is also complicated by the distance (see pages 14–15) between individual decisions and the execution of the firm's strategy. For example, at Greene's Grocery the purchase of flooring materials seems

routine. At first glance, the decision appears to fall into cell III: nonstrategic/consensus (see page 41). While the association between the selection of flooring materials and the courtesy component of its value proposition is distant, the decision contributes to the execution of the strategy. Complete decisions are also financially challenging. At Greene's, nonskid, easy to clean, and attractive flooring materials are costly, especially while at the same time the firm is paying for a large inventory and staff.

Unintended Consequences

Figure 5.8 (see page 84) indicates that decisions interact, and the interactions determine the clarity of the competitive strategy that emerges from the bottom of the funnel. Given the interactions, managers are challenged to consider the unintended consequences of their decisions. In Figure 5.10, a technology firm increases R & D spending to add features to its primary product. However, there are unintended consequences: more calls to the help desk and a grow-

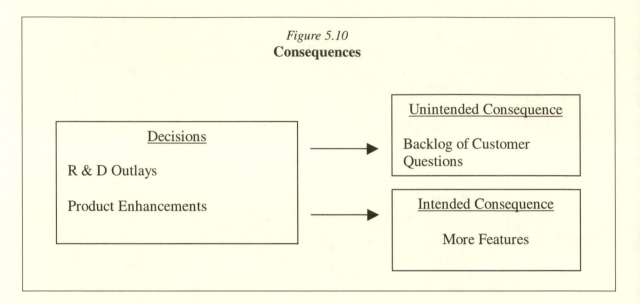

Figure 5.10
Consequences

ing backlog of requests for assistance. The failure to consider the unintended consequences leads to incomplete decisions and the ineffective execution of the firm's strategy.

Gelle's Building Products: Unintended Consequences

The easy payment policy may be intended to create a competitive advantage over rivals. However, an unintended consequence could be that the strategy attracts buyers who have weak cash flows or are bad credit risks. Inadvertently, Gelle's could be on a path that leads to an undesirable mix of customers.

The analysis highlights key themes:

- A firm's strategy emerges from its prior and current decisions.
- The strategy may be carefully executed through consistent and complete decisions or may be the end result of disjointed and inconsistently guided choices.

- Decision making is a continuous activity. The consistent application of a strategy lens over time and across an organization strengthens the competitive position of the firm and builds a cohesive management team.

Exercise 5.4

Identify an important decision in your firm, one with which you are familiar, school, case study, or simulation. Describe a consistent and complete set of decisions and possible unintended consequences.

A similar exercise is provided in the Instructor's and Student's Simulation Guide, question 17.

Summary

This chapter completes a measurable path from a firm's decisions to the execution of its competitive strategy and to the realization of financial returns. The decision-making methodology relies upon the firm's strategy as a lens, and the measurable path allows the firm to monitor the execution of its strategy.

Key Themes and Terms

Complete Decisions

Complete decisions occur when all operations, policies, and practices that contribute to a desired outcome are aligned. (See pages 86–87.)

Consistent Decisions

Consistent decisions align operations with the firm's strategy. Consistent decisions include responding the same way to the same problem at different times and to the application of a single strategic lens to different problems. (See page 86.)

Financial Performance Measurements

Financial performance is the lagged consequence of the design and execution of the firm's strategy. (See page 82.)

Interim Outcome Measurements

Interim outcome measurements monitor events between the execution of the value proposition and the realization of financial returns. (See pages 81–82.)

Interim Performance Measurement

Interim performance measures monitor the cause-effect sequence between decisions and the execution of the value proposition. (See pages 72–73.)

Performance Measurements

Performance measures quantify the execution of the firm's value proposition. (See pages 70–71.)

Unintended Consequences of Decisions

When considering a decision to achieve a desired outcome, strategy-specific decision makers ask the following: what else may happen? (See pages 87–88.)

Discussion Questions

1. Why is financial performance often a misleading indicator of the quality of a firm's decision making?
2. How can interim performance measurements be used as a diagnostic tool?
3. What is a muddied strategy? How can a muddied strategy be cleansed?
4. Discuss the importance of complete and consistent decisions.
5. What are the different categories of measurements, and why is it important to classify them properly?
6. Why are managers frequently second-guessed, and why is morale low in many organizations?
7. Why are employees often skeptical of new managerial initiatives?

End-of-Chapter Exercises

1. Refer to Case 2, Don Batts. Guide his data-gathering responsibility by using the following measurement concepts:
   a. Interim performance measures.
   b. Performance measures.
   c. Interim outcome measures.
   d. Financial performance measures.
   e. Feedback measures.
2. With reference to Rockwell's Health Club, Case 4, identify one heavily weighted variable in the firm's value proposition. Identify the areas of the firm that contribute to the execution of its strategy and develop a list of complete and consistent decisions.

3. Build an action plan to integrate strategy-specific decision making into your organization. Write a memo to your boss making the suggestion. If you are engaged in a simulation, direct the memo to your teammates.

4. Provide an example where individual decisions mix together and affect the value proposition actually delivered to buyers.

5. Find a print advertisement. What messages are implied about the firm's value proposition?

6. If you are engaged in a simulation, how is your firm structured to assure complete and consistent decisions? How are unintended consequences considered?

Notes

1. Paul R. Niven, *The Balanced Scorecard Step-by-Step* (New York: Wiley and Sons, 2002), p. 57.

2. Edward Russo and Paul J. H. Schoemaker, *Decision Traps: 10 Barriers to Brilliant Decision-Making and How to Overcome Them* (New York: Fireside Press. 1999), pp. 2–4.

3. Niven, *Balanced Scorecard Step-by-Step*, p. 66.

4. Ibid.

5. Larry Bossidy and Ram Charan, *Execution: The Discipline of Getting Things Done* (New York: Crown Business, 2002), p. 64.

6. Michael Porter, "What Is Strategy?" *Harvard Business Review* 74 (November–December 1996): 12.

7. James Heskett, Earl Sasser, and Leonard Schlesinger, *The Service Profit Chain* (New York: Free Press, 1997), p. 87.

8. David Maister, *True Professionalism* (New York: Free Press, 1997).

9. Heskett, Sasser, and Schlesinger, *The Service Profit Chain*, p. 95.

10. *Managing Customers for Profit* (Boston: Harvard Business School Press, 1998).

11. Heskett, Sasser, and Schlesinger, *The Service Profit Chain*, p. 126.

12. Roland Rust, Valerie Leithaml, and Katherine Lemon, *Driving Customer Equity* (New York: Free Press, 2000), pp. 3–5.

13. Marc J. Epstein and Robert A. Westbrook, "Linking Actions to Profits," *MIT Sloan Management Review* 42, no. 3 (Spring 2001): 39–50.

6

Strategy-Specific Decisions and Management Control Systems

The first five chapters established the concept of strategy-specific decision making and built a performance measurement system to guide and monitor the execution of a firm's strategy. This chapter integrates strategy-specific decision making into management control practices to improve the execution of a firm's strategy.

Upstream and Downstream Analysis

A firm's competitive strategy is defined by its theme-based and weighted value proposition, but the execution of the strategy cannot be mandated by management. An appliance manufacturer that competes on the basis of product durability cannot rely upon issuing orders to their employees to execute the strategy. Rather, the advantage based upon low maintenance costs and a long useful life is the result of effective decisions involving product design, procurement, equipment selection, inspection system, quality control practice, training, personnel selection, and compensation plan.

Downstream analysis applies a strategic lens to assess options and make decisions that execute the firm's value proposition. For example, the appliance manufacturer must select an electrical system for one of its refrigerators. Several options are available. Electrical systems differ by manufacturing costs, life expectancy, the technical demands placed on workers, reliability, and ease of installation. Each criterion makes sense. However, trade-offs exist, and a strategy lens is needed to make a selection. The manufacturer chooses an electrical system based upon its contribution to the life expectancy of the appliance. Given the firm's competitive strategy, extending the useful life of the product takes precedence over, for example, reducing costs or improving the aesthetics of the appliance. A manufacturer who brings a different value proposition to market appropriately chooses another electrical system.

Gelle's Building Products: Strategic Lens

John Chudovas received conflicting advice about the management of the accounts receivable. Each recommendation is reasonable. John needs a strategy lens to evaluate the options.

Upstream analysis applies strategy-specific decision making to shape its marketing initiatives. For the appliance manufacturer, the marketing message can emphasize price, delivery time, life expectancy, or operating costs. Promotional pieces can be placed in different media outlets. The firm can choose among alternative vendors, mixes of inside and outside sales personnel, print media, electronic advertising, trade show displays, and outbound logistical systems. Given the manufacturer's competitive strategy, marketing messages emphasize durability and are placed in appropriate media formats. Vendors are chosen by the fit between their buyers' expectations and the manufacturer's product.

Firms that consistently apply a strategy-specific decision lens both downstream and upstream realize several benefits.

- Internal discussion is focused; only strategy-specific argument is relevant.
- Healthful debate is facilitated and unhealthy debate discouraged.
- Functional area operations are integrated around the common requisites of implementing the firm's competitive strategy.
- Problems are detected before the firm's financial performance deteriorates.
- Managerial stress levels and second-guessing are reduced and morale improves.
- Internal and external communications present clear and consistent themes.
- The firm's competitive strategy is effectively executed, strengthening its competitive position.

Practicing Strategy-Specific Decision Making

Organizational Structure

Organizations are groups of people who work together to achieve common objectives, and strategy-specific working relationships help to achieve the common purpose efficiently and effectively.[1] However, organizational structures and practices sometimes create impediments. Strategy-specific working relationships remove bureaucratic obstacles, coordinate activities across an organization and over time, and yield complete and consistent decisions that execute the firm's competitive strategy.

Organizations divide work to capture the benefits of specialization and the division of labor. However, once work is divided, coordination problems arise. Building a product, completing a complex service, or preparing a team presentation involve more than assembling specialized contributions. Coordination requires aligning each component with the firm's strategy and assembling them into a complete and cohesive final product.

Complex organizations build hierarchies and control systems to align the work of specialists. Figure 6.1 displays a common organizational structure that divides work by function. Reporting to the CEO are vice presidents of each major functional area of the firm. In turn, for example, directors of training, employee benefits, and regulatory compliance report to the vice president of human resources.

A functional structure works well in a firm that offers a single product or a narrow group of products. A senior officer coordinates the functional specialists. However, risks abound. One danger is that each operating area defines its performance responsibilities and their own objectives to take precedence over the execution of the firm's strategy. Decisions are neither consistent nor complete. Over time, problems compound as the strategy lens gets cloudier. A second danger is that reporting channels create a bureaucracy that is slow to respond to changes in technology, buyer preferences, or competitor initiatives while pushing decisions uphill and away from those closest to and most knowledgeable about a process, client, or problem.

Multidivisional structures are appropriate in firms that are diversified by either product groups or geography.[2] Reporting to the chief executive officer (CEO) are product (or regional) managers. In this structure, two critical coordination challenges arise. First, the firm needs a mechanism to allocate scarce organizational resources among its divisions. Second, multidivisional firms must define the intended relationships between its divisions.

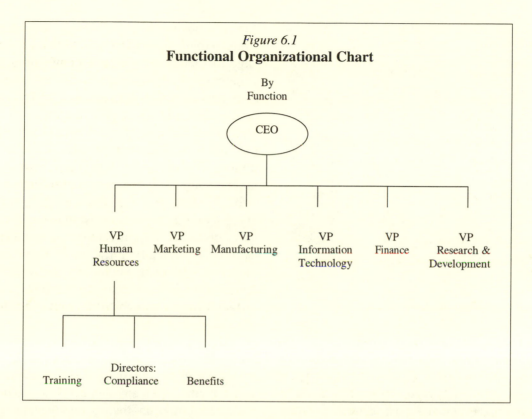

Figure 6.1
Functional Organizational Chart

By Function

CEO

VP Human Resources | VP Marketing | VP Manufacturing | VP Information Technology | VP Finance | VP Research & Development

Directors:
Training   Compliance   Benefits

Matrix structures arise in a large and complex organization where multiple products and projects require skills and resources from diverse parts of the organization.[3] Within a matrix organization, multiple reporting structures develop; for example, functional area operations serve multiple products. Engineering staff report to a vice president for product development and also to project managers.

Regardless of an organization's structure, management guides and coordinates individuals and specialized units to execute the firm's strategy. As discussed in chapter 1 (see pages 9–14), the required guidance and coordination is strategy-specific. For instance, the restaurant that emphasizes speed of service designs individual activities to serve quickly a standardized product. This restau-rant requires minimal coordination between work-stations that cook and that assemble an order, though a manager assures that the workflow between stations is appropriate for the volume of customers. In contrast, the custom-focused sandwich restaurant differently designs individual activities, and this restaurant depends upon effective communication between order takers, cooking crews, and assemblers.

- Decisions must be consistent across operating areas and over time to execute a firm's strategy.
- Decisions must be complete to execute effectively a firm's strategy.
- The coordination responsibility includes anticipating the *unintended consequences* of decisions.

Exercise 6.1

For your employer, a firm with which you are familiar, or your firm in a case study or simulation, draw an organizational chart. In addition, do the following:
1. Delineate responsibilities and assign tasks.
2. Explain how the structure facilitates consistent and complete decision making.
3. Explain the processes and mechanisms for allocating resources among competing uses.

A similar exercise is provided in the Instructor's and Student's Simulation Guide, question 10.

Cross-Functional Teams

Cross-functional teams facilitate making *consistent* and *complete* decisions and anticipate *unintended consequences*. Cross-functional teams comprise individuals representing different areas of an organization that form a standing or ad hoc group.[4] The specific composition of a team depends upon the task and the strategy-specific dependencies between individuals and departments. By nature and purpose, cross-functional teams bypass the constraints of the vertical chain of command to improve collaboration across lines of authority.

In building cross-functional teams, managers consider:

- Who contributes to an outcome?
- Who is affected by a decision?
- What else may happen?

Figure 6.2 builds a cross-functional team around the requisites of implementing the firm's strategy. The figure refers to Greene's Grocery, and the breadth of selection component of their value proposition is measured by the number of stock-keeping units (SKUs). The team is responsible for managing the number of SKUs and is comprised of representatives of each operating area that contributes to executing the firm's value proposition and those who are affected by it. Decisions involving procurement, finance, logistics, and human resources (HR) execute this component of the firm's value proposition. The number of SKUs impacts information systems (who must manage the data involving invoices and price), finance (who must manage the firm's cash, given its large inventory), and marketing (who must attract Type I Buyers). Some departments are both contributors to a decision and affected by it (such as HR and procurement), though different individuals may be responsible for the specific functions.

Students, developing managers, and employees frequently engage in team projects. Teammates often divide the project into discrete components. One team member does the finance and accounting, another is responsible for the marketing issues, and another tackles the personnel concerns. These teams operate as if in a functional organizational structure (see Figure 6.1). However, these teams cannot overlook the critical responsibilities of management. Someone must assure that the individual assignments are completed on time, in accord with the firm's strategy, and assembled into a complete and consistent report.

Management Control Systems

Strategy-specific decisions make operational a firm's value proposition, and the practice of strategy-specific decision making occurs through ongoing management control systems. Strategic control systems guide and monitor the execution of a firm's strategy.[5] Strategy-specific decision mak-

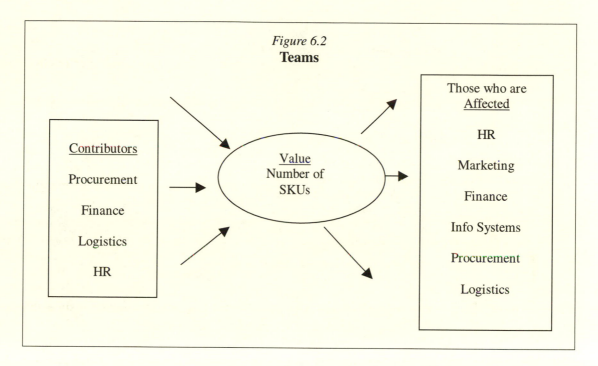

Figure 6.2
Teams

ing is integrated into the following management control systems:

- Strategic planning
- Performance reviews and audits
- Sales forecasting
- Financial planning and control systems
- Scheduling and work flows
- Human resource management
- Information systems
- Continuous improvement initiatives
- Building an organizational culture

Strategic Planning

Most organizations engage in strategic planning, though formality, sophistication, scope of participation, and ongoing commitment to the process vary widely.[6] Strategic planning involves more than a vision of the firm's future. Effective plan-

ning is action-oriented and directs the implementation of the firm's competitive strategy. The focus on execution of the firm's strategy implies four criteria for evaluating an organization's strategic plan: (a) a clear mission statement, corporate strategy, and line of business strategies, (b) a clearly stated value proposition for each narrow group of products, performance measurements, and target values, (c) operational guidelines for each functional area, and (d) time-specific action plans.

A useful outline for a firm's strategic plan is shown in Figure 6.3. In Part I, the firm's mission statement (see pages 51–54) is reviewed; the corporate-level strategy (see pages 12 and 136–142) and lines of business strategies (see pages 7, 18, 25, and 45) are stated. Each line of business strategy is translated into a theme-based and weighted value proposition. The strategy is assessed relative to the firm's abilities (internal

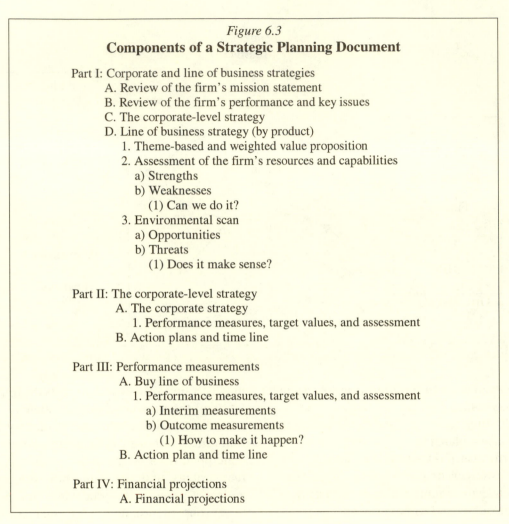

Figure 6.3
Components of a Strategic Planning Document

Part I: Corporate and line of business strategies
    A. Review of the firm's mission statement
    B. Review of the firm's performance and key issues
    C. The corporate-level strategy
    D. Line of business strategy (by product)
        1. Theme-based and weighted value proposition
        2. Assessment of the firm's resources and capabilities
        a) Strengths
        b) Weaknesses
          (1) Can we do it?
        3. Environmental scan
        a) Opportunities
        b) Threats
          (1) Does it make sense?

Part II: The corporate-level strategy
    A. The corporate strategy
        1. Performance measures, target values, and assessment
    B. Action plans and time line

Part III: Performance measurements
    A. Buy line of business
        1. Performance measures, target values, and assessment
        a) Interim measurements
        b) Outcome measurements
          (1) How to make it happen?
    B. Action plan and time line

Part IV: Financial projections
    A. Financial projections

analysis) and the compatibility of the firm's environments with that strategy (external analysis). Part II focuses on the corporate-level strategy, including the specification of the intended relationship between the product groups, performance measurement, and key operating decisions. Part III is completed for each narrow group of products and establishes performance measurements, target values, an action plan, and an assessment schedule. Part IV states financial projections.

Exercise 6.2

1. Obtain the most recent strategic planning report for your organization, one with which you are familiar, school, or firm in a simulation exercise. Evaluate the report in terms of the criteria stated above.
2. For those readers engaged in a simulation exercise, prepare a strategic plan for your firm.
3. Review and revise the plan after each round of the simulation.

Table 6.1
Performance Appraisal and Audit

Performance Measure	Target Value	Actual Value	Gap
Number of SKUs	4,300 units	4,290 units	– 10 units
Time to shelf	1.25 hours	2.45 hours	– 1.25 hours
Time in line	5 minutes	7.5 minutes	– 2.5 minutes

Performance Reviews and Audits

Performance reviews and audits assess the execution of a firm's competitive strategy. Audits are a continuous activity conducted on both a clock-time and strategic-time basis. Clock-time audits occur with the availability of data. For example, at Greene's the number of stock-keeping units (selection) is recorded at the end of each day, combined for a weekly average, and assessed relative to the target value. Similarly, the frequency of buyer repurchases is measured on a monthly basis and compared with its target value.

Strategic-time audits group and examine measurements in their cause-effect sequence. For Greene's, interim performance measures (percentage of on-time deliveries) are grouped separately from performance measures (number of stock-keeping units), interim outcome measurements (percentage of buyers who repurchase within one month), outcome measures (profit), and feedback measures (end-of-year cash balance). Grouping the data by strategic time reflects the cause-effect linkages from decisions to outcomes and helps to anticipate and diagnose problems.

Tables 6.1, 6.2, and 6.3 comprise a strategic-time audit for Greene's Grocery. The first column of Table 6.1 lists three performance measures from Greene's value proposition: the number of stock-keeping units (SKUs) (selection), time to shelf

(freshness), and time in line (courtesy). The other columns identify the target values, the actual performance levels, and the performance gaps.

The data are unambiguous. Greene's is not achieving the target values for its performance measures. The number of stock-keeping units is ten items below the target; the time to shelf is 1.25 hours longer than the target value, and the average time in the checkout line is 2.5 minutes longer than the target. Despite these problems, Greene's Grocery is profitable; it enjoys a favorable retail grocery market. If Greene's examines only outcome measures (profit and equity valuation), it is at risk. Changes in the rate of growth of industry sales, the entry of new competitors, or competitor upgrades can quickly alter the fortunes at Greene's.

The performance audit in Table 6.1 invites Greene's to take corrective action. But who or what is at fault? What can be done? Table 6.2 guides the diagnosis of the problem by examining interim performance measures for one performance measure: freshness. Similar tables examine the other performance measures: selection and courtesy. With reference to the freshness criterion, the interim performance measures include the timeliness of deliveries, the percentage of fully staffed crews, and labor productivity (see pages 72–73). The data in Table 6.2 indicate that Greene's exceeds its target for staffing its crews. The shortfall in labor productivity (three units per hour) is modest. The failure

Table 6.2
Interim Performance Measurements: Audit

Performance Measure	Interim Measure	Target Value	Actual Value	Gap
Time to shelf	Percent timely delivery	95%	80%	– 15%
	Percent fully staffed crews	90%	91%	+ 1%
	Labor productivity	200 units / hr.	197 units / hr.	– 3 units / hr.

to receive timely shipments is the culprit. Only 80 percent of the shipments are received as scheduled, fifteen percentage points below target.

Table 6.2 identifies that the lack of timely deliveries is the problem. But why are the shipments not received in timely fashion? The slow deliveries could be the result of poor vendor selection, the slow payment of invoices, poorly scheduled deliveries, or awkwardly located stores. Additional strategy-specific data is needed to correct this operational problem at Greene's.

Looking upstream from the execution of the value proposition, a performance audit of the interim outcome and outcome measurements provides additional insights. Table 6.3 refers to Greene's Grocery and one outcome measurement: the profit-to-sales ratio.

The first row of Table 6.3 indicates the firm seeks a 0.8 percent return on sales. But Greene's Grocery is realizing only a 0.5 percent rate. Before corrective action can be taken, Greene's must determine the cause by examining the interim outcome measures, including the repurchase rate, frequency of repurchase, the cost of goods sold, average bill, the number of new customers per week, and actual spending as a percentage of budgets. The data reveal that the firm is operating within established budget limits, but buyers are spending less than the target value per visit to

the store. The average bill is $22 below the target. Why?

The data does not provide a complete explanation. But Greene's Grocery is challenged by the following questions. Why are the buyer repurchase rate and the number of new buyers per month meeting targets, but the average shopper spends less per trip to the store than targeted? Is the shortfall a result of the firm's failure to meet its freshness standard? Or do buyers purchase nonperishable items from lower-priced retailers and freshness-sensitive merchandise from specialty shops? Additional study is needed.

Performance audits do not assure a firm's success. However, the audits provide the following benefits:

- The audits shift emphasis from assessing financial performance to evaluating the effectiveness of the execution of the firm's strategy.
- The audits establish a system of accountability tied directly to the execution of the firm's strategy.
- The audits define a road map of the events from decisions to financial performance. The expected cause-effect linkages permit managers to monitor the immediate consequences of their decisions and to diagnose problems.

Table 6.3
Outcome Measurement: Performance Review and Audit

Outcome Measurement	Interim Outcome	Target Value	Actual Value	Gap
Profit-to-sales ratio		0.8%	0.5%	– 0.3%
	Repeat purchase percentage	85%	85%	0
	Frequency of repurchase	1 per week	1.1 per week	+ 0.1 per week
	Average bill ($)	$75	$53	– $22
	Number new customers/week	20	21	+ 1
	Spending/budget	98%	96%	+ 2 %

Exercise 6.3

Build a performance assessment and audit process for your firm or firm in a case study or simulation. Be specific!

A similar exercise is provided in the Instructor's and Student's Simulation Guide, questions 2 and 14.

Sales Forecasting

Sales forecasting is a complex process. This section does not discuss mathematical forecasting techniques. Such is left to statisticians and econometricians. This section discusses the importance of accurate forecasts and builds a strategy-specific approach to sales forecasting.

A poor sales forecast creates many problems. Overly conservative projections result in too little production and lost sales. Importantly, lost sales allow rivals to attract new buyers, earn their loy-alty, and their repeat purchases. Lost sales involve the lifetime value of each customer captured by rivals. Optimistic forecasts generate other problems. Unsold goods drain cash, threaten a liquidity crisis, and depress a firm's stock price and bond rating. The adverse effects of unsold goods are not a one-time phenomenon. Unsold goods, poor profits, and liquidity constraints force firms to scale back intended product upgrades, training, quality initiatives, and marketing plans. In ensuing periods products lag those of rivals. At worst, unsold goods weaken the firm's execution of its strategy in ensuing periods and threaten the solvency of the business. At best, the firm needs several periods to implement a turnaround and improve its position relative to rivals.

Strategy-Specific Forecasting: Two Steps

Strategy-specific sales forecasting limits the amount of lost sales or unsold goods and involves two steps. The first step calculates a firm's potential sales: its current sales increased by the expected growth rate of the market. This calculation assumes the company maintains its market share. But this calculation is not the sales forecast. Rather, it is a first step and reality check. Potential sales do not consider the effects of changes in price, competitor initiatives, product upgrades, changes in buyer expectations, or changes in marketing. However, potential sales are a reality check, and a sales forecast that deviates from the potential must be explained by the second step of the forecasting process.

Exercise 6.4

1. Based on current market share and the market's expected growth rate, calculate potential sales by product and by time period.
2. Compare potential sales to current capacity. Identify the period for each product when capacity constraints become a problem.
3. When capacity constraints develop, what options are available to the firm? Identify the different costs.

A similar exercise is provided in the Instructor's and Student's Simulation Guide, question 7.

The second step examines the expected strength of a firm's strategy relative to rivals and to buyer expectations. It determines if and by how much sales are expected to deviate from the potential sales. This complex step involves two considerations. First, a company must anticipate the shift of buyer expectations and determine the attractiveness of its value proposition (see pages 19–24). Second, a firm must anticipate actions of rivals, including product upgrades, price changes, and marketing initiatives. This step allows a firm to determine if it is becoming a stronger or weaker competitor.

Offering, relative to rivals, a more favorable value proposition allows a firm to grow faster than its market; however, the firm must have enough units to sell. Therefore, the company must also evaluate its ability to produce and deliver the expected volume of goods. The same assessment must be made of rivals to determine if competitors face capacity or distribution channel constraints.

Gelle's Building Products: Competitive Advantage

Rebecca Green believes that the firm should reduce the time from receipt of an order to the delivery of the product. Assume Rebecca is correct and that changes are made. In turn, Gelle's believes that its relative competitive position will improve and its sales will grow faster than the market.

Figure 6.4 displays the analysis and refers to the general user's segment for desktop computers. Buyers are sensitive to the technical sophistication and price of competitive products. The asterisks (*) represent the price and sophistication coordinates of each product. The downward-to-the-right pattern of the asterisks indicates: (a) different firms offer different value propositions, and (b) the trade-off between price and technical sophistication.

The arrows slope upward and to the right and show the expected direction and magnitude of change in position for each product for the next selling period. Each firm knows the sophistication and price it intends to offer in the next period. Competitor intelligence anticipates the changes in price and sophistication of each rival. Competitor analysis is based upon the each rival's historic behavior, financial capability, and prior investments in R & D, products development, training, marketing initiatives, and cost reductions.

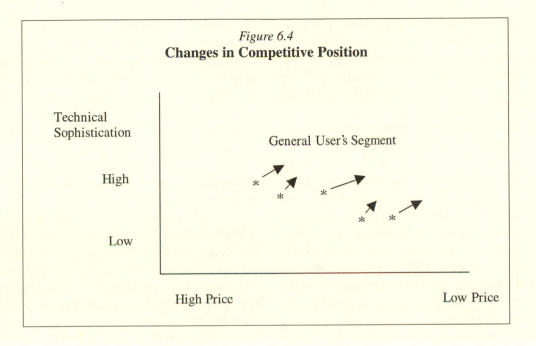

Figure 6.4
Changes in Competitive Position

As seen in Figure 6.4, each product is expected to become more sophisticated and lower priced, albeit at different rates. The different changes in price and technical sophistication indicate that some firms will become relatively more competitive while others will lose competitive strength. In turn, some companies will grow faster than the market while others grow slower.

Figure 6.4 is speculative. The actions of rivals are uncertain, though examination of their historic behavior and strengths and weakness clarify the range of options. The key idea is that anticipated changes in product attractiveness determine the firm's ability to grow faster than the market or constrain the firm to growing slower than the market.

Evaluating the Forecast

Sales forecasting, albeit critically important, is an imperfect science. Trying to anticipate buyer pref-erences, initiatives of competitors, and the economy as a whole is filled with risk and uncertainty. Regardless, forecasts must be made, and the review of each forecast is a learning opportunity. The review and assessment of a sales forecast is based upon the following considerations: the end-of-period inventory, the profit margin, marketing dollars expended, and competitor intelligence.

First, the end-of-period inventory partially reflects the accuracy of the forecast; however, a zero end-of-period inventory is not the objective. Stocking out of merchandise may mean that the firm (a) lost selling opportunities; (b) underpriced their product; (c) spent more than necessary in marketing. In contrast, excessive inventory may result from: (a) an overly optimistic forecast; (b) poor product positioning relative to rivals and buyer expectations; (c) overpricing or undermarketing; (d) an unattractive market characterized by an abundance of products; or (e) the incorrect anticipation of the actions of rivals.

The desired end-of-period inventory depends upon several factors, including the unit cost of production, the cost of storage, the good's loss of value over time, the firm's cash position, and the implicit interest costs of carrying inventory. An end-of-period inventory of approximately 5 to 7 percent of sales is an appropriate, albeit generalized, target.

Diagnosing the outcomes of a selling period helps the firm build skills. Looking back over the period to identify what was done correctly and what was done incorrectly helps decision makers improve their ability to forecast sales; manage inventory levels, cash, capacity, and marketing outlays; and price products. Over time, the organization that learns more rapidly than rivals and improves their management control systems gains a relative advantage.

Exercise 6.5

1. For those readers engaged in a simulation, what variables will you examine to evaluate your sales forecast?
2. Build a template to evaluate your products' positioning relative to rivals. Update the template after each round of the simulation.

A similar exercise is provided in the Instructor's and Student's Simulation Guide, questions 15 and 16.

Implications of the Forecast

A firm's sales forecast sets other forces in motion. Following Figure 6.5, the unit sales forecast combined with the unsold goods from the prior period and the desired end-of-period inventory determine the rate of production for the upcoming period. The firm's pricing decisions must be consistent with the unit sales forecast and market conditions.

The production and pricing plans allow the firm to forecast revenues and build budgets.

Budgets for the upcoming period are developed with the sales forecast. Budget development also responds to the cash and borrowing capacity that are the result of the firm's prior success. Budget development is considered in the following section.

Financial Planning and Control Systems

Budgets are resource allocation mechanisms that coordinate and control operations. Several different types of budgets exist. A *capital* budget specifies expenditures and sources of financing for plant and equipment, and capital budget analyses determine if, for example, a proposed capacity expansion is expected to yield a rate of return that exceeds the firm's cost of capital. *Operating* budgets allocate resources among functional areas, including marketing, information technology, and human resources and must be sufficient to execute the firm's strategy. *Cash* budgets allocate the firm's liquid assets to assure that funds are available at the right time.

A capital request for plant capacity, new or replacement tools, or the automation of an assembly line must be justified by a capital budget.[7] A capital budget compares the present value of the expected stream of earnings (or savings) attributable to an investment with its cost. A capital budget is based upon the cost of the new plant and equipment and the forecast of increased sales revenues and costs attributable to the investment. The net change in earnings per period over the life of the investment is discounted to present value at the firm's cost of capital. The investment increases the value of the firm only if the present value of the increase in earnings exceeds the cost of the investment.

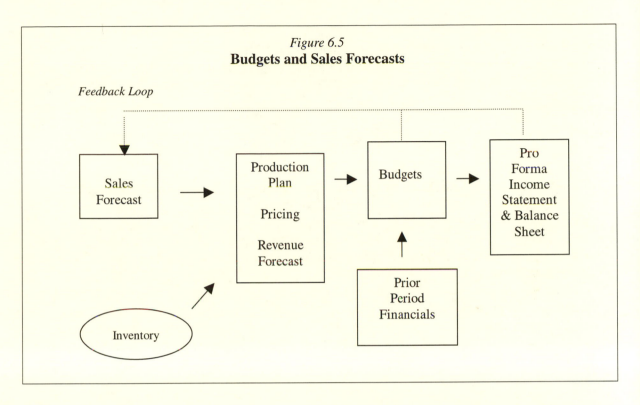

Figure 6.5
Budgets and Sales Forecasts

Exercise 6.6

For any capital project in your firm or firm in a simulation or case study, outline a capital budget to determine if the present value of the expected earnings exceeds the investment.

A similar exercise is provided in the Instructor's and Student's Simulation Guide, question 8.

Within many firms, operating budgets "bubble-up" from functional areas. Figure 6.6 indicates that functional area managers screen multiple options. For example, a marketing manager examines alternate spending options, including print advertising, trade show displays, and electronic marketing. Each option sounds good. At the same time, the human resources manager examines alternative compensation systems, leave policies, health insurance plans, and training programs. The strategy-specific assessment requires consideration of the opportunity costs, and a strategic lens prioritizes the options. The strategic lens assures each request meets strategy-specific needs.

Figure 6.6 indicates that budget requests are reviewed by higher levels of management who filter competing requests through a strategy lens. Requests for revisions may occur before the final allocations are determined. The final budget allocations are based upon a careful assessment of opportunity costs and consistent with the execution of the firm's strategy.

Table 6.4 (page 105) is a budget development tool that applies a strategy lens and links performance reviews and audits to the budget process. With reference to Greene's Grocery, the first two columns dis-

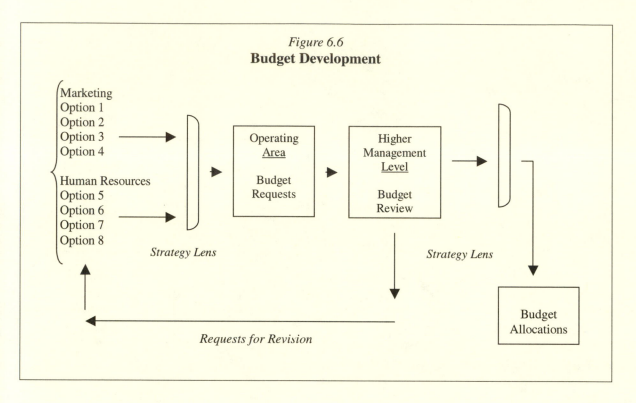

Figure 6.6
Budget Development

play weighted performance measures derived from the firm's value proposition. The measures include the number of stock-keeping units (selection), the time spent in the checkout line (courtesy), and time to shelf (freshness). For the upcoming budget year, Greene's sets a target value of 4,300 stock-keeping units. The target value is 300 units above the (current) actual number, reflecting a performance gap. Greene's Grocery is challenged to allocate resources to close this gap to execute effectively its competitive strategy.

The last two columns in Table 6.4 provide operational guidance. In the next to last, all of the operating areas that contribute to executing the value proposition and that are affected are identified. This step leads to complete and consistent decisions. The final column includes the dollar amounts needed to implement the intended value proposition. The re-

maining step requires decision makers to assess the opportunity cost of the proposed outlays.

The budget process is cumbersome. However, several benefits are realized:

- All requests must be justified in terms of the firm's competitive strategy to assure a consistent focus on the firm's strategy.
- By considering all that contribute and all that are affected, decisions and budget allocations are complete.
- Capital budget allocations meet the firm's cost of capital and raise the value of the firm.
- Non-strategy-specific requests are minimized and readily denied.
- Opportunity costs are assessed and resource allocations effectively implement the firm's strategy.

Table 6.4 Greene's Grocery						
Performance Measure	Percentage Weight (%)	Target Value (units)	Actual Value (units)	Gap (units)	Those Who Contribute & Are Affected	Budget Action ($)
Number of SKUs	0.40	4,300	4,000	– 300	Finance Procurement Human Resources Information Technology	Dept: $ Dept: $ Dept: $ Dept: $
Time in line	0.30					
Time to shelf	0.30					
Total	100%					

Pro Forma Financial Statements

Upon completing the sales forecast and budgets for the following period, examining the pro forma financial statements offers a reality check. Pro forma statements are projections of what the financial statements will look like at the end of the forecast period, assuming the sales and expenditure forecasts are correct. Scrutiny of the pro forma financial statements allows the firm to examine, for example, the profit and cash implications of the forecast. Scrutiny of these statements requires target values for such variables as the ending cash position and profits. For instance, a firm may want the pro forma to show an end-of-period cash position of approximately 5 percent of gross sales in order to prevent a liquidity crisis if sales fall short of expectations. A larger percentage is appropriate if the firm lacks confidence in its forecast.

Following the review of the pro forma statement, revisions to the sales forecast, production schedules, prices, budgets, dividend payments, or borrowing can be made. However, changes must be made judiciously. Sales forecasts cannot be changed to improve the pro forma statement unless justified by the firm's competitive strengths; similarly, budgets cannot be cut to improve the financial statements if such changes undermine the execution of the firm's strategy.

Scheduling and Work Flows

Scheduling and work flow management systems are control mechanisms that coordinate parts of an organization. Work and information flows between departments must meet the requirements of implementing the firm's strategy. One aspect is timing. The flow of materials, information, and events must coincide with the firm's operations. For example, a manufacturer must effectively schedule procurement, the completion of intermediate-stage products, the assembly of final products, and outbound logistics.

Additional aspects of scheduling and work flows involve the coordination that leads to complete and consistent decisions. For a manufacturer, interdepartmental needs extend beyond schedules. Information, work in progress, systems, policies, and practices must compile to consistent and complete decisions that effectively execute the firm's strategy. Strategy-specific scheduling and work flow management necessitate answering the following questions:

- Who needs what from whom?
- When is it needed?

Scheduling and work flow coordination requirements are affected by a firm's decisions and can be a source of competitive advantage. For example, precise scheduling allows firms to deliver products more rapidly and/or to work on promised schedules. Both consequences improve the process quality component of the company's value proposition.

Human Resource Management

Human resources management issues are sensitive and often generate unhealthy debate. After all, there are many alternative, and rational, human resources management practices. Any decisions personally affect each employee, heightening levels of concern. Everyone has self-interest motives and an opinion. For instance, a professional services firm's compensation and reward system can assign different relative weight to seniority, equality, or performance. Performance can be measured in terms of gross billing, work quality, origination of new business, or contributions to the overall well-being of the firm. In the absence of strategy-specific human resource management to guide and explain decisions, unhealthy debate prevails.

Strategy-specific human resources management decisions follow triangle 3 (Coworkers) in the Cycle of Success (see Figure 6.7).

Figure 6.7 indicates that the requisite skills and attributes required to complete a job successfully are defined by the firm's strategy-specific operations. Even within the same industry, employees appropriate for one firm are inappropriate for another, given differences in their competitive strategies. These differences occur even if the job descriptions are similar. Consider two software development firms. One produces and supports standardized programs for nontechnical users whereas the other emphasizes state-of-the-art and customized products whose features respond to the expressed needs of buyers. The different competitive strategies require their programmers to hold a different skill and attribute set. A programmer may be effective for one employer but not another.

Hiring

Strategy-specific hiring applies weighted selection criteria based upon the firm's strategy. Table 6.5, for example, refers to a building supplies and home repair retailer whose competitive strategy heavily weights customer service. The deliverers of the service are front-line sales personnel who listen to customer needs, help them buy the right merchandise to complete a project, and teach them how to complete the project. For this firm, service is more than a process quality variable. Service interacts with the price variable in the value proposition because sales personnel help customers select the right merchandise; service also interacts with results as customers are instructed how to complete projects.

Gelle's Building Products: Type I Employees

Sandy Koopmans is well trained and competent. But she is a source of contention.

John Chudovas could be at fault. He may not clearly articulate the firm's competitive strategy, creating an environment conducive to unhealthy debate.

Alternatively, Sandy may be uncomfortable working without tight financial management practices. Despite her technical skills, she may be a poor fit with Gelle's competitive strategy.

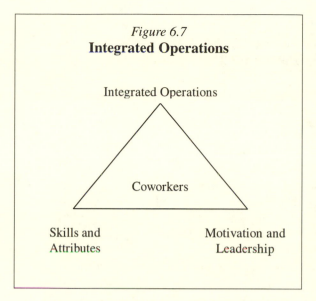

Figure 6.7
Integrated Operations

Integrated Operations

Coworkers

Skills and
Attributes

Motivation and
Leadership

For this firm, employee selection, training, and rewards are critical to the effective execution of the firm's competitive strategy, and Table 6.5 guides new employee selection by linking hiring criteria to the requisites of implementing the firm's strategy.

The first two columns show the firm's theme-based and weighted value proposition. The emphasis on customer service is reflected by the 50 percent weight assigned to process quality; however, this firm believes its process quality interacts with the results and price components of the value proposition. Given the firm's strategy, the requisite skills and attributes for a customer service representative include product knowledge and the ability and interest in teaching. The final column shows the percentage importance of each skill and attribute.

The hiring practice depicted in Table 6.5 (page 108) is an important management control system. An organization's claim that it seeks employees who fit in to its strategy is made operational by the selection process. The fit is defined in terms of the firm's competitive strategy, and strategy-specific hiring leads to Type I Employees: those who have the skills and attributes to implement the firm's strategy. If there is a lack of agreement about the company's strategy or the requisite skills and attributes, the organization is troubled. The process of selecting new employees is flawed, and the lack of consensus about the firm's strategy will manifest itself through unhealthy debates across the firm.

Figure 6.5 leads to an applicant screening device. Table 6.6 (page 109) refers to the building and home repair retailer. The first two columns list the weighted skills and attributes based upon the requirements to implement the firm's strategy. The next column provides space to score each candidate, using a ten-point system, where ten is the highest score and one is the lowest score. The final column is the product of the weight times the score. The products are summed and provide each applicant with a final score. The applicant with the highest score is chosen.

Strategy-specific hiring provides important benefits. The process assures fairness because each candidate is evaluated according to the same strategy-specific criteria. Also, the process assures that employee selection contributes to the firm-wide understanding of the competitive strategy, the clarity of the decision-making lens, and to the effective implementation of the strategy.

Table 6.6 does not eliminate the stresses of hiring new employees. Several complexities remain. Despite evaluating each candidate according to common criteria, subjectivity remains. Those engaged in the selection process may differently assess candidates. After all, different people see and react differently to common stimuli. Also, new employee selection is based upon incomplete and imperfect information and an uncertain future. However, strategy-specific hiring limits the range of debate.

Strategy-specific hiring is not a panacea. After hiring the right people, they must be trained, retained, motivated, and equipped. Therefore,

Table 6.5
From Value Proposition to Strategy-Specific Hiring
Customer Service Representative

Value Proposition	Percentage Weight (%)	Skills and Attributes	Percentage Weight (%)

Results
  Selection of
  merchandise
	0.25	Ability to recommend
		  appropriate products
			15

Process Quality
Service
  Helpful
  Return policy
  Teaching
  Encourages buyers
	0.50	Technical knowledge
		Inventory knowledge
		Patience
		Teach/Explain
		Work with multiple buyers
		Subtotal
			10
			15
			10
			20
			10
			65

Price
  Materials
  Credit
	0.20	Offers cost-efficient
		  solutions
		Wage requirements
			10

Cost of acquisition
  Time to service
	0.05	Complete explanations:
		  Others wait turn
			10

Total	100%		100%

consistent and complete decisions extend to compensation and training practices and to providing each employee with the tools needed to do their job effectively.

Exercise 6.7

For your firm, one with which you are familiar, or school, identify a job. List and weight the requisite skills and attributes, relating the skills and attributes to the firm's competitive strategy. In the candidate screening process, how are the skills and attributes evaluated?

Reward Systems

The weighted criteria system for hiring also applies to decisions regarding promotions, pay raises, and other rewards. In Table 6.7 (page 110) the skills and attributes and relative weights for a particular job are listed in the first two columns. The third column provides space to score each candidate on the job-specific criteria, applying a ten-point scale. The final column is the product of the relative weight multiplied by the score, and these products are summed at the bottom of the table. Rewards are based upon relative performance levels as determined by the firm's competitive strategy.

Strategy-specific compensation is a cumbersome process. It takes time to develop and apply the weighted scoring system. Rewards are merit-based, and merit is defined in terms of the firm's strategy. As with hiring practices, the crucial step involves agreeing upon the firm's competitive strategy and the association of the weighted skills and attributes of each individual.

| | | *Table 6.6* | |
| | | **Strategy-Specific Hiring Grid** | |
Skill/Attribute	*Percent Weight (%)*	*Score (1 = Low to 10 = High)*	*Product (Percent times Score)*
Technical knowledge	35		
Teach/Explain	30		
Patience	25		
Other: Ability to learn	10		
Total	100%		Sum =

The system described in Table 6.7 assures that a single set of evaluation criteria is applied to individuals in comparable positions. Rewards for different positions are based on weighted skills and attributes determined by the position's contribution to the execution of the firm's strategy. Subjectivity remains, but the strategy-specific process reinforces the firm's commitment to its competitive strategy, and strategy-specific rewards support a culture consistent with the requisites of implementing the strategy.

Compensation systems are not limited to pay and benefits. Success is recognized and rewarded in many different ways and also includes employee recognition awards, inclusion on work teams, and subtle signs of respect. For each reward, the selection criteria are strategy-specific. Because of the importance of rewards on the motivation and behavior of employees, they must be closely tied to the firm's strategy. The visibility and sensitive nature of compensation issues demands consistent, strategy-specific decision making.

Strategy-specific hiring and reward systems do not eliminate important differences between individuals in an organization. Everyone should not think and act alike. Different compositions of skills and attributes are useful, and the weighted skills and attributes allow employees to excel at different things. The range of differences is, how-

ever, limited by the requisites of executing the firm's strategy. For example, two staff accountants for a CPA firm differ according to technical skills, interpersonal skills, interest in developing younger professionals, writing skills, and client relations. But, assuming the hiring and rewards processes are managed correctly, neither staff accountant is weak in any area important to the execution of the firm's value proposition. At the same time, particular skills and attributes differ, and both accountants are expected to engage in healthy debate.

Exercise 6.8

1. For your firm, one you are familiar with, or a firm in a simulation exercise, describe the human resources practices. Assess its consistency with the requisites of executing the firm's strategy.
2. What changes do you propose?
3. Have the human resources practices favorably affected the execution of the firm's value proposition?

Coaching and Personnel Development

Coaching and staff development programs are control mechanisms because they reinforce ap-

	Percent Weight (%)	Score (1= Low to 10 = High)	Product (Percent times Score)
Table 6.7			
Strategy-Specific Compensation Grid			
Skill/Attribute			
Technical knowledge	35		
Teach/Explain	30		
Patience	25		
Other	10		
Total	100%		Sum =

propriate skills and behaviors within the firm. Coaching and personal development programs are not limited to large organizations. Coaching and development opportunities arise whenever large or small groups collaborate on a task. Someone must assume a strategic leadership role, and this responsibility includes assuring that participants understand the organization's strategy. Those who persist in offering non-strategy-specific positions must be coached and, if the attitude persists, replaced.

Gelle's Building Products: Organizational Cultural

The case provides only a few hints about the organizational culture at Gelle's. But, for John Chudovas's immediate staff, the current experience is unfavorable. The unpleasant and unproductive atmosphere is attributable to the lack of a common belief system.

Rules, Policies, and Procedures

Rules and defined procedures are a management control mechanism because they direct and limit employee behaviors. But organizations must define their rules and procedures in compliance with the execution of the firm's strategy. Con-

sider a financial services organization whose value proposition heavily weights enduring relationships between service providers and clients. Given the strategy, compensation policy rewards seniority and client retention. A firm that heavily weights process quality in their value proposition establishes rules that lead to the prompt return of phone calls and meeting promised schedules. A firm that emphasizes state-of-the-art products in their value proposition establishes policies that allow employees to stay current in their disciplines. Rules and procedures that are not strategy-specific constrain behaviors, but employees are likely to wonder why such rules are needed. In turn, non-strategy-specific rules may lead to unhealthy debates within an organization.

Information Systems

All management systems are dependent upon information, and information technology coordinates diverse parts of an organization by making information available. Accounting systems are one means through which data are collected and disseminated across an organization, and the timely access to information can be both management control and coordination and a vital element to implement a firm's strategy. For example, a firm's ability to gain a relative advantage based upon process quality may depend upon customer service reps having immediate access to client data.

A firm's information system is also a key ingredient in its ability to monitor the effectiveness of the execution of its strategy and to diagnose problems. The sets of measurements in sequence from interim performance measurements to outcome and feedback measurements are crucial to guide decision making. However, the ability to assemble this data in a timely manner is a result of the firm's information system, and the ability to design and manage a strategy-specific information system is a source of competitive advantage.

Continuous Improvement Practice

Continuous improvement practices fall under many labels, including Total Quality Management and Six-Sigma Processes, and are a management control system.[8] Continuous improvement processes are methods for responding to the myriad of factors that affect a firm's success. One aspect of this coincides with performance audits (see page 97). In addition to determining if target measures have been met, they identify and assess the activities that contribute to the execution of the firm's strategy.

A second aspect of continuous improvement practices are forward-looking and coincide with the periodic revision of target values for performance measures. The practices anticipate changes in buyer requirements and competitor capabilities, revise the target values, and redesign activities across the firm to facilitate meeting the revised targets. Effective continuous improvement practices help the firm alter the trade-offs in its value proposition by finding new processes or tools.

Building an Organizational Culture

Strategy-specific decision making builds an organizational culture aligned with the requirements to execute the strategy, and the culture affects individual behaviors. Where a strong corporate culture exists, behaviors are modified, and each individual has the opportunity to "nag" their colleagues. A strong corporate culture mitigates the need for rules because everyone knows their responsibilities. Furthermore, no rule book can address all situations. A strategy-based culture provides proper guidance, even when no formal rule is in place, and the culture becomes a self-reinforcing control mechanism.

Summary

This chapter developed the strategy lens as a decision-making tool. Each day, large and small organizations make many decisions. Some are small and seemingly inconsequential; others are more complex and daunting. But the clarity of the firm's strategy and the effectiveness of the execution of that strategy depend upon the degree to which a common strategy lens is applied. A carefully articulated strategy facilitates decision making because competing ideas are evaluated on the basis of agreed upon criteria.

Students or trainees who are engaged in case study analysis of a management simulation are urged to practice strategy-specific management control systems. The decision-making procedures discussed over the preceding pages require more work than seat-of-the-pants actions. But, the discipline of evaluating and explaining choices in terms of the firm's strategy pays enormous dividends. Wise choices are made, and a culture is built to sustain the focus on implementing the strategy. Accordingly, explaining a decision becomes a simple task.

Key Themes and Terms

Management Control Systems

Management control systems refer to day-to-day operations and practices through which the firm conducts its business, including budgeting, hiring, and rewarding personnel. (See pages 94–111.)

Strategic Planning

Strategic planning is the periodic review of the firm's intentions to gain a competitive advantage over rivals. Strategic planning is made operational when management selects performance measures that reflect the firm's value proposition and actions are guided in terms of the requisites of implementing the strategy. (See pages 95–96.)

Discussion Questions

1. Do you think strategic planning leads to superior financial performance?
2. Would you choose a job based on the employer's mission statement?
3. What are the obstacles to applying the strategy lens to management control practices?
4. Why are budgets an essential management control system?
5. Distinguish between operational effectiveness and competitive strategy. Why are both vital to a firm's success?
6. What are the benefits of strategy-specific management control practices? What difficulties are expected while trying to implement strategy-specific controls?
7. Why is it important to forecast sales?
8. Discuss the variables and conditions to evaluate a sales forecast.
9. Discuss the problems of designing and implementing strategy-specific human resources practices.

End-of-Chapter Exercises

1. Prepare a memo to Timothy Ryan (see Case 7). Indicate which of the three candidates you propose hiring and why. Offer additional advice as appropriate.
2. Assume the role of Timothy Ryan. Prepare a memo to your boss. Forward your recommendation with explanation.
3. Refer to Case 5, Specialo and Family.
   a. Develop an annual review program and propose an annual compensation adjustment system.
   b. Assume Raymond Specialo has allocated $20,000 for salary increases for the managers. Distribute the monies among these employees.
   c. Draft, for Raymond, two memos. First, write to all employees and describe the compensation system. Second, write to each of the managers, stating their pay increase and the justification.
4. Refer to Case 4, Rockwell's Health Club. Draft the following:
   a. A mission statement.
   b. A theme-based and weighted value proposition.
   c. A set of performance measurements.
   d. List interim outcome measurements.
   e. Discuss the ways in which items (a) through (d) are used as management decision-making tools.
5. For Rockwell's Health Club, Case 4, develop a strategic lens to filter the budget requests.
6. Obtain the most recent strategic plan for your organization or school. Evaluate the plan.

Notes

1. Gregory Bounds, Gregory Dobbins, and Oscar Fowler, *Management: A Total Quality Perspective* (Cincinnati: South-Western Press, 1995), p. 276.

2. Michael Hitt, R. Duane Ireland, and Robert Hoskissin, *Strategic Management,* 2nd ed. (New York: West Publishing, 1996), pp. 342–75.

3. Samuel C. Certo and J. Paul Peter, *Strategic Management* (New York: Random House, 1988), pp. 125–29.

4. Charles W.L. Hill and Gareth R. Jones, *Strategic Management Theory: An Integrated Approach*, 5th ed. (Boston: Houghton Mifflin, 1999), pp. 407–411.

5. Hill and Jones, *Strategic Management,* p. 420.

6. Cornelius A. De Kluyver, *Strategic Thinking* (Upper Saddle River, N.J.: Prentice Hall, 2000), p. 7.

7. J. Fred Weston and Eugene F. Brigham, *Managerial Finance,* 7th ed. (Hillsdale, Ill.: Dryden Press, 1978), pp. 394–451.

8. John A. Pearce and Richard B. Robinson Jr., *Strategic Management* (New York: McGraw Hill, 2002), pp. 330–34.

7

From Value Proposition to Outcomes

Chapters 1 to 4 established the concept of *strategy-specific decision making* and built a performance measurement system to guide and monitor the execution of a firm's strategy. In chapters 5 and 6 the strategy lens guided *complete* and *consistent* decision making and considered the *unintended consequences* of managerial choices. In chapter 6, strategy-specific decision making was integrated into management control practices to direct *downstream* decisions that execute the firm's value proposition. This chapter applies strategy-specific decision making *upstream*. Beginning from the firm's value proposition, upstream analysis defines the firm's Type I Buyers, and strategy-specific decisions determine the place and promotion aspects of the marketing mix. Interim outcome measures monitor the execution of the firm's strategy in sequence from the firm's value proposition to its financial returns.

Upstream Analysis

Overview

Figure 7.1 repeats the schematic depicting *upstream* and *downstream* analysis (see page 71) to establish the context for this chapter. For brevity and simplicity, the analysis of Figure 7.1 is divided into five steps, rather than the nine steps in chapter 5.

Step 1: From Mission to Performance Measures

Reading from the top of Figure 7.1, the analysis begins with the firm's mission statement and moves to its subsequent translation into a theme-based and weighted value proposition. For Greene's Grocery, the mission statement (see page 51) emphasizes the freshest meats and produce, widest selection, and utmost courtesy. The value proposition defines the firm's strategy, and performance measures quantify the execution of the strategy (see pages 55 and 57).

For Greene's Grocery, performance measurers include the number of stock-keeping units, time to shelf, and the average number of minutes in the checkout line. From the left side of Figure 7.1, strategy-specific downstream decisions execute the firm's strategy, and these decisions include the selection of vendors, staff size, the management of accounts payable, the number of hours of training, equipment selection, procurement practices, shelf space allocations, compensation, and motivation practices (see page 63).

From the left side of Figure 7.1, the effects of strategy-specific downstream decisions are initially observed in interim performance measures (see pages 74–76). For Greene's Grocery, the initial effects of selecting vendors, choosing the size of the staff, and the selection of equipment include

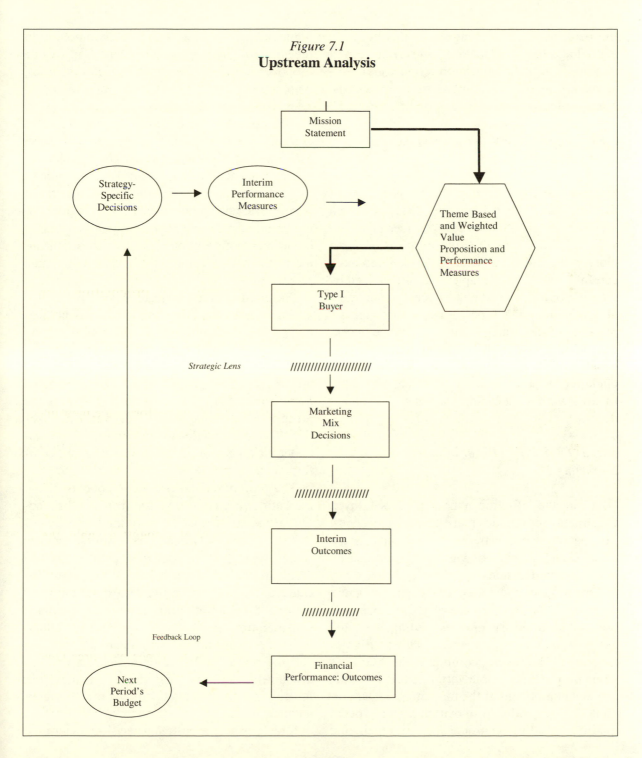

Figure 7.1
Upstream Analysis

the percentage of stocking crews that are fully staffed and the percentage of deliveries received on time. In turn, the value proposition leads to performance measures, including freshness and the breadth of selection.

Step 2: From Value Proposition to the Type I Buyer

Upstream analysis begins from the execution of the firm's value proposition. The first step upstream identifies the firm's Type I Buyers (see page 79), who are those whose value proposition most closely align with the seller's. As explored more carefully later in this chapter, they are defined by their use of the product and by demographic variables. Defining the Type I Buyer extends the application of the strategic lens to allow the firm to market its product efficiently and effectively. The benefits of a high percentage of these buyers include repeat purchases, referrals, and the ability to work within established activities and procedures.

Step 3: From Type I Buyer to the Marketing Mix

Following the definition of the firm's Type I Buyer, the strategy lens guides marketing mix decisions. The marketing mix is frequently referred to as the four Ps[1] and consists of variables controlled by management decisions.[2]

This product component of the marketing mix refers to important features: quality, technical precision, durability, options, styling, size, and ease of use of a good or service. These variables are part of the results component of the firm's value proposition. Some variables related to the product component of the marketing mix are included in the value proposition under process quality, including technical support, repair, and

maintenance services. The price component in the marketing mix is also part of the firm's value proposition and includes the list price, discounts, maintenance costs, credit terms, and the operating costs.

The promotion component of the marketing mix comprises activities that inform buyers, raise awareness, and sustain interests. They include selecting from advertising, personal selling, publicity, and other options. Promotion variables make buyers aware of a product and contribute to building brand identity and buyer loyalty. By building brand recognition, promotion decisions contribute to the results component of the firm's value proposition.

Place considerations make a good or service available at the right time and in convenient locations. Place decisions include selecting from distribution channels, account management, the selection of locations, geographic coverage, inventory management, and transport system options. Some aspects of the place variables are part of the process quality component of the value proposition. The favorable location of an office or retail outlet makes a transaction easier and more comfortable to complete.

The promotion and place components of the marketing mix consist of the firm's selling activities and are directed toward the firm's Type I Buyers. Greene's Grocery, for example, selects its advertising message and media outlets to communicate with its Type I Buyers. Stores are located and hours of operation established to meet their needs. For other firms, promotion and place considerations include the selection of vendors, the mix between inside and outside sales personnel, the relative reliance upon distributors and account management, and the logistical system for moving finished goods to buyers in a timely manner.

Strategy-specific upstream decisions determine

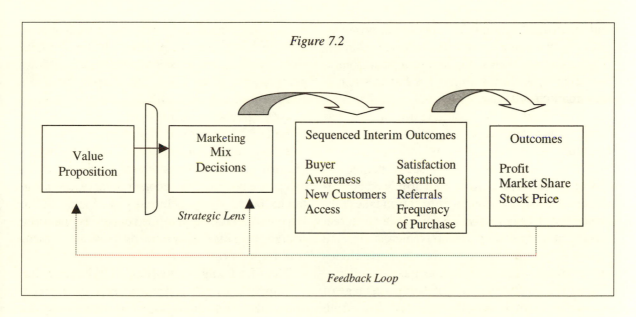

Figure 7.2

the marketing mix and yield important benefits that include the following:

> *Marketing is efficient:* Costs are minimized because promotion and place activities are targeted and directed toward the Type I Buyer. Efficiency measures include gross sales revenue per marketing dollar and product awareness per marketing dollar.

> *Marketing is effective:* Promotion and place decisions direct strategy-specific messages to the most likely buyers of the firm's good or service. Effectiveness measures include the percentage of Type I Vendors, access to the product, and the number of Type I Buyers reached per marketing dollar expended.

The discussion of downstream and upstream analyses suggests the decisions are made separately and in a time sequence. This view is a useful simplification but incorrect. Many decisions are both upstream and downstream at the same time. For example, a manufacturing firm offers a product with features and a price similar to competitors. To gain an advantage, the firm's competitive strategy emphasizes the ease of access to its products. The firm's

exemplary vendor and distributor relationships result from downstream decisions (to achieve process quality) and upstream decisions (that execute the marketing mix). Similarly, a textile company competes on style and image. Its promotion decisions create real or imaginary product differences to enhance the results component of the firm's value proposition. In both examples promotional decisions are upstream and downstream. The decisions contribute to the effective delivery of the firm's value proposition and the marketing of the product. Recognizing that some decisions are both is not surprising. The overriding theme of strategy-specific decision making is that choices across a firm are commonly directed.

Step 4: From Marketing to Interim Outcomes and Financial Performance

Promotion and place decisions execute the firm's selling efforts and lead to the firm's financial performance. However, as displayed in Figure 7.2, events occur between marketing mix activities and the firm's financial performance. *Interim outcome measurements* occur in sequence. Gaining buyer awareness, attracting new buyers, and building distribution channels precede buyer satisfaction, repurchases, and the referral of new buyers.

All firms do not monitor the same interim outcome measures nor assign equivalent importance to common measurements. While every firm is interested in the number of new clients per month, this measure is compelling for a firm in an emerging market whereas customer retention takes precedence in mature markets. Similarly, a restaurant located at a highway rest stop is interested in the percentage of travelers that stop to make purchases and the percentage of repeat purchasers. This restaurant is not concerned about their percentage of a customer's total spending on meals away from home. In contrast, a CPA firm that focuses on integrated tax, financial planning, and investment management is concerned with their percentage of a client's financial services spending.

Step 5: Feedback

The feedback loop from the firm's financial performance to strategy-specific decisions results in spirals of organizational success or failure. Successful firms direct earnings from one year to execute their strategy in the following year. Successful firms make a complete set of decisions to continue to earn superior returns. Feedback measurements include the firm's ability to raise funds (debt-to-equity ratio, times interest earned, the price-to-earnings ratio, and the bond rating), new products under development, buyer awareness, employee productivity and loyalty, and customer satisfaction.

The Fifth P

The marketing function facilitates meeting the firm's financial objectives by achieving profitable sales. Marketing managers make many decisions, and the traditional perspective involves the four Ps of the marketing mix. The analysis that follows pursues an expanded path based upon the Cycle of Success and adds a fifth P (practices), referred to as *integrated operations*.

Figure 7.3 reproduces Triangle 1 of the Cycle (see page 26). The upper corner of this triangle is the firm's competitive strategy, expressed by its value proposition. The second corner targets a particular buyer group, referred to in Figure 7.3 as buyer expectations. The third corner is integrated operations. This corner extends the analysis to the fifth P (practices).

The fifth P aligns activities with the requisites of implementing the strategy, including downstream decisions that lead to the execution of the firm's value proposition and the upstream marketing and logistical decisions that deliver the right messages to the right buyers and get the goods or services in the right places at the right time.

To highlight the strategy-specific aspects of the fifth P, consider a small manufacturer of exterior metal-based lighting fixtures, railings, and decorative items.[3] In its early years, the firm manufactured a small number of standardized products. The products were sold through small family-owned hardware stores, and nonexclusive field reps were paid on commission. The products were fully functional, durable, traditional in design, and inexpensive.

Gelle's Building Products: Practice

Gelle's results include product durability, weather resistance, and ease of installation. Price includes the accounts receivable policy.

Rebecca Green wants to accelerate the delivery of orders. Quicker delivery is a place variable, and Rebecca's proposal would alter the firm's value proposition.

(continued)

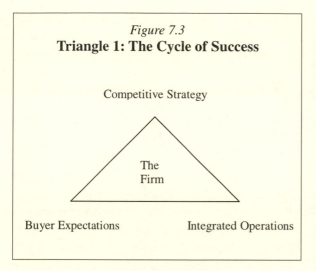

Figure 7.3
Triangle 1: The Cycle of Success

Competitive Strategy

The
Firm

Buyer Expectations   Integrated Operations

Adopting Rebecca's suggestion requires changing many of the firm's practices. Manufacturing would have to adapt to shorter production runs; outbound logistics would have to respond to less than full truckloads.

Given the firm's strategy, the manufacturing department emphasized long production runs to minimize production costs. In the sales department, the reps made periodic visits to retail accounts to take orders and restock inventory. The reps did not require intensive product training; territories were large because field reps spent little time with individual accounts, and quotas were established in relation to a territory's population and income. Aside from submitting orders promptly and in accord with established company procedures, the field reps required little communications with the home office or other functional areas of the firm.

Over time, the growth of large home building product retailers put many family-owned hardware stores out of business. The manufacturer lost its distribution channel, and its small size prevented it from capturing shelf space at the large retail outlets. As a result, it shifted its strategy from low-

priced standardized products to customized and highly priced items sold through real estate developers, architects, and custom builders. The change in strategy requires the redesign of the fifth P.

The product variables in the marketing mix change with the competitive strategy. Products are revised from standardized, low-priced items to customized shapes, size, designs, materials, and colors. Many operations are managed differently, including manufacturing practices, research and product development, inventory management, and the development of the firm's human resources. Pricing practices change with the costs of production, customization of the products, and competitiveness of the new market segment. Promotions are redesigned to present the new products to new buyers through different marketing channels. The standardized products were promoted through a catalog and the outside sales force made periodic visits to individual accounts. In contrast, personal selling efforts are needed to promote the customized product. Finally, place variables changed with the strategy. The standardized products were still sold through family-owned hardware stores, whereas the custom products are marketed through architects, home builders, and remodelers.

Practices

The strategy-specific change in practices, the fifth P, occurs across the firm and is highlighted by considering selected responsibilities of the sales manager, including the specification of sales territories, vendor selection and distribution channels, training, and employee selection.

Sales Territories

When selling standardized products, territories were large. Reps spent little time with individual accounts, and they served a large number of hardware stores. Under the new strategy, the personal selling requirements increase the time per account and shrink the appropriate size of the sales territories.

Vendor Selection and Distribution Channels

Under the original strategy of selling low-priced standardized products, the primary distribution channel was small family-owned hardware stores. Under the new strategy, customized products are sold through selective architects, builders, and developers. In addition to new selling channels, the sales reps need a new set of skills involving greater demands for product knowledge and the personal skills to interact effectively with new customers.

Training

When selling the standardized products, product knowledge requirements were limited. More extensive training is needed when the reps sell custom products to informed buyers. Also, sales reps need new tools to carry out their responsibilities. Under the old strategy, the reps submitted orders to restock a store's inventory. Under the new strategy, closer communications between sales rep and the home office is important to answer quickly buyer questions about production abilities, shipping dates, and prices. The new strategy also requires that the sales reps be equipped with contemporary communication devices to have access to production schedules, production capabilities, and the status of an order.

Employee Selection

Given the change in strategy, sales reps need a new set of skills and attributes. As training regimens change, so too do the hiring criteria. The designs of activities change to implement the new strategy.

The fifth P yields a holistic view of the firm. The firm's competitive strategy guides the design of all activities across the firm.

> ### Exercise 7.1
>
> Refer to your firm, one with which you are familiar, or a firm in a simulation, to describe the five Ps and evaluate the consistency.

Upstream Analysis and Trade-offs

Upstream decision making involves several trade-offs. As discussed in chapter 1, these occur when one action limits (or prevents) some other. For example, given existing materials and technology, reducing the weight of a vehicle increases fuel efficiency but reduces safety and comfort. The firm's competitive strategy prioritizes efficiency or safety and guides management's responses to the exchange. Several trade-offs occur in upstream decision making and involve prioritizing buyer groups and choosing from among alternative promotion and place options. The strategy lens that prioritizes fuel efficiency relative to safety also prioritizes upstream options.

Three such trade-offs are examined: (a) the selection of the Type I Buyer, (b) the nature of the buyer-seller relationship, and (c) the composition of the promotion and place components of the marketing mix.

Type I Buyers

Following Figure 7.1 (see page 115) the firm's value proposition leads to the definition of its Type I Buyer. For example, Greene's Grocery offers the widest selection, the freshest meats and produce, and the utmost courtesy. Greene's defines its Type I Buyer by demographics, including income, ethnicity, age, and education. The definition also includes product use variables, including the frequency of hosting family, friend, or business gatherings, the formality of meals, and the joys of preparing interesting meals.

In determining these buyers, a firm implicitly declares other groups to be less attractive. Non–Type I Buyers are more costly to attract and serve and are less likely to repeat their purchases. For example, grocery buyers whose value proposition emphasizes price may shop at wholesale markets. These consumers are unlikely to make frequent and substantial purchases at Greene's. Greene's strategy lens does not direct its promotion and place activities toward those unlikely to be loyal shoppers. The more carefully Greene's focuses promotion and place decisions, the more effective and efficient the marketing outlays.

Two questions facilitate defining the Type I Buyer: (a) What are the characteristics of the target buyers? (b) What are the benefits sought by the target buyer? Figure 7.4 highlights the questions.

Buyer characteristics are demographic variables, including age, income, sex, and ethnicity. Benefits-sought characteristics refer to the buyer's use of the product. For example, those who choose to fly on discount air carriers are defined by demographic characteristics, perhaps age and income. Alternatively, they are classified by the benefits sought: low price. Similarly, those who regularly consume yogurt products are defined by demographic variables or by dietary benefits sought. The two classifications overlap, but are not identical. Both approaches are important, though creativity and judgment are required to determine the most useful definition.

It is important for a firm to identify its Type I Buyers. The definition guides promotion and place decisions. However, the definition also facilitates evaluating the *design* of a firm's strategy. A firm's

strategic planning seeks superior and sustained returns; therefore, the target buyer group must be evaluated in terms of the profit potential. The following assessments are critical to evaluating the design of a firm's strategy:

- How large is the target buyer group?
- What is their purchasing power?
- How important is our value proposition to them?
- How rapidly do buyer preferences change?
- How stable are the buyers' needs and purchasing capabilities?

The questions imply that not all competitive strategies are equally attractive. Certainly, within any industry, value propositions differ in terms of the difficulties and costs of execution. But different value propositions appeal to buyers with different willingness and ability to make recurring purchases.

Exercise 7.2

Define the Type I Buyer for your firm, one with which you are familiar, school, or firm in a case study or simulation. Discuss the difficulties and inefficiencies associated with selling to non–Type I Buyers

A similar exercise is provided in the Instructor's and Student's Simulation Guide, question 12 .

Segmentation Analysis

The identification of the Type I Buyer involves segmentation analysis, a process that divides a market into groups. Segments are defined by demographic characteristics of buyers and/or by the benefits sought. For example, purchasers of a particular athletic shoe are defined by their age and

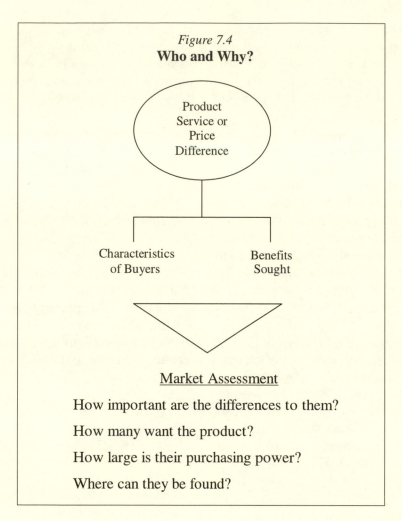

Figure 7.4
Who and Why?

Product
Service or
Price
Difference

Characteristics
of Buyers

Benefits
Sought

Market Assessment

How important are the differences to them?

How many want the product?

How large is their purchasing power?

Where can they be found?

income and/or by their use of the shoes and the benefits sought. Segmentation variables include the ones discussed below.

Demographics

One set of variables that segregates buyers is demographics. Buyer age, sex, ethnicity, income, education, occupation, marital status, family size, lifestyle, and religion are among those variables that differentiate buyers and may define Type I

Buyers. Each socioeconomic group exhibits different consumption patterns and responds differently to promotion and place decisions.

Geographic Variables

Geographic variables like climate, terrain, population density, cultural variables, and geography-determined lifestyle patterns contribute to the definition of Type I Buyers. Geographic segmentation guides promotion and place decisions.

Psychological Variables

These buyer differentiators include personality characteristics, lifestyle qualities, or personal values. If a product's price, characteristics, or service align with particular psychological variables, promotion and place are properly directed.

Behavioral Variables

Markets are also segmented by behavioral characteristics of buyers. These differences include determining who buys the product and uses it, and how a product is used. For example, purchasers of a motorcycle are defined by those who seek low-cost transportation or want a distinctive recreational vehicle.

Benefits Sought

Buyers are also defined by the benefits received. For example, a vehicle manufacturer's value proposition heavily weights acceleration. It requires spark plugs with particular capabilities. A high-performance spark plug manufacturer appropriately directs marketing efforts. Similarly, consider a manufacturer of exercise equipment. It distinguishes between workout enthusiasts who value product durability and caloric use versus buyers who want an easy-to-use and inexpensive device. Upstream decisions rely upon the definition to prioritize alternative promotion and place outlays.

Gelle's Building Products: Type I Buyers

The Type I Buyer can be defined in two ways, assuming their competitive strategy emphasizes flexible credit policies.

One definition is based on demographic variables, including the contractor's gross sales, geographic location, or years in business.

In terms of the benefits, Gelle's targets those contractors who compete for customers on the basis of convenient credit terms.

For Greene's Grocery, the commitment to offer the freshest meats and produce, the widest selection, and the utmost courtesy suggests that the Type I Buyer is defined by income and wealth. But the definition of this buyer is not limited to economic variables. Greene's commitment to offer the widest selection raises the possibility that particular racial and ethnic groups define the Type I Buyer. Other variables include age, education, dietary needs, frequency of entertaining at home, and gourmet lifestyles.

Greene's must be very careful how it defines its Type I Buyer. Different definitions necessitate different compositions of foods that comprise its widest selection of products. For example, the definition determines the mix of ethnic foods, dietetic, diabetic, and organic foods on the shelves. The selection of promotional messages and media outlets differ based upon the definition of the buyer. Doubtless, the size of the buyer group, the group's purchasing power, and the group's frequency of recurring need contribute to the assessment of the Type I Buyers.

Exercise 7.3

For your employer, firm with which you are familiar, or firm in a case study or simulation, briefly review the competitive strategy and evaluate alternative marketing outlays. How will you filter the marketing options?

A similar exercise is provided in the Instructor's and Student's Simulation Guide, question 11.

Buyer-Seller Relationship

The definition of the Type I Buyer implies a second upstream trade-off regarding the nature of the buyer-seller relationship. These associations are grouped into three categories: intrinsic, extrinsic, and strategic.[4] The proper classification clarifies the seller's value proposition and shapes the decision-making lens. Because each buyer-seller bond calls upon different strengths and activities within a firm, the pursuit of one type of relationship inhibits its ability to pursue others simultaneously.

Intrinsic Relationships

Intrinsic customers define value in terms of the qualities of the product and its price. Intrinsic buyers know what they want. They choose a seller who delivers the right product at the right time at the right price. There is little dialogue between the buyer and seller beyond the exchange of information about product qualities, price, and delivery schedule. Intrinsic relationship sellers are cost and price conscientious while staying acutely responsive to their customers' needs. Firms who target intrinsic value customers use their strategic lens to filter promotion and place options and select catalogs over trade shows, and inside sales personnel over outside sales reps.

Extrinsic Relationships

Extrinsic value customers differ. They seek solutions. They expect vendors to provide advice and help them execute their value proposition. In extrinsic relationships, the results and process quality variables in the value proposition interact and enhance the benefits received. For example, the manufacturer of an intermediate-stage product invests time to learn their customers' business. This producer designs a product that enhances their buyers' value proposition.

> ### Gelle's Building Products: Buyer–Seller Relationships
>
> Kirk Davis believes Gelle's is an intrinsic value seller that offers attractive products based upon their weather resistance and durability. Contractors know how to select their construction materials. Once the physical criteria are met, price and availability determine their selection.
>
> Gelle's becomes an extrinsic seller upon offering advice and instruction to do-it-yourselfers.

Extrinsic sellers emphasize service, consultation, responsiveness, and customization in their value proposition. Downstream decisions include the selection and training of front-line personnel and the flexibility in their production processes to accommodate custom requests. Upstream decisions involve building an outside sales force and fostering communications between field reps and R & D and production.

Strategic Relationships

Strategic-value customers seek more than a product and advice. They seek partners. Strategic relationship buyers desire a level of cooperation that leverages the skills of the buyer and the seller to create extraordinary value for the end user. Consider a pharmaceutical firm that provides medical offices and hospitals with sterile supplies and tools. It requires a packaging firm to design and assemble treatment packs that include sterile devices in quick and easy-to-open packages. Many different treatment packs are needed, and the packs change periodically as treatment procedures and devices change. The pharmaceutical firm also requires quick and accurate shipments to reduce the end users' need to stock a large inventory. In strategic relationships, suppliers and buyers are indistinguishable. Each commits to collaboration. The value propositions are dependent upon one another, and each designs activities in accord with the skills and abilities of their strategic partner.

Exercise 7.4

For the firm considered in Exercise 7.1, describe the nature of the relationship between the buyer and the seller.
1. Discuss the implications for the firm's operations.
2. Discuss the buyer-seller relationship.
3. Discuss the management and marketing implications.
4. Describe the buyer-seller relationship in your firm or firm in a simulation exercise.

Marketing Mix

A third set of upstream trade-offs relates to promotion and place decisions. These decisions involve the allocation of finite resources among alternative marketing mix allocations. For example, firms choose their marketing message and media outlets. They select a mix between attending trade shows, upgrading electronic marketing, building an outside or inside sales force, and relying upon account managers or distributors, vendors, and outbound logistical systems. Figure 7.5 displays the application of a strategy-specific lens to guide these decisions.

To highlight the application of the strategy lens, consider a firm whose value proposition emphasizes technically advanced products. This firm's strategic lens prioritizes trade shows, electronic marketing, and outside sales people. In contrast, a rival who offers a standard, lower-priced product relies upon print media and distributors. Promotion and place decisions are strategy-specific!

Upstream Measurements

An important aspect of management control is the ability to monitor the results of marketing mix decisions. *Interim outcome* and *outcome measurements* (see pages 117–118) monitor the sequence of events from the execution of a firm's competitive strategy to the realization of financial returns. The starting point of this discussion is the strategy-specific promotion and place decisions that occur following the definition of the Type I Buyer.

Marketing Efficiency and Effectiveness Measurements

The definition of the Type I Buyer guides the promotion and place decisions, and these decisions are assessed by efficiency measures, including the number of Type I Buyers reached and the promotional cost per Type I Buyer reached.

- Number of Type I Buyers reached by message
- Frequency of promotion messages received by Type I Buyers
- Percentage of recipients who are Type I Buyers
- Dollars expended per Type I Buyer reached
- Cost to service vendor or distributor
- Inventory turnover per vendor or distributor
- Percentage capacity use: outbound logistic
- Percent Type I Vendor or Distributor
- Promotion or place dollars per sales dollar

The variables in this list are strategy-specific measures of the efficiency of promotion and place outlays. The measures are strategy-specific because they require a definition of the firm's Type I Buyer.

Marketing efficiency and effectiveness must be assessed relative to marketplace conditions. For example, in a market characterized by rapid growth and a shortage of products, firms can minimize marketing outlays. In contrast, where there is an

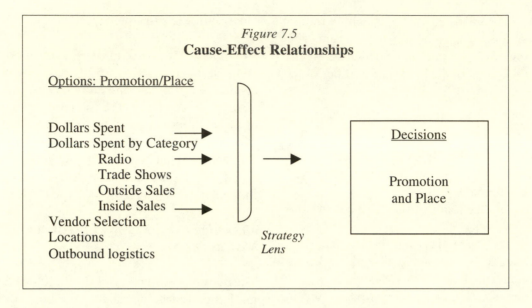

Figure 7.5
Cause-Effect Relationships

abundance of units available, larger marketing out-lays are needed (all else being equal) to capture the same market share. Also, if a firm holds a strong product feature or service or price advantage over rivals, it expends fewer marketing dollars.

Interim Outcome Measurements

Figure 7.6 identifies interim outcome measurements that follow from the execution of the firm's value proposition and of the initial place outcomes. The interim outcome measurements occur in sequence (see Figure 7.6).

In sequence, the interim outcome measurements lead to the firm's financial performance. Before one examines the firm's financial outcomes, the execution of the firm's strategy leaves footprints in the firm's financial data. The following list identifies selected financial indicators that reflect the current financial health of the firm.

- Asset utilization rate
- Inventory turnover

- Gross margin
- Contribution margin
- COGS to sales
- Interest to sales
- Inventory to sales

The following list indicates *outcome* measures that are the lagged consequences of the design and execution of the firm's strategy.

- Profit and profit margins
- Rate of return on capital or equity
- Price-to-earnings
- Stock price
- Market share

Feedback Measurements

A firm's ability to sustain its financial performance is related to the strengths it brings forward from one period to the next, and Table 7.1 offers a list of measurements that monitor a firm's ability to sustain a competitive advantage. The

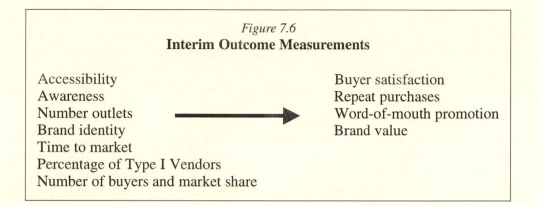

Figure 7.6
Interim Outcome Measurements

Accessibility
Awareness
Number outlets
Brand identity
Time to market
Percentage of Type I Vendors
Number of buyers and market share

Buyer satisfaction
Repeat purchases
Word-of-mouth promotion
Brand value

Table 7.1
Feedback Variables

Infrastructure Measures	Financial Measures
Products under development	Stock price
R & D spending	Bond rating
Available productive cpacity	Cash balances
Labor skills	Debt to equity
Product awareness and access	Product awareness
Cycle development time	Unit costs
Buyer loyalty	

feedback measures reflect the firm's financial and infrastructure strengths that it brings forward to the next year.

The firm's end-of-period cash balance is important to examine, and firms need to establish a target value. Certainly it is important to avoid a liquidity crisis that results in the need to acquire emergency credit. However, too much cash represents lost earning opportunities. Cash is a nonearning asset, and the firm is losing the opportunity to earn interest income. Additionally, the firm must examine the opportunity cost of its cash balances. There are many alternative uses, including the payment of dividends, the reduction of debt, repurchase of stock, the in-

vestment in new plant and equipment, or R & D spending.

Target Values

The analysis distinguishes between performance measurements that monitor the execution of the firm's strategy (time to shelf) and outcomes measurements (buyer satisfaction followed by repeat purchase followed by profit) and feedback measures. For each measurement, target values are set for planning, guiding decisions, motivating personnel, assessing the actual measurements, and rewarding achievement. The firm's competitive strategy determines the selection of variables to be measured, and the strategy is the basis for determining the target values.

For the outcome measurements, target values are established with caution, and they permit the firm to monitor and assess the results of the design and execution of the strategy. Target values for outcome measurements are firm, strategy, and market-specific. For example, consider two companies that produce a mechanical component of a larger and more complex product. One competes on the basis of high performance and customization whereas the other offers less-sophisticated and lower-priced units. The customized product manufacturer, all else being equal, targets a smaller number of customers, a higher rate of repeat purchase, and a more consulting-like relationship with buyers. In contrast, the manufacturer of the standardized, lower-priced product targets a larger number of customers and expects a lower rate of repeat purchase. The competitiveness of the marketplace also affects the firm's profit performance, given the effectiveness of the execution of its strategy.

Target values for outcome measurements are specified in absolute and efficiency terms. The outcome of a firm's advertising efforts are measured in absolute terms: the number of Type I Buyers it reaches. The associated efficiency measure is the advertising cost per Type I Buyer. Efficiency targets are firm- and strategy-specific.

The specification of financial performance targets creates a special set of problems. This book's focus is on the execution of a firm's strategy, and little attention has been paid to the design of the strategy. Chapter 8 examines the firm's strategy relative to the firm's competitive strengths and the attractiveness of its selling environment.

Upstream Analysis: Summary

Several important implications emerge from Figure 7.1:

- Marketing mix decisions are strategy-specific.
- The firm's financial performance is the lagged consequence of the design and the execution of its strategy. A well-crafted strategy is insufficient. An effective and complementary marketing program contributes to financial success.
- The management of the firm's financial outcomes occurs through the design and the execution of its strategy.

- The firm's competitive strategy is the decision-making lens that allows managers to engage in theme-based marketing.
- Interim outcome measures allow the firm to monitor the expected sequence of events from the execution of the firm's strategy to its financial performance.
- Successes breed success, and failures breed failure. The firm's financial performance determines its ability to allocate funds, and the budgets affect the firm's ability to execute its value proposition. A firm forced to cut budgets as a result of poor financial performance undermines its ability to execute its strategy, threatening a negative spiral.
- Functional areas of operations are guided by the requisites of a common competitive strategy. Parochial departmental concerns must be sacrificed in favor of common strategic concerns, and strategic leaders apply a common strategic-specific decision-making lens across the entire firm.

Summary

This chapter extends strategy-specific decision making *upstream* from the execution of the value proposition. Strategy-specific analysis guides decisions that determine the marketing mix. In turn, the upstream analysis is translated to sequential outcomes that allow the company to monitor the effectiveness of the strategy. Students or trainees engaged in case study analysis or simulation are urged to explain their marketing mix decisions and outcomes measurements in terms of their firm's strategy.

Key Themes and Terms

Interim Outcomes Measurements

Interim outcome measures monitor the effectiveness of upstream decisions and precede the firm's financial performance. These measures include the rate of buyer satisfaction and the repeat purchase rate. (See pages 117–118.)

Outcome Measurements

Outcome measures include profit, stock price, and market share and are the result of the design and execution of the firm's value proposition. (See pages 117–118.)

Strategic Marketing

Strategic marketing is a process that evaluates product, price, promotion, and place and practices options in terms of the requisites of implementing the firm's strategy. (See pages 124–125.)

Type I Buyer

Type I Buyers have a value proposition that closely aligns with that offered by the firm. These buyers are likely to be loyal, repeat buyers that allow the seller to work efficiently within their existing procedures and skills. (See pages 120–121.)

Discussion Questions

1. Why is it important to have repeat buyers?
2. Do you want to work for a firm that has intrinsic or extrinsic relationships with customers? Why?
3. Is marketing a matter of enticing buyers to purchase a product?
4. Discuss the connections between a firm's value proposition, its marketing mix, and the fifth P.
5. Why is it important to distinguish between a firm's financial performance and the design and execution of its value proposition?

End-of-Chapter Exercises

1. Build a marketing plan for Randolph Hooke, see Case 3.
2. Refer to the Rockwell Health Club, Case 4. For Rockwell's:
   a. Discuss the uncertainty of their value proposition and problems defining their Type I Buyer. Is Rockwell's guilty of straddling markets?
   b. Determine a value proposition for Rockwell's.
   c. Build sequential performance measurements.
   d. Prepare a memo to Steve Rockwell and outline the marketing mix.
3. For a full-service grocery and a convenience store:
   a. Explain differences in their value propositions and discuss the differences in their performance measurements.
   b. Discuss differences in their outcome measurements.
   c. How are the different strategies reflected in financial statement ratios? Be specific!
4. For Nancy's Women's Shoppe, Case 1, discuss the problems establishing the Type I Buyer and fifth P of the marketing mix. How are the confusions associated with the lack of a clear competitive strategy?

Notes

1. William Price and O.F. Farrell, *Marketing: Concepts and Strategies*, 8th ed. (Boston: Houghton Mifflin, 1993), p. 21.

2. J. David Hunger and Thomas L. Whalen, *Strategic Management* (New York: Addison-Wesley, 1993), p. 299.

3. William G. Forgang, *Competitive Strategy and Leadership* (New York: Rowman and Littlefield, 2001), pp. 9–13.

4. Neil Rackham and John DeVincentis, *Rethinking the Sales Force* (New York: McGraw Hill, 1999).

8

Performance Measurements and the Multiple Products Firm

The methodology of strategy-specific decision making established in chapters 1 to 7 applies to a single line of business and the execution of its value proposition. This chapter extends strategy-specific decision making in two ways. First, it shows how these decisions guide the firm toward meeting its long-term objectives. Second, it demonstrates how to execute the firm's corporate-level strategy.

Goals and Objectives

One issue has not yet been raised: What is the intended outcome of the execution of a firm's value proposition? Business strategy texts frequently distinguish between goals and objectives.[1] *Goals* are open-ended general statements that include surviving, being profitable, and providing satisfactory incomes and a balanced lifestyle to owners and employees. *Objectives* are more specific and include target values for a firm's stock price, market share, rate of return on sales, and assets or equity. Table 8.1 lists areas in which companies set goals and objectives.

Many firms show little day-to-day concern for their goals and objectives. Daily tasks and emergencies take precedence. However, some goals and objectives conflict with one another and impose a trade-off. Managers need a strategic lens to guide their choices. For example, in any time

Table 8.1
Goals and Objectives

Goals	Objectives
Survival	Return on assets
Being profitable	Stock price
Risk avoidance	Market share
Technological leadership	Return on equity
Reputation	Asset use rates
	Growth
	Efficiency

period a firm must choose (at the margin) between spending on R & D to gain technological leadership or on improving current profits. Similarly, there is a trade-off between current and future profits. A firm also may defer maintenance to raise current profits or surrender some current profits by lowering their prices to increase market share. Other firms may choose to minimize risks rather than pursue potentially lucrative but uncertain returns.

Carefully prioritized goals and objectives are a decision-making lens when specified *in advance* of taking action. They cannot be established after results have been observed and then applied to justify decisions. Therefore, students or developing managers engaged in case study analysis or a simulation must set weighted goals and objectives before making any operating decisions. It is crucial to understand the weighted determinants of the goal and objectives. For example, if a firm's sole objective is stock price maximization, decision makers must understand the relative importance of current and cumulative profits, dividends per share, the debt-to-equity ratio, liquidity, and expectations of future earnings. For those engaged in a simulation, the weighted determinants are specific to their class exercise, thereby making it crucial to study the user's manual.

Exercise 8.1

For your firm, one with which you are familiar, or a firm in a case study or simulation, state the following:

1. The weighted goals and objectives. One goal or weighted set of goals may be set for all teams by the instructor.
2. Discuss any trade-offs between the goals and objectives.
3. List and estimate the relative importance of the determinants of each goal and objective.
4. Discuss how the goals and objectives and their determinants affect decision making.

A similar exercise is provided in the Instructor's and Student's Simulation Guide, questions 6 and 14.

Strategic Business Units and Grand Strategies

Strategic Business Units

The value proposition defines the specific mix of product features, service, and price that comprises a firm's strategic business unit (SBU)— the competitive strategy for a particular prod-

uct or narrow range of products. An SBU has three characteristics:

- The single product or narrow set of products comprise a distinct administrative unit.
- A manager is responsible for the profit performance of the product or set of products.
- Grouped products share a common competitive strategy, personnel, fixed assets, distribution channels, or buyers.

The grouping of products into an SBU can be complex and cause intense (unhealthy) debate. Controversies must be resolved to build the appropriate reporting structure and to execute effectively the competitive strategy of each SBU. For example, a manufacturer offers five varieties of a product. Each targets a particular market segment, and each segment differently weights the same buying criteria. The buying criteria include the technical sophistication of the product, price, durability, customized features, timely delivery, access, and ease of use.

Gelle's Building Products: Line of Business

Gelle's manufactures a variety of products, but it serves a single market, relies upon a common technology, and shares a coating machine among its products. Though not stated in the case, Gelle's Building Products is managed as a single strategic business unit.

For this manufacturing firm, each buyer has specific needs and purchases only one grade of the product. With the exception of shared administrative support (accounting, human resources, computing systems, legal services, and public relations), fixed assets and personnel are dedicated to individual products and are not shared across the five products.

For this manufacturer, one market segment is price sensitive. In other segments the buying criteria are weighted differently. This firm aligns the value proposition for each product with the segment's weighted buying criteria. It organizes as five strategic business units. Each unit is headed by a product manager (or vice president) who is accountable for the unit's functional operations and financial performance. Revenues are pooled, and budget allocations to the individual business units come from the common pool. A formal system allocates resources among the units based upon the firm's cost of capital and the competitive strength and the attractiveness of each market.

In contrast, a competitor also offers a product in each of the same five market segments. However, this firm does not align each product's value proposition with the weighted criteria in each market. It pursues a common low-price (or technical sophistication, or ease of use, or date of release) strategy in each segment.

This firm's success depends upon the development of a core competence that, for example, lowers the cost of production for each product. The competence is developed over time through strategy-specific decisions involving product designs, procurement practices, selection of equipment, scheduling, logistics, continuous improvement practices, or human resource practices that increase productivity. The core competence alters the trade-off between components of value for each of the firm's products and allows it to offer a value proposition more attractive than its rivals. For instance, in the segment where buyers heavily weight technical sophistication, this firm offers a technically capable product at a relatively lower price.

In contrast to its rival manufacturer, this firm organizes as a single strategic business unit. It assigns a manager to each of the five products, but the managers have limited authority. They operate with the constraint of the firm's competitive

strategy, and a central authority makes decisions that build and maintain the core competence.

Exercise 8.2

For your employer, a firm with which you are familiar, or a firm in a case study or simulation exercise, respond to the following:
1. What core competencies can be built and how can those competencies improve the value proposition for each product?
2. How important is each possible core competence in building a competitive advantage?
3. What decisions build each core competence?

A similar exercise is provided in the Instructor's and Student's Simulation Guide, question 2.

The Single Business Unit Firm

The single business unit firm offers one good or service or a narrow set of products, and the strategic management of the firm raises three issues: (a) grand strategies, (b) the intended relationship among the products, and (c) the allocation of resources among the products.

Grand Strategies

Grand strategies refer to major actions through which a firm's long-term goals are achieved. For the single line of business company, three grand strategy options will be discussed: (a) market penetration, (b) market development, and (c) horizontal integration.

Market Penetration

Consider a firm with a narrow group of products in a single market who seeks long-term expansion in sales and profits. Deeper market penetration is one grand strategy option and includes pursuing more custom-

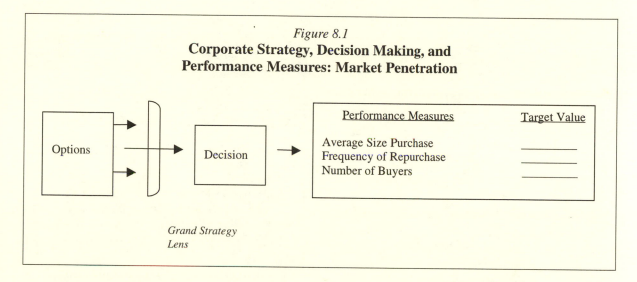

Figure 8.1

**Corporate Strategy, Decision Making, and
Performance Measures: Market Penetration**

ers within a market and/or more sales per customer. This option involves trade-offs. If resources are allocated to penetrate more deeply a market, they are unavailable to develop new products or new markets. Also, front-line personnel must be directed, at the margin, toward spending time and other resources to develop new accounts or more sales per account. External environmental forces influence the choice. In rapidly growing markets, obtaining new accounts takes precedence. In a slower growth market, buyer retention and sales per account are the priorities. Regardless, decision makers who assign sales personnel, implement a reward system, and select among promotion and place decisions need a strategic lens.

The effectiveness of the execution of a market penetration grand strategy is monitored by tracking the average size purchase, the number of buyers, and the frequency of repurchase (see Figure 8.1). Target values for each of the measures allow a firm to assess its execution of its market penetration strategy.

Market Development

Market development includes geographic expansion and the creation of new uses and users of the product. Market development is pursued by developing new product features to extend the life of a product or the range of uses, by developing quality variations, or new models of existing products. For example, aspirin makers realized a market development opportunity when their headache remedies were found to lower heart attack risks. Similarly, yogurt makers enjoyed market development when their products migrated from the health food market and assumed various forms with a wide array of food and drink uses.

Gelle's Building Products: Grand Strategy

Gelle's has options to pursue market penetration, including building a larger buyer base within its sales regions or achieving larger and more frequent purchases from existing accounts. New geographic markets are also an option.

Market development could involve finding new uses for their products.

The expansion paths are not mutually exclusive. But trade-offs exist. Pursuit of one path draws resources away from other uses.

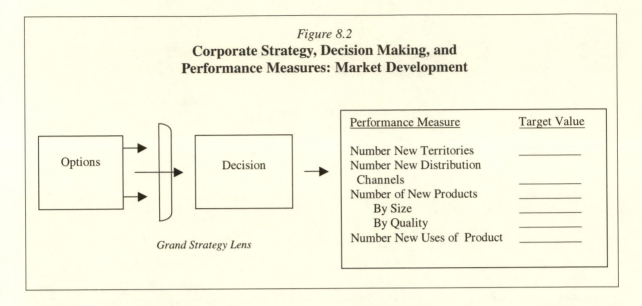

Figure 8.2
**Corporate Strategy, Decision Making, and
Performance Measures: Market Development**

Firms that pursue a market development strategy make decisions to achieve particular outcomes. For example, the commitment lessens the importance of introducing new products. Market development measurements are listed in Figure 8.2 and include the number of new territories and the number of new products. The market development grand strategy serves as a decision-making lens that prioritizes alternative uses of finite organizational resources.

Horizontal Integration

This grand strategy option is characterized by the acquisition of competitor firms. These acquisitions eliminate competitors and allow the acquiring firm to expand, consolidate production and marketing, and capture economies. Horizontal integration prioritizes the use of resources; Figure 8.3 lists appropriate performance measures to monitor the execution of the grand strategy.

The grand strategies discussed above (market penetration, market development, and horizontal inte-

gration) lead the firm toward its goals and objectives. The three grand strategies are not mutually exclusive. Aspects of each can be pursued at the same time. But, there are trade-offs. A firm who adds sales reps to develop territories loses the opportunity to direct those same individuals or financial resources to pursue deeper penetration of existing territories. It is advantageous to have a weighted path to allow the firm to remain focused on its grand strategy and eliminate nonstrategic options.

The Intended Relationship between Products

A single business unit that offers several closely related products or services must define the intended relationships among its products to allocate resources. For example, an athletic shoes manufacturer offers many sizes and models at different prices. Similarly, a printing firm handles newspapers, shopping guides, advertising flyers, business letterhead, envelopes, and annual reports. The multiple products impose trade-offs. Re-

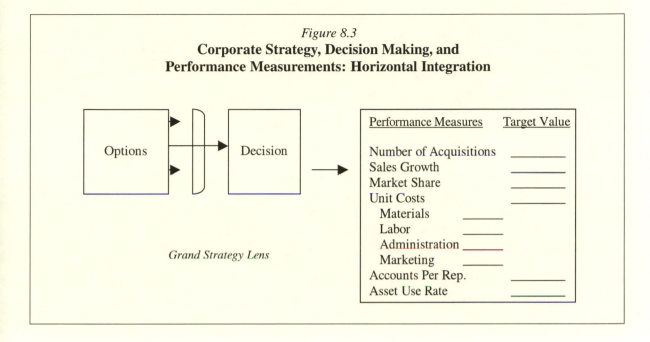

Figure 8.3

**Corporate Strategy, Decision Making, and
Performance Measurements: Horizontal Integration**

Performance Measures	Target Value
Number of Acquisitions	_____
Sales Growth	_____
Market Share	_____
Unit Costs	_____
Materials	_____
Labor	_____
Administration	_____
Marketing	_____
Accounts Per Rep.	_____
Asset Use Rate	_____

Grand Strategy Lens

sources allocated to one product are unavailable to the others, and the multiple products business unit needs a strategic lens that clarifies the intended relationship between the products.

Before resources are allocated among products, the firm must determine if each product is expected to stand alone as a profit source. Alternatively, to satisfy the complete needs of buyers, some products are offered to complement others but are not profitable on their own. These products are evaluated by their contribution to the retention of customers who purchase a variety of goods. Other products are offered to raise the asset use rates and lower average costs for all products. These products are expected to cover only the marginal costs.

Resources Allocation

A single business unit firm with multiple products allocates resources among alternative uses and among products. Allocation mechanisms are dis-

cussed more thoroughly with regard to the management of the multiple business unit firms (see page 18). But critical allocation problems occur within a single business unit firm that affect resource allocation, scheduling, marketing, research, and the assignment of personnel.

One resource allocation system prioritizes requests for resources based on profitability. To allocate resources this way, revenues and costs must be properly assigned, but the task is not simple. On the revenue side, consider a manufacturer who produces a low-volume product. The revenues attributable to this product are deceptive. At first glance, the revenue is simply the number of units sold multiplied by the price, less any discounts. But are customers attracted and retained because this infrequently used product is available? If the availability of this product completes a buyer's needs, the revenue attributable to this product is more than its price times quantity.

Similarly, costs are difficult to assign. For example, how are office space, administration, and equipment costs allocated by product? These costs can be assigned on a pro rata basis. If one product uses 5.0 percent of the assembly line time, it assumes 5.0 percent of those costs. However, a small-volume product may be produced only when the assembly line is not otherwise used. For this product, the opportunity cost of the use of the assembly line is zero. The decision to allocate costs on a pro rata basis or to assign the opportunity costs affects the profitability of the product. Despite the difficulties of assigning revenues and costs to individual products within a business unit, a formal asset rationing system is necessary.

The Multiple Strategic Business Units Firm and Corporate Strategies

The multiple business units firm creates additional management challenges and opportunities. Two ideas are explored below—grand strategies and corporate-level strategies.

Grand Strategies

The multiple business units firm has grand strategy options that are unavailable to the single line of business entity, including product development, conglomerate diversification, concentric diversification, and vertical integration. The grand strategies are a decision-making lens and prioritize options.

Product Development

This strategy involves the introduction of new products or the substantial modification of existing products. This grand strategy option extends beyond that available to the single business unit firm. For the multiple business units firm, product development offers a wider set of options that includes a new business unit and distantly or unrelated products.

Conglomerate Diversification

Conglomerate diversification is a grand strategy associated with firms comprised of multiple strategic business units. A firm's goals and objectives are met through the expansion into or acquisition of unrelated business units. A firm chooses a conglomerate corporate-level strategy to redeploy assets from a slow growth or unattractive market to higher yield opportunities. Conglomerate diversification is discussed later in this chapter as one of the possible relationships between a firm's strategic business units.

Concentric Diversification

Concentric diversification is an expansion path that develops or acquires new products that are related to the existing operations in terms of technology, markets, or products. For example, a manufacturer of snow skis diversifies into related items, including other ski equipment (poles, goggles, ski racks) and winter clothing. This grand strategy is discussed more thoroughly in the corporate strategy section regarding the relationship between multiple business units (see pages 141–142).

Vertical Integration

This expansion path involves the development or acquisition of business units that either provide inputs to an existing business or are users of the firm's output. For example, a beef cattle slaughterhouse vertically integrates *backward* when it develops or buys feedlots to stabilize the supply and price of animals. It integrates *forward* if it develops or acquires restaurants or butcher shops to stabilize the market for its product. The slaughterhouse may make a more limited forward integration and complete meat-processing steps previously done at the grocery store or butcher shop. This step may substitute low-wage slaughterhouse workers for unionized butchers and reduce the grocery's net cost of beef on the shelf. Forward integration may involve the acquisition of a restaurant chain to stabilize the demand for the product.

Corporate-Level Strategies

This section recognizes that the multiple business units firm creates additional management challenges involving the coordination between multiple business units under common ownership. A firm's corporate-level strategy refers to the intended relationship between its various units. By defining the possible relationships between product lines, the following benefits accrue:

- Firms clarify the relationship between meeting their long-term objectives and the corporate-level strategy.
- Firms enjoy the benefit of a lens to evaluate new business opportunities.
- Firms gain a decision-making lens to guide the implement of the corporate-level strategy.
- Firms enjoy the benefit of a performance measurement system to assess their execution of the corporate-level strategy.

Three generic corporate-level strategies are discussed below: (a) conglomerate relationships, (b) hygienic relationships, and (c) leveraged strategies. The three corporate strategies are not mutually exclusive. It is possible to conduct both a hygienic and a leveraged strategy at the same time.

Conglomerate Relationships

A conglomerate corporate strategy is the weakest option. A conglomerate relationship occurs when a firm's business units are unrelated in terms of technology, distribution channels, users, and productive capabilities. Consider, for example, a family-owned golf course. After years of building the course; upgrading the clubhouse, locker areas, and food service; and developing a successful business, the golf enterprise generates more cash per year than needed to sustain the business. The family seeks investment opportunities.

After examining several options, the family chooses to purchase a convenience store franchise. The two business units (golf course and convenience store) comprise a conglomerate corporate-level strategy. Though commonly owned, the individual businesses operate separately from one another. The businesses serve different buyers. The tools, equipment, and personnel do not move between the business units. This conglomerate corporate-level strategy is not unreasonable. Perhaps the return on any incremental investment in the golf course or related activity does not meet the opportunity cost of capital. For example, the best golf course investment project is expected to yield a 7 percent return, whereas the convenience store offers the prospect of 11 percent. In this situation, redeploying assets into a convenience store franchise makes sense and defines a conglomerate diversification.

The businesses operate independently, but several dependencies cannot be avoided. First, the cash generated by one business is available to finance the other. Second, the businesses may be differently sensitive to the business cycle or seasonal fluctuations and thus smooth the earnings over time. Finally, an investment in one business unit may have favorable tax implications for the entire firm. Though the business units operate individually, a conglomerate corporate strategy requires the allocation of resources between the units.

Resource Allocation

One asset rationing system is based upon each business unit's market attractiveness (see Table 8.2) and relative competitive strength (see Table 8.3).

Table 8.2
Market Attractiveness

Variable	Percent Weight (%)	Score (1 = Low to 10 = High)	Product (Percent times Score)
Number and size of competitors	35		
Average profitability	30		
Market growth	20		
Seasonal volatility	5		
Market size	10		
	100%		Sum =

Table 8.2 displays the weighted criteria that define the attractiveness of one market within which the firm competes. The same weighted criteria and process is applied to each of the other business units. For the firm in question, the number and relative size of competitors, average profitability, and growth in sales are the heavily weighted criteria. The firm scores each criterion on a ten-point scale, with ten representing the most attractive and one the least attractive circumstance. Scores are recorded in the table. The right-hand column is the product of the weight multiplied by the score. These entries are summed, creating a composite value that reflects the attractiveness of the market.

The value at the bottom of the column provides valuable information when the process is applied to more than one market. Comparing the sums reflects the relative attractiveness of individual markets. The comparison is a guide for allocating resources among competing products.

Other firms, even in the same industry, select different criteria to define the attractiveness of a market. For example, a firm that is short of cash heavily weights expected cash flow, whereas a firm with unusually vibrant research and development is attracted to technologically dynamic markets. Firms also apply different market attractiveness criteria when evaluating an ongoing line of business compared with a possible start-up. For instance, when considering the start-up of a business, several variables are crucial, including the size of the initial investment, the time to break even, cash requirements over time, risk, and ease of entry for new competitors. For an ongoing business, profit margins, stability of earnings, and reinvestment needs are particularly important. A partial list of market attractiveness criterion is offered in Table 8.3.

Exercise 8.3

Build a weighted index to define the attractiveness of a market for your firm, one you are familiar with, your school, or firm in a case study or simulation. Score the variable, using a ten-point scale, where ten is high and one is low. Repeat the exercise for each business unit in the firm. Explain.

A similar exercise is provided in the Instructor's and Student's Simulation Guide, question 15.

Table 8.4 on page 140 applies the same methodology to establish a firm's relative competitive strength within each of its markets. In the table the firm measures its competitive strength in terms of market share, financial strength, and product awareness.

Firms select and weight competitive strength

Table 8.3
Market Attractiveness Criteria

Ongoing Business	Start-up Business
Cash generation	Capital requirements
Industry profit margin	Time to break even
Stability of earnings	Barriers to entry
Relies upon established distribution channels	Risk
Reinvestment needs	

criteria differently, based upon their competitive strategy, market characteristics, and other variables to define a firm's competitive strength:

- Knowledge of customers and the market
- Technological capabilities
- Products under development
- Relative costs
- Labor capabilities
- Fixed assets in place
- Managerial strengths

Exercise 8.4

Assess the competitive strength of the firm discussed in Exercise 8.3. Repeat this exercise for each line of business. Score each variable using a ten-point scale where ten is high and one is low. Explain.

A similar exercise is provided in the Instructor's and Student's Simulation Guide, question 15.

Tables 8.2 and 8.3 establish the attractiveness of each market within which the firm competes (or is considering entering) and the firm's relative competitive strength. Figure 8.4 combines the calculations into a four-quadrant matrix.[2]

The four-quadrant matrix guides the allocation of corporate resources among competing business units. Business units are classified by their competitive strength and the attractiveness of their market, and their positioning in the quadrant diagram serves as a decision lens.

Cell I: Attractive Market/Strong Competitor: Cell I includes products or business units that are in attractive markets and are strong competitors. Cell I units are stars and have a priority claim on the organization's resources.[3]

Cell II: Attractive Market/Weak Competitor: Cell II products or business units create uncertainties. The market is attractive, but the firm is a weak competitor. It is a question mark.[4] A business unit that falls into this cell does not hold a priority claim. Cell II units must validate their claim on organizational resources by explaining their path to achieve a competitive advantage. In the absence of a convincing explanation, these units are candidates for elimination.

Cell III: Unattractive Market/Weak Competitor: Cell III products or business units are the weakest. They are classified as dogs, reflecting their weaknesses in unattractive markets.[5] Investment in these business units is minimized, and the divestment of these units is proper.

Cell IV: Unattractive Market/Strong Competitor: Cell IV products or business units are strong competitors in unattractive markets. These business units are harvested.[6] Investment in the business units should be limited to preserving the competitive strength and emphasis placed on harvesting the earnings and cash flow.

Exercise 8.5

Given the calculations in Exercises 8.3 and 8.4, complete the four-quadrant diagram, and discuss the management implications. This exercise should be repeated after each round of a simulation. Explain.

A similar exercise is provided in the Instructor's and Student's Simulation Guide, question 15.

Table 8.4			
Competitive Strength: Market A			
Variable	Percent Weight (%)	Score (1 = Low to 10 = High)	Product (Percent times Score)
Market share	40		
Financial strength	35		
Product awareness	25		
	100%		Sum =

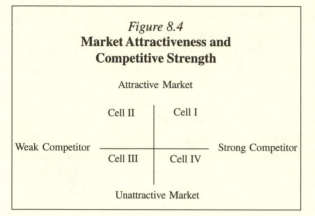

Figure 8.4
Market Attractiveness and Competitive Strength

Performance Measures and Corporate-Level Strategy

Firms that operate with a conglomerate corporate-level strategy apply performance measures to assess their portfolio of business. Measures of the current performance include profit by strategic business unit, rate of return on invested capital, and cash flow, as shown below:

- Profit
- Cash flow
- Market share
- Cash requirements
- Product age
- Contribution margin
- Risk level

Hygienic Relationships

A hygienic corporate strategy differs from a conglomerate strategy, and the effective collaboration between the business units enhances returns through greater efficiencies. Consider, for example, a fast-food restaurant specializing in lunch and dinner sandwiches. The diversification into serving breakfast provides more than another income stream. The morning meal service raises the rate of utilization of the firm's fixed assets. Revenues in excess of the incremental costs add to the firm's profits. Similarly, a tax preparation firm diversifies into consulting services to raise the average monthly use rate of professional personnel.

A hygienic corporate-level strategy has implications for the execution of individual line of business strategies. For example, consider a manufacturing firm that competes on the basis of price. A single line of business is unable to utilize fully its fixed plant and professional and administrative personnel. Introducing a new strategic business unit that shares plant and personnel increases the asset utilization rate. This firm becomes a more effective price competitor in each of its markets. Similarly, a new strategic business unit makes use of another's waste or by-products and converts a disposal cost into a revenue stream. The effectiveness of the execution of the

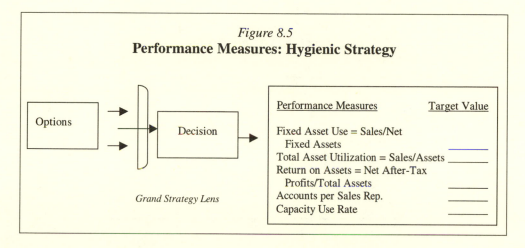

Figure 8.5
Performance Measures: Hygienic Strategy

Options → Decision →

Grand Strategy Lens

Performance Measures	Target Value
Fixed Asset Use = Sales/Net Fixed Assets	
Total Asset Utilization = Sales/Assets	
Return on Assets = Net After-Tax Profits/Total Assets	
Accounts per Sales Rep.	
Capacity Use Rate	

hygienic corporate-level strategy is measurable in several ways, as listed in Figure 8.5.

The successful execution of a hygienic corporate strategy requires strategy-specific decision making. Sought-after efficiencies do not occur automatically, nor are hygienic benefits the result of managerial mandates. A manufacturing firm that seeks to share fixed plant costs across products must schedule accordingly and avoid dedicating resources to particular products. Similarly, an accounting company might seek to develop consulting practices to supplement its tax practice. In order to raise the utilization of personnel over a calendar year, it must hire and train in accord with the hygienic corporate strategy.

Firms that seek hygienic strategy but fail to execute it properly waste profitable opportunities. In effect, the failure to manage correctly the hygienic strategy reduces the strategy to a conglomerate relationship. For example, a manufacturer seeks a higher fixed asset utilization rate and introduces a new product line. After gaining experience with the new product, it realizes that its existing plant and personnel are poorly adapted. In response, they build new production facilities, and the intended hygienic strategy deteriorates to a conglomerate relationship.

Leveraged Relationships

A leveraged corporate-level strategy provides additional opportunities to enhance profitability of the multiple strategic business units firm. Whereas a hygienic strategy focuses on efficiencies attributable to multiple business units, leveraged relationships extend an organization's core competence over multiple products.[7]

Consider a CPA firm that concentrates on tax preparation for upper-income households. Given the firm's access to confidential data and the earned trust of its clients, it diversifies into financial planning and investment services. The diversification provides an opportunity for leveraged benefits if the value proposition of each line of business is enhanced by the related services (see Figure 8.6). For example, the diversification allows the firm to share client knowledge across lines of business and provide integrated advice. At the same time, the client discloses personal and sensitive financial information to only one service provider. The leveraged benefits do not preclude hygienic benefits. The accounting firm's diversification into estate planning and financial management services may also increase asset utilization rates.

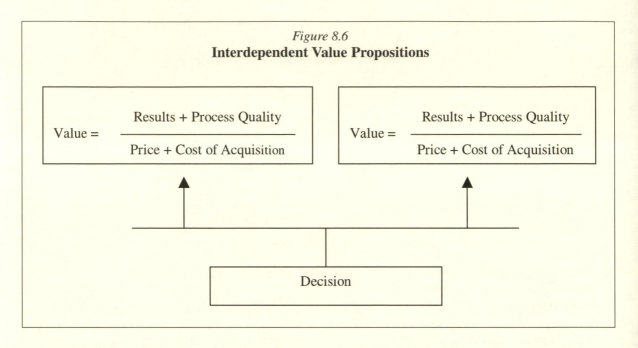

Figure 8.6
Interdependent Value Propositions

Leveraged benefits can be measured, albeit with some difficulty. One measure is the number of purchasers of multiple products (see Figure 8.7). Consider the lawn and garden firm that diversifies into snow removal (see pages 18–19). For this firm, the leveraged corporate strategy relies upon earning the trust and confidence of buyers who purchase multiple services.

The importance of the leveraged corporate-level strategy to buyers is more difficult to measure but more important. The key to the success of the strategy is the improvement in value extended to buyers. For the lawn and garden firm, their buyers gain the convenience and savings associated with working with only one outdoor maintenance firm. The CPA that diversifies from tax services to financial planning and business consulting offers clients an array of services. But what is the additional value for buyers? Is the integrated advice better? How important is it to disclose confidential data to only one service provider?

Exercise 8.6

For a hypothetical firm or firm in a case study or simulation, describe multiple lines of business and how a leveraged corporate-level strategy may be developed. Discuss the key management challenges to assure that the strategy does not deteriorate to a conglomerate relationship.

Summary

This chapter extends the concepts of strategy-specific decision making to the multiple lines of business firms. These complex organizations pursue several levels of strategy at the same time. Each line of business offers its own value proposition, requiring strategy-specific decision making to execute the strategy. In addition, the multiple lines of a business firm define the intended relationship among its business units, decision making must allocate resources among

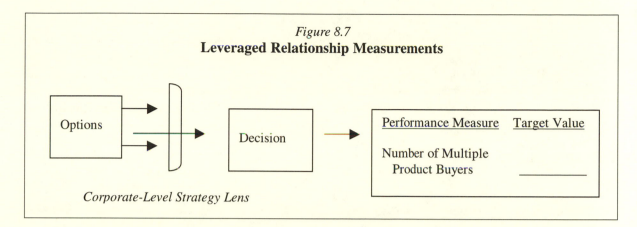

Figure 8.7
Leveraged Relationship Measurements

Options

Decision

Performance Measure	Target Value
Number of Multiple Product Buyers	_____

Corporate-Level Strategy Lens

the units, and decisions must be directed toward achieving effective execution of the corporate-level strategy.

Key Themes and Ideas

Business Unit

A business unit refers to a single product or narrow group of products. (See pages 131–132.)

Corporate-Level Strategy

A firm's corporate-level strategy refers to the intended relationship between its multiple business units. Three generic corporate strategies exist and are conglomerate, hygienic, and leveraged. (See pages 140–142.)

Conglomerate Relationships

A conglomerate relationship between multiple business units within a firm is the weakest corporate-level strategy. With conglomerate relationships, individual business units operate independently and do not share assets for efficiency or leverage technological skills or relationships with clients. (See pages 137–140.)

Hygienic Relationships

A hygienic corporate strategy occurs when multiple business units share assets to increase operating efficiency. (See pages 140–141.)

Leveraged Relationship

A leveraged corporate strategy provides the greatest opportunity to improve organizational profitability by extending capabilities or customer relationships over multiple products. (See pages 141–142.)

Measuring the Corporate Strategy

The success of corporate-level strategies is reflected in carefully selected performance measures. (See pages 138–142.)

Discussion Questions

1. What factors determine the attractiveness of a market?
2. What factors determine a firm's competitive strengths?
3. Why is it important to have an asset allocation mechanism in a multiproduct or multiple lines of business firm?

4. What are the differences between a line of business and a corporate-level strategy?
5. How can the firm's corporate-level strategy affect its lines of business strategies?
6. Why is it important to develop reporting relationships in a firm that coincide with the line of business and corporate-level strategy?

End-of-Chapter Exercises

1. Refer to Case 5, Raymond Specialo and Family. The firm is considering an expansion of services.
   a. Describe the intended corporate-level strategy.
   b. What are the challenges facing decision makers?
   c. Establish performance measures to monitor the execution of the firm's corporate-level strategy.
2. Describe a hypothetical firm engaged in each of the following:
   a. A conglomerate corporate strategy
   b. A hygienic corporate-level strategy
   c. A leveraged corporate-level strategy
3. For the firms described above, describe, explain, and justify how you propose organizing the business units.
4. Refer to Rockwell's Health Club, Case 4. What are the different corporate strategy options available to this firm?

Notes

1. Cornelius De Kluyver, *Strategic Thinking: An Executive Perspective* (Upper Saddle River, N.J.: Prentice-Hall, 2000), pp. 10–11.

2. Philip Kotler, *Marketing Management*, 8th ed. (Englewood Cliffs, N.J.: Prentice-Hall, 1994), p. 69.

3. Gary Hamel and C.K. Prahalad, "Strategic Intent," *Harvard Business Review* 67 (May–June 1989).

4. John A. Pearce and Richard B. Robinson Jr., *Strategic Management*, 8th ed. (New York: McGraw Hill, 2002), pp. 227–28.

5. Ibid.

6. Ibid.

7. Ibid.

9

Leadership and Strategy-Specific Decision Making

The previous eight chapters developed decision-making tools to execute effectively a firm's competitive strategy. This final chapter extends strategy-specific decision making into a profile of strategic leaders.

Winning and Losing

Whether real businesses or firms in a simulation exercise, some outperform others, and winning is the preferred outcome. There are many ways to account for differences in performance, including luck and good fortune. In environments of uncertainty, the effects of risk taking and risk avoidance are pervasive. But the evidence indicates that firms who carefully plan[1] and effectively execute their plans enjoy superior performance.[2]

Strategic leaders do not rely upon good luck. They achieve superior performance for themselves and their organizations through strategy-specific decision making. Akin to the photographer who relies upon accurate measurements of light and distance and a clear lens, strategic leaders apply a measurement system and a strategic lens to evaluate options, make a choice, monitor performance, explain their actions, and motivate others to act in accord with the firm's strategy. Strategic leaders are winners because their decision-making methodology effectively executes the strategy. The firm's financial performance is strong, and strategic leaders earn the trust and confidence of colleagues, welcome healthy debate, and reduce the debilitating effects of chronic second-guessing.

Characteristics of Strategic Leaders

Strategic leaders possess a number of traits in common.

Visionary

Strategic leaders have a clear vision of their firm. They have a five- to ten-year time horizon that encompasses the organization's goals and objectives, and the firm's competitive strategy defines the path to achieve the goals and objectives. For example, a strategic leader envisions being the industry's market-share leader by extending superior customer service. Strategy-specific decisions execute the firm's value proposition and lead to superior performance.

Superior performance, however, requires that the vision must be realistic and effectively implemented. Strategic leaders *design* a competitive strategy consistent with their firm's resources, abilities, and external environments. Strategic leaders *execute* their firm's strategy through a decision-making lens that evaluates trade-offs and aligns operations with the strategy.

Decisive and Consistent

Strategic leaders make decisions! They understand that not acting is (often) the greater risk. Strategic leaders gather and analyze data; they consult with others, examine risks, and evaluate trade-offs. But strategic leaders are not distracted by unhealthy debate or non-strategy-specific data. They rely upon a strategic lens to see issues clearly, allowing them to make decisions, explain their actions, and motivate others.

Strategic leaders make consistent decisions. By relying upon a clear lens, strategic leaders are fair. They respond to similar problems in the same way across departments, people, and time. Additionally, strategic leaders apply the same decision-making lens to different problems. Choices made in different parts of an organization and over time are commonly directed by the firm's strategy. Strategic leaders consistently explain their decisions in terms of the priorities of the firm's strategy and guide others to make commonly directed decisions.

Systems Thinkers and Complete

Strategic leaders move beyond consistent decisions and make complete decisions. As systems thinkers, they understand the cause-effect connections within their organizations. They understand the dependencies among operating areas, policies, processes, and individuals and the linkages to the execution of the firm's strategy. Strategic leaders act upon these dependencies, align the details of the firm's operations, and make complete decisions.

Teachers and Motivators

Strategic leaders rely on others to execute effectively the firm's strategy. They develop strategic leaders at all levels of the organization, accepting the responsibilities to teach, motivate, and reward others. As teachers, strategic leaders reduce the debilitating effects of unhealthy debate and chronic second-guessing while creating an environment conducive to inquiry and healthy debate.

Strategic Leadership and Simulation Exercises

Students and developing managers engaged in a strategic management simulation have opportunities to sharpen their strategic leadership skills. Success in a simulation is contingent upon: (a) a carefully *designed* competitive strategy, (b) the effective *execution* of the strategy through complete and consistent decisions across functional areas of the firm and over all of the rounds of the simulation, (c) the ability to align and motivate teammates with the firm's strategy, and (d) the clear communication of the logic of decisions to coworkers up, down, and across their organization.

After leaving the classroom or management development workshop, these strategic leadership skills are immediately applicable in the workplace. While young employees are not positioned to design a firm's strategy, they contribute to the execution of the strategy in several ways. Their daily tasks are part of the fabric of activities that delivers the intended value proposition. Working in accord with the requisites of the firm raises an individual's value to their company. Also, young employees offer information and make recommendations. As strategic thinkers, individuals do not contribute to unhealthy debate. Rather, the input of young employees contributes to healthy debate and helps others make strategy-specific decisions. Finally, everyone in an organization has the ability to influence the behaviors of others, and young employees who think strategically contribute to building an organization compatible with the firm's strategy.

> ### Exercise 9.1
>
> Reflect upon your work situation or experience with the simulation exercise.
> 1. Describe the opportunities to implement strategy-specific decision making and strategic leadership.
> 2. Evaluate your effectiveness as a strategic leader.

Strategic Leadership, an Extension

The concepts and practices of strategic leadership extend beyond decision making within for-profit or not-for-profit organizations. The application of a decision-making lens allows individuals to be principles-centered.[3] A person's moral and ethical standards, or sense of right and wrong, help to accomplish this. Personal choices are made and explained by filtering options through a decision-making lens. The lens allows individuals to make complete and consistent decisions based upon their values.

Summary

Managers make decisions, and the success of individuals and their organization depend upon the effectiveness of their choices. Some managers struggle to make decisions, and many organizations struggle with low morale and the chronic second-guessing of their decision makers.

In contrast, strategic leaders guide the effective implementation of their firm's competitive strategy by making complete and consistent decisions through a strategic lens. (See pages 83–88.) Their organizations enjoy high morale, trust and confidence in decision makers, and superior performance.

Discussion Questions

1. Discuss the concepts of strategy leadership that apply to guiding your personal decisions.

2. Discuss whether or not personal charisma is essential for being an effective strategic leader.
3. Discuss the importance of complete and consistent decision making.
4. What are the two aspects of consistent decision making? Do you agree that both are equally important?
5. Discuss the parallels between strategy-specific decision making and principle-centered leadership.

End-of-Chapter Exercises

1. Reflect upon the simulation exercise. What were the lessons learned? What strategic leadership skills were developed? How are these skills directly applicable to the workplace?
2. Consider Rockwell's Health Club, Case 4. Identify three decisions that Steve Rockwell must make. Identify consistent decisions.
3. Prepare a memo to yourself. Evaluate your strategic leadership skills and (as appropriate) develop an action plan to improve your strategy-specific decision-making skills.
4. For your organization, one you are familiar with, or your firm in a course simulation, outline a new staff orientation program or a staff training program. Be specific.
5. Refer to Case 1. What principle-centered decisions challenge Nancy? What strategic decisions challenge her? How do the principle-centered and strategic decisions merge?

Notes

1. James C. Collins and Jerry I. Poras, *Built to Last* (New York: Harper Business, 1994).

2. Larry Bossidy and Ram Charan, *Execution: The Discipline of Getting Things Done* (New York: Crown Business, 2002).

3. Stephen Covey, *Principle-Centered Leadership* (New York: Summit Books, 1990).

APPENDIXES

Appendix I

Review of Gelle's Building Products Case

(See pages xv–xvii)

1. Reread your memo to John Chudovas.
2. Upon reflection, list major changes in your advice, explanation, and tone of reply.
3. Rewrite the memo.

4. Explain why the revised memo is more useful to John Chudovas.
5. Discuss the lessons learned from the case.

Appendix II

Instructor's and Student's Simulation Guide

Teaching and learning through a simulation is effective and enjoyable. However, the rewards come only *after* successfully completing a complex and stressful orientation. For students, the start-up responsibilities include familiarization with the rules and mechanics of the simulation, understanding strategic design and execution, bridging the concepts of strategic management with the simulation, and developing strategy-specific decision-making skills. Other challenges are attitudinal.

Students and developing managers who are assigned a simulation exercise must invest considerable energy to get started. Once the simulation begins, trying to catch up later does not work. Also, a strategic management simulation is a capstone

learning experience. Consulting texts from prior courses will be necessary. Finally, be responsible. If you work in a team with classmates, contribute! Take decision making in the simulation seriously and be accountable for your actions.

Instructors face the challenge of designing and leading the orientation to strategic management and to a simulation. Two objectives are noted. One is to get every learner ready to make their first set of decisions. Each individual contributes to the learning of others. When one ineffectively designs or executes their strategy, a simulation loses the rigor of a tightly contested market. The outcomes of the simulation are distorted. The friendly selling environment minimizes the importance of competitor intelligence, and the consequences of misjudgments are minimized. A second goal is to create a collaborative learning environment within which students comfortably explore ideas, take acceptable risks, and enjoy developing decision-making skills.

In the world of real businesses, mulligans—second chances—do not occur. The same is true in a simulation. There is no reset button. Also akin to the world of real business, decisions in a simulation have lingering effects. Mistakes are difficult to overcome. Whereas real businesses fail, poor performance in a simulation puts an exciting learning opportunity at risk. Individual learners (or teams) who make early-round errors lose interest. The simulation becomes a depressing semester-long burden rather than a vibrant learning experience.

Getting ready to play the simulation is a shared instructor and student obligation. When both succeed, the rewards are significant. This Instructors and Students Simulation Guide seeks to help learners and instructors meet their responsibilities, and it is divided into Pre- and Post-Simulation Activities. The activities help to bridge the gap between the concepts of strategic management and a simulation and require consulting the simulation's user manual.

The Pre-Simulation Activities involve questions to be completed prior to making any decisions in the simulation. Instructors may use the questions for class discussion or written assignments. Students may use them as self-tests. The questions link the concepts of competitive strategy, strategy-specific decision making, and the simulation.

The Post-Simulation Activities include more questions and an outline. The questions prompt learners to diagnose and explain the results of each round of their simulation. The outline guides the preparation of written reports at the end of selected rounds and at the end of the simulation. Instructors may use the questions and outline for class discussion or as writing assignments following

each round of the simulation.

Many of the questions in the Guide are asked for a second time. The questions initially appeared as chapter exercises. This redundancy is intentional. As chapter exercises, the reader responds when the relevant text material is freshest in mind. However, as the reader progresses through the book, additional information may prompt new ideas and suggest revisions. Reexamining the questions permits revision of the initial answers.

Part A: Pre-Simulation Activities

Students or developing managers are urged to answer the following questions *prior to* making first-round decisions. If formal replies are not required by your instructor, write your answers anyway. Create a record of your thinking to assure that your actions are consistent and strategy-directed. It is time consuming, but the payback is real. You will make more effective decisions during the simulation and prepare more insightful reports on your actions and the outcomes.

Question 1: (See Exercise 1.1 and page 5.)

a. Compile a list of the ways to differentiate products within your simulation to gain a competitive advantage.
b. Identify and explain the trade-offs among the differentiators.
c. Review the weighted buying criteria in each market and evaluate the importance of the differentiators by product or market segment.
d. Propose a line of business strategy for each of your products. Be prepared to make revisions after defining the corporate-level strategy.

Question 2: (See Exercise 2.1 and 8.2 and pages 18 and 32.)

a. Explain the concept of a firm's corporate-level strategy and the relationship with lines of business strategies. What corporate-level strategy options are available to you in your simulation?
b. What core competencies can be built within your simulation? (See page 141.)
c. What decisions build the core competencies?
d. How will the corporate strategy affect the line of business strategy for each product? Return to Question 1, part d, and revise the value propositions as appropriate. (See page 18.)
e. Develop a set of performance measures to monitor the execution of your firm's corporate-level strategy. (See pages 137–142.)
e. How do you think rival teams will compete? Why? Do you want to rethink the lines of business strategies and the corporate-level strategy?

Question 3: (See Exercise 4.1 and page 52.)

a. Write a mission statement for your firm. (See pages 51–54.)
b. Evaluate your mission statement. (See pages 51–54.)
c. Translate the mission statement into a theme-based and weighted value proposition for each product offered. (See page 54.)

Question 4: (See Exercises 4.1, 4.3, and 5.2 and pages 54, 58, and 78.)

a. Translate the theme-based and weighted value proposition (see Question 3) into performance measurements. Complete this question for each of your products.
b. Develop interim performance measures. (See pages 74–76.)
c. How will you audit the execution of your firm's strategy? (See pages 97–99.)

Question 5: (See Exercise 3.4 and 5.1 and pages 42 and 73.)

a. Relate specific decisions in the simulation to the execution of the firm's corporate-level and lines of business strategies. Work by functional area to assure your decisions are consistent and complete.
b. How does the corporate-level strategy improve the value proposition for each product?

Question 6: (See Exercise 8.1 and pages 130–131.)

a. List and weight long-term goals of your firm. (See page 131.)
b. Relying upon the simulation's manual, what variables affect the goals?
c. How do the weighted goals affect your decision making?

Question 7: (See Exercise 4.5 and pages 99–100.)

a. Project the size of the market for each product in each round of the simulation.
b. Assume each of your products retains its beginning market share. Calculate the potential sales by product by selling round. (See pages 99–101.)
c. At what points in time (by product) do you run out of plant capacity and require overtime or a second shift?
d. What factors allow your firm to grow faster than the market? What factors make it grow slower?

Question 8: (See pages 99–102.)

a. Estimate the cost of producing additional units by increasing plant capacity (without overtime) compared with increasing production with overtime or a second shift.
b. Outline a capital budget analysis to evaluate

the desirability of adding plant capacity. Explain the decision rule to invest or not invest? (See page 102.)

Question 9: (See Exercise 4.4 and pages 64 and 99–102.)

a. Estimate the changes in buyer expectations by product and by time period.
b. Based upon your firm's competitive strategy and the expected changes in buyer requirements, identify the desired positioning of each of your products for each selling period. (See pages 99–102.)
c. How do you expect rivals to position their products?
d. What problems do you anticipate in upgrading your products?

Question 10: (See Exercise 6.1 and pages 92–94.)

a. Draw an organizational chart for your firm (team). Designate positions and reporting relationships. Assign team members to specific tasks. (See page 93.)
b. Explain the logic of your organizational structure in terms of the firm's lines of business strategies and the corporate-level strategy.
c. Who is responsible for the coordination of decisions?

Question 11: (See Exercise 4.1 and pages 51–54.)

a. Does the simulation allow you to characterize your firm's Type I Buyer?
b. Specifically in terms of the simulation, what are the benefits of buyer loyalty? Is this realistic in your opinion?
c. What are the different ways to market your products? List each of the options and evaluate each in terms of the line of business strat-

egy. Do this for each product. How will you allocate marketing dollars by product and by marketing option?

Question 12: (See Exercise 7.2 and pages 120–125.)

a. Can you identify and characterize your firm's Type I Employee?
b. What decision options influence your hiring? In your opinion, are the options realistic?
c. What are the potential costs and benefits of each human resources option in the simulation? Build a model that identifies the costs and benefits of each possible decision.

Question 13: (See pages 105–106.)

a. What are pro forma financial statements?
b. How do pro forma financial statements provide a reality check before finalizing decisions?
c. What are the critical variables to examine in pro forma financial statements?
d. What cautions are to be taken before changing decisions based upon the analysis of the pro forma financial statements?

Part B: Post-Simulation Activities

Each team plays the simulation to "win" within their class. However, it is advantageous for instructors to separate a learner's grade from the results of the simulation. For many reasons, the results of the simulation are an imperfect indicator of a learner's achievement at the end of the simulation. A student's or developing manager's ability to explain their decisions, diagnose outcomes, and explain how things should have been done differently are more compelling than their firm's financial performance.

Diagnosing the results of each round of the

simulation is an important part of the learning process. Debriefing each round of the simulation may include class discussion and written assignments. To facilitate the debriefing, the Post-Simulation Activities include questions and an outline. Instructors may use the questions to prompt class discussion, and the outline may help to organize written reports.

Question 14: (See Exercise 8.1 and pages 56–59.)

a. After each round of the simulation, update the performance of your firm based upon the weighted goals. Evaluate your performance relative to prior periods and relative to rivals.
b. After each round of the simulation, update key financial ratios. Evaluate the financial health of your organization.
c. After each round of the simulation, update the execution of your competitive strategy, referring to performance measures, interim performance measures, outcome measures, and measures of the execution of your firm's corporate-level strategy. Develop a template that allows you to record and monitor the competitiveness of your products compared with rivals. (See pages 99–102.)
d. Which outcomes surprised you? What are the implications for the next round of decisions?
e. What occurred as expected? How does this affect your decision making in the next round?
f. Did you alter the line of business strategy for any product or the firm's corporate-level strategy? If "yes," explain.

Question 15: (See Exercises 6.5, 8.3, and 8.4 and pages 137–140.)

a. Build models to determine the competitive strength and market attractiveness for each product. (See page 140.)

b. How will this model help your firm allocate resources among products?
c. Redo parts (a) and (b) after each round of the simulation.

Question 16: (See Exercise 6.5 and pages 99–102.)

a. Develop criteria to evaluate your sales forecasts (See page 99.)
b. Evaluate your sales forecast.
c. Project sales by product for the next selling period. List your assumptions about rival behaviors and buyer expectations.

Question 17: (See Exercises 5.4 and 6.6 and pages 83–88.)

a. List all of your decisions in the most recent round of the simulation. Evaluate the decisions accord in terms of consistency and completeness. Were unintended consequences considered? What, if anything, should have been done differently?
b. Complete a capital budget for each of the projects. Were the right decisions made?

Question 18: (See Exercise 9.1 and pages 145–147.)
Look back over the entire simulation and consider the following:
a. What did you learn?
b. What actions proved to be wise and what actions were unsuccessful?
c. Which decisions of rivals were wise and which ones unwise?
d. Given the benefits of hindsight, what should you have done differently?
e. As you look forward to building a successful career, what strategic leadership lessons will you put into practice?

Debrief Outline

I. Executive summary
II. Review of financial results and progress toward long-term goals
   A. Highlights of financial status of firm
   B. Assess sales forecast and production schedule
III. Restatement of firm's mission and strategy
IV. Performance review and audit by product or market segment
   A. Presentation of performance and interim measurements
      1. Assessment of the execution of the line of business strategies
   B. Presentation of corporate-level strategy measurements
      1. Assessment of execution of corporate-level strategy
   C. Discussion of functional area decisions to execute strategy
      1. Assessment of completeness and consistency of decisions and unintended consequences
   D. Competitive assessment
      1. Strengths/weakness of rivals
      2. Market opportunities and threats
   E. Justification of capital and operating budget decisions
      1. Capital budget analyses of prior round capital outlays
      2. Allocation of resources
         a. between functional areas
         b. between products or market segments
   F. Impending major decisions
      1. Capital expenses needed by future round
      2. Shifts in strategy
      3. Other
   G. Financial ratio summary
   H. Lessons learned

CASES

CASE 1
NANCY'S WOMEN'S SHOPPE

Nancy Campbell, owner of a women's clothing store, is enjoying a leisurely dinner with her husband, Bob. They are discussing Nancy's meeting with her accountant, John Malch.

Nancy's Women's Shoppe

The Shoppe is located in the downtown district of historic Gettysburg, Pennsylvania. Nancy has sold women's clothing for almost forty years. Her client base has changed over time. Originally, her buyers were women who sought conservative styles, responsive service, and the convenience of a local retailer. Over the years, the cycle of high school and college proms, country club, civic, and charitable galas were a big part of the business. As the community grew and as more women entered the labor force, her customers changed. More recently, new hotels and a conference center have created new market opportunities.

Nancy has enjoyed running the business. Though not the family's sole source of income, it has been a vital supplement. The business allowed her to pay college tuition for her two children, provide extras for the family, and assure a comfortable retirement. Nancy still enjoys working with longtime customers and doing the buying for the store but does not want to be in the store sixty hours a week.

Nancy has considered three options: (a) giving the business to her daughter, but Nancy is uncertain if Abigail is really interested, (b) selling the store to two of her long-term employees, or (c) continuing to run the business while limiting her hours in the store.

Nancy's Thoughts Expressed to Bob

Several weeks ago, John completed the taxes for the store, and he noticed that the profits are largely unchanged over the last four years. Though sales grew about 7 percent per year, the profits are up by less than 2 percent over the period. So I asked John to take a closer look at the business and provide some advice. I met with John this morning to go over his recommendations. He suggested several things.

First, he thinks the rent is too high. The downtown location near the courthouse, a hotel, and the hospital is too costly. Medical, legal, and accounting offices and restaurants are pushing the rents higher. He thinks I should relocate, even if only a few blocks away. I am really not sure this is a good idea. The store gets a lot of walk-in business from professional women and those who are downtown for any number of reasons. Also, with the large number of tourists who come downtown, the location helps us.

He also suggests that we trim the inventory. He says we have almost $125,000 of merchandise on the floor at any time, and the carrying costs affect our profits. He thinks that stricter inventory practices will help the bottom line. To facilitate the inventory management, he suggests we acquire new computing capabilities for inventory management. He says it will allow us to identify the slow- and fast-moving styles and sizes. He believes the new system will pay for itself in about two years through tighter inventory control. But I'm just not sure that such strict inventory management is smart. Since we're the only specialty women's store in town, I need a variety of sizes and styles. Also, with charity galas as well as school and college proms and formals, I must stock what are by nature slow-moving items. The tourists' purchases are different, and I must have merchandise to meet their needs. If I limit the inventory, I'll lose sales.

He recommends that I cut the hours of operation, reduce the size of the staff, or handle more of the hours myself. Again, I'm just not sure. Because many of our shoppers seek advice and high-touch service, having fewer sales assistants will change the character of the store. Yet I don't want to spend more hours in the shop.

Finally, John says that I should try to allocate some of the savings to an increase in advertising. I don't know what to think. Everyone in town knows me. They know the store. I would rather give more money to the hospital than increase advertising. Supporting the hospital is the right thing to do, and I know the business benefits from the exposure and goodwill.

I'm just not sure what to do. I paid John a good bit of money for his advice. He knows more about business than I do, but his ideas are outside of my comfort zone. What do you think?

Bob's Reply

Nancy, the store has been great. You have done a remarkable job. If it's time to sell the business, let's do it and spend more time traveling. My schedule allows it.

If you want to stay with the store for a few more years, I'm supportive. But use the years to build the value of the business. I know you want to support the hospital and some of the local charities. I agree. The beneficiary will be the community. But this goal requires the same attention to business detail as trying to make money for us.

John Malch has interesting recommendations, but I always worry about those who are too technically trained. Often they see problems too narrowly. And you're clearly troubled. Don't rush to decide.

End-of-Case Exercise

Identify the major decisions Nancy must make. List the pros and cons. Discuss how a decision-making lens could weight the arguments and lead to a decision.

CASE 2
DON BATTS

Don Batts has recently been appointed to the newly created position of chief information officer for Reeder's Video, a nationally franchised chain of video stores. Don, trained in finance and accounting information systems, is on the staff of CEO Jeff Gubbiette.

Chief Information Officer

Mr. Gubbiette created this position to help senior managers in their decision-making choices. In this increasingly competitive and shrinking-margin business, Mr. Gubbiette acted on his long-held belief that easy access to industry and firm-specific data helps managers make better decisions. But managers often find it time-consuming and costly to maintain data files. Individual projects often entail some combination of re-creating data or relying on the firm's conventional wisdom without the benefit of supporting data.

Mr. Gubbiette has also been frustrated by the lack of systematic information. On a daily basis he receives sales data. On a monthly and quarterly basis he receives financial reports. But between these financial reports he is unable to monitor the pulse of the organization. Though his immediate staff provides frequent briefings, the reports lack continuity and hard data.

By centralizing the collection of data and maintenance of management information, Mr. Gubbiette believes that analysis and decision making can be more professional and based upon the best information possible.

In creating this position, Mr. Gubbiette personally prepared the following job description:

The Chief Information Officer serves on the President's staff and is responsible for the following: (a) designing and maintaining the firm's information system, (b) staff training, and (c) assisting area managers by providing regular data reports to Tax, Accounting and Finance, Sales, Human Resources offices, and other offices as requested.

Don Batts

Don is excited about his new job. After earning a BA and an MBA from the University of Maryland, he worked for ten years with a large multinational consulting firm. After a series of promotions and assignments involving information management and strategic planning, Don became increasingly restless. He wanted to spend more time with his family, and he wanted to get closer to the operations and decision making in a single organization. Consulting challenged Don but left him dissatisfied. When one project was completed, he moved to a new one and did not have to "live with" his recommendations.

His new position is attractive. It makes full use of his finance, accounting, and information management background. Though he has no direct line authority, the position charges him with maintaining data in support of decision making. As discussed with Mr. Gubbiette, Don is expected to support area managers. Part of this responsibility is collecting and maintaining data files to monitor, to anticipate, and to diagnose problems.

Reeder's Video

Reeder's Video is a nationwide franchised chain that rents videos. Organized in the early 1980s,

Reeder's grew rapidly, relying upon franchising to facilitate growth as the country embraced the VCR technology. The growth helped the firm capture scale economies in promotion and film acquisition. Many small "Mom and Pop" outlets could not compete as the number of Reeder's members grew rapidly.

More recently, Reeder's growth rate has slowed. Though they continue to franchise new retail units in the United States, the marketplace is saturated, even though most households are VCR owners. Reeder's has extended its inventory to include DVDs, and they have expanded the breadth of the products to include snack food, toys, video games, and music. The firm also has been opening stores abroad, and this international expansion has been moving forward.

Getting Started

Eager to please, Don wants to get off to a fast start. However, managers and franchisees do not know what data they need until a project comes up. Don needs their cooperation, but they usually suggest only a laundry list of items that includes the number of stores, sales, number of employees, new films purchased, and total payroll.

End-of-Case Exercise

Prepare a memo to Don. Advise him on several items. First, prepare a theme-based and weighted value proposition for Reeder's (as you think appropriate for a large video rental business). In turn, indicate the data series that you believe are important for him to gather. Design reports that will go to Mr. Gubbiette and his senior staff.

CASE 3
RANDOLPH HOOKE

Randolph Hooke is the newly appointed vice president for marketing for McGlade's Tube Products.[1] He has been charged to develop a business and marketing plan to improve the firm's profitability, market share, and customer satisfaction. He has thirty days to complete a report. The short time period is not threatening. Hooke is familiar with the firm, its products, and the industry.

McGlade's Tube Products

McGlade's Tube Products is approximately ten years old and billed $13 million last year. The business is profitable, but it seems as if each time McGlade's gains a new buyer it loses one of its established customers. Sales revenues have been stagnant for three years, and the firm's profit margins have declined despite favorable market conditions.

McGlade's manufactures tubes that hold and dispense a variety of consumer products (toothpaste and foodstuffs), industrial and construction materials (caulk and glue), as well as medicinal products (salves and ointments). Tubes are produced in a wide variety of shapes and sizes. Most of the tubes are plastic but some are coated paper. There is a wide variety of strength and density of the tubes; the tubes also differ by the size, shape, and the precision of release of the contained materials. Several different caps to the tubes are offered. McGlade's, as requested by the purchaser, imprints the product name, instructions for use, and cautions on the tube.

McGlade's has two groups of clients, each requiring distinct distribution routes. The large accounts, major consumer products companies, are few in number but generate more than 75 percent of the firm's sales. These large accounts are not price sensitive but require prompt delivery; they frequently have customized requirements, and they seek new, attractive ways to package their products. Full-time personnel service these large accounts. The firm also serves small customers who, in total, generate about 25 percent of the sales. The small accounts are price sensitive, persistently press for discounts, and are served through distributors.

At McGlade's unit costs decline with the length of the production run, and long production runs facilitate scheduling and keep machine use rates high. But long production runs frequently conflict with just-in-time demands of some buyers and the customization requests of others. Also, R & D complains its budgets are inadequate to keep pace with the changing needs of buyers. Marketing struggles with pricing issues and with the trade-offs between supporting the individual account managers compared with serving the distributors.

Randolph Hooke

Randolph Hooke has enjoyed a successful career. Following a West Point education and twenty years military service, Major Hooke served as a project manager for a consumer products firm that had a relationship with the suppliers of tubing products.

The Marketing Plan

As Randolph thinks about the marketing plan, he knows it must include a sales forecast and a budget for advertising, promotion, and personnel. He must also address pricing issues. As Randolph begins work, he is troubled by the prospect of missing key points.

End-of-Case Exercise

Prepare a memo to Randolph Hooke. Outline the problems he must solve before developing a marketing plan.

Note

1. *Managing Customers for Profit* (Harvard Business School Press, Interactive Simulation, HBSP/insimseries.htm).

CASE 4
ROCKWELL'S HEALTH CLUB

Rockwell's Health Club

Rockwell's Health Club is a modern exercise facility located on a high-traffic street in a densely populated affluent suburb of Charlotte, North Carolina. During 2002, Rockwell's monthly memberships averaged 600 men and women whose basic fee is $800 per year. Gross revenues amounted to nearly $600,000, comprised of membership fees, supplemental personal trainer and class fees, equipment purchases, and food sales from the club's snack bar. During the year, the club experienced 5 percent growth in their average monthly membership; however, there was considerable turnover in their membership.

Steve Rockwell owns 55 percent of the club. Five of his friends divide the remaining 45 percent. The minority shareholders are passive investors. Steve relies upon his "draw" from the business as his primary source of income. The minority owners seek the tax advantages from the depreciation of the building and equipment.

Annual Planning Retreat

Since opening the club in 1996, Steve Rockwell assembles his senior staff annually for a planning retreat. The retreat is an opportunity to reflect upon the prior year and to begin formulating plans and goals for the upcoming year. Steve schedules the retreat about sixty days prior to establishing budgets for the upcoming year.

The retreat is informal. Everyone speaks freely. Before open discussion and brainstorming, Steve asks everyone to comment briefly about their area of operation.

The Staff and Reports

Colin Prevost, Director of Physical Training and Program Coordinator

As seen in the data in Case Table C4.1, the net revenue from the aerobics and other classes has grown about 5 percent to almost $60,000. The growth is attributable to an increase in the number of classes and the fees per course. Enrollment relative to class capacity has declined since 1999.

In my opinion, we had a good year, especially given the expansion of the YMCA and the enormous amount of public attention it received. Looking forward, I have several suggestions. We should replace our aging equipment, add new workout stations, improve the audio and visual equipment in the exercise rooms, and organize training regimens for the local road races and triathlon.

Our capital equipment needs for the upcoming year are shown in Case Table C4.2.

The request to replace and upgrade equipment sounds like a lot of money. But the equipment has a five-year life. If we retain and attract fewer than twenty members each year, the devices will pay for themselves. The investment is important. We have a lot of members who want to use the most contemporary equipment and who need the distraction of audio and visual equipment to make their workouts more pleasurable.

I also think we have an opportunity to build a rehabilitation business. The local hospital has added several new orthopedic surgeons and cardiac specialists. There is a shortage of physical therapists and locations for supervised rehabili-

Table C4.1
Enrollment Data

	1999	2000	2001	2002
Number of workouts	79,102	82,372	88,550	93,600
Number of class hours	423	440	473	520
Class fees	$63,524	$67,679	$71,136	$74,880
Percent class enrolment	55%	54%	52%	48%
Expenses: Trainers and supplies	$11,421	$12,320	$14,190	$15,600
Net contribution	$52,103	$55,359	$56,946	$59,280

Table C4.2
Capital Requests

Item	Dollars	Explanation
Replacement Aerobic machines (5)	$30,000	These new machines will give us top-of-the-line exercise equipment for those who want strenuous workouts.
Cardio theater TVs, sound system, and transmitters (6)	$7,000	The video and sound systems will help attract and retain members who need diversion with their workouts
Expansion Weight machines (5) Cardio machines (3)	$4,000 $18,000	These new machines are easy to use and safe. The designs and resistance levels serve older members and those rehabilitating from illness or injury.
Additional maintenance	$10,000	
Total	$69,000	

tation, and the situation is getting worse. Also, this community has experienced rapid growth in the number of retired citizens. Within five miles of our facility, there are seven senior-living complexes. The independent-living facilities have golf courses and out-of-door swimming pools. But none has an indoor pool, exercise center, trainers, or therapists. This is a market we can quickly capture.

In addition to the equipment, here are my three recommendations: (a) We should expand into rehabilitation services and physical training for se-

Table C4.3 Aquatics Data				
	1999	*2000*	*2001*	*2002*
Lap hours available	24,000	24,000	24,000	22,500
Number of lap swimmers	13,200	14,100	15,225	16,250
Rental income	$1,200	$1,575	$1,750	$2,660
Lesson income	$4,500	$6,600	$9,300	$12,500

nior citizens. We will need to add a certified trainer and a therapist. The two positions may cost approximately $65,000 per year, plus fringe benefits. (b) Develop classes associated with local marathons and triathlons. (c) Expand our personal training opportunities.

Nancy Toppel, Director of Aquatics

I am very excited about the Aquatics Center. In the last year, revenues grew about one-third, attributable to more specialty classes for senior citizens, swim lesson fees, and rental incomes from birthday parties and church-group youth days. I am excited about the increased use. Swimming is a great activity for people of all ages, and I believe we have a great facility. I want to see it used. (See Table C4.3.)

Here are my recommendations: (a) More classes for children of all ages. (b) Advanced training classes for those who want to compete. (c) More rentals: birthday parties, corporate family days. (d) Host a water polo team, and (e) Host swim meets of area schools.

There are three problems in my area to discuss. First, scheduling pool activities is increasingly difficult because of the intensity of its use. Some members are complaining about the lack of availability of lap swim hours. Second, participants in the mid-morning water aerobics and arthritis therapy classes are complaining the water is too cold. The lap swimmers complain if the water is too warm. Finally, with the more intensive use of the pool, there are problems in the locker rooms, including the lack of privacy, noise, cleanliness, and parents with children of the opposite sex. People are complaining, and I am not sure what to do.

Eddie Reynolds, Director of Facilities, Marketing, and Membership Services

The local market for health club memberships is very competitive. There are many facilities that compete for members, and home exercise equipment is popular. To boost memberships and member retention, we need to work on two things:

First, we have to make coming to this club more fun. Just exercise is not enough. We need to draw young and athletic members to create an environment that makes this club a part of their social life. Health clubs are like dentists: people think they need to go but don't enjoy it. We need to make it fun. Parties, game nights, group events, awards, and competitions will help. Also, we need to upgrade our lounge and snack bar. These investments will improve member retention and attract new members.

Second, we have to cut our prices. Young members struggle to pay their car and rent bills and make payments on their school loans. The YMCA is considerably cheaper, and we will lose potential members. I suggest cutting our monthly fee by 20 percent.

Chuck Betz, Director of Personnel and Business Manager

We are in pretty good shape financially, but there are developing stresses. The growth in revenues is not fast enough to match our rising expectations for equipment and services. We have to make careful choices because the budget simply will not support all that we want to do.

End-of-Case Exercise

Prepare a memo to Steve Rockwell, helping him interpret and filter the advice. What should Steve do?

Specialo and Family

Specialo and Family is a midsize regional accounting firm. During 2002 its gross billings totaled almost $18 million. Despite operating in an intensely competitive market, the firm's revenue has grown 5 percent per year for the last decade. Its steady expansion is the result of unusually high client retention, increased billings to its long-term clients, some new clients, and, recently, offering management consulting services.

Raymond Specialo is one of five partners and the third-generation managing partner of the firm. Raymond's grandfather, Vincent, opened the practice in 1945. As the practice grew, Vincent's younger brother joined the company. Each had a son join the practice in the 1970s. Raymond joined in 1995 and assumed the leadership role in 2001. Six younger Specialo family members work in the firm, which employs a total of sixty-three persons.

The Firm

The firm is highly regarded in the region based upon the quality of the work and the courtesy of personnel. The firm is proud of its long-term relationships with clients. The practice also enjoys the loyalty of its employees. The turnover rate is very low relative to the industry, and Raymond cites the following reasons: "We don't hire a lot of people straight from school. We let them gain some experience elsewhere where they clarify their professional aspirations. Those who come to us are choosing this type of firm. Once they are here, the experience is positive. We work hard, but we help each other. There is a positive spirit of working together."

The Challenges

Raymond is faced with two challenges. The immediate task is the annual salary review and awarding of bonuses. The partners have allocated $150,000 for payroll adjustments. This sum is in addition to the firm's covering all increased costs of the medical and dental insurance. He has not yet determined how to distribute the money among the staff.

The second problem is less immediate but is still pressing. One partner has announced his retirement next year, and Raymond would like to promote one of the current managers.

Raymond's third problem is longer term. He recognizes the industry is growing increasingly competitive, and the profitability of tax and audit work is diminishing. Some members of the firm are urging him to increase the rewards to those who bring in new business, even if this widens the disparities in compensation. Others believe that the long-term relationships with clients necessitates that people stay with the firm, and a seniority-based compensation system is important. A third group wants the firm to push aggressively into consulting services.

The Data

The data in Table C5.1 refer only to the firm's five managers. The data are compiled from company records and from the assessment of the other partners. Raymond has decided to allocate

$75,000 of the $150,000 to the managers for salary adjustments.

End-of-Case Exercise

Prepare the following memos to Raymond:
1. Recommend a bonus for each of the five managers.

2. Draft a letter to each of the five seniors. Report their bonus and other information deemed useful.
3. Recommend the promotion of one of the managers to partner, and explain.

Table C5.1
Senior Management Analysis

	Lisa Reade	José Garcia	Steve Whittmann	John Campbell	Michael Tolwe
Years in firm	10	6	9	17	26
Years in grade	5	4	9	11	15
Years experience	14	10	12	23	34
Current salary	$66,000	$62,000	$73,500	$75,000	$83,500
Billing rate per hour	$165	$170	$210	$180	$200
Billed hours	1,400	1,825	1,220	1,500	900
Percent collected	85%	93%	98%	94%	100%
Client relationships	Does well, especially with women clients	Great with clients; very active in town	Smartest tax guy around; likes unusual problems	Nice guy; clients trust him	Well liked; long-term relationships
Work quality	Slow but accurate	Works hard; good work	Brilliant; likes complex work	Very good	Very good
New Clients					
Total	50	45	30	96	112
Last year	7	10	4	12	5
3-yr. retention	80%	93%	35%	90%	98%
Entrepreneurship	Has interest in consulting with businesses owned by women	Natural business developer; pushing IT consulting	Not an active business developer; has MBA	Active in business and social groups; well liked	Slowing down; very good with younger staff; delegates and oversees
Internal role	Mentors recruits; forms committees as needed	Tops in IT; helped redesign firm's new system	Not active; not well liked; helps only if asked	Serves as firm's financial officer	Wise; knows the firm, the business, and clients
Outlook	Only female in senior role; capable of growth	A star in the making.	Has high expectations	An important member of the firm	A valuable senior member of firm
Age / Race	40 / Caucasian	34 / Hispanic	36 / Caucasian	50 / Caucasian	60 / Caucasian

CASE 6
KARL'S OF MAINE

"Karl's Famous Ice Cream" has been producing a premium product at its Belgrade Lakes, Maine, plant since 1951. Karl's uses predominantly local ingredients, and sales are concentrated in the New England states. About one-half of the sales originate from six family-owned shops located in tourist areas in coastal and central Maine. The shops sell ice cream, and the attached restaurants offer light meals with a local flavor. Specialty items include lobster rolls and fish chowder. The other half of the sales occur through nonfamily-owned specialty stores, selective restaurants, and a few grocery stores. The market extends as far north as Bar Harbor, Maine, and south to Boston. Karl's does not extend westward to New Hampshire or Vermont.

Karl's ice cream is regarded as a special treat and is priced accordingly. Its primary feature is fresh local ingredients, including cream and fruit. Some staple ingredients, such as vanilla, chocolate, and sugar, are not produced locally and so are "imported." However, Karl's prefers to limit the flavors rather than lose the local character. Karl has, for example, rejected producing a peach product and several nut-based flavors because the principal inputs are not local. Karl's ice cream flavors rely upon local berries and other fruits; a unique maple ice cream is also available.

The Market

Karl's geographic market scope and distribution channels are limited. Within the market there are many competitors. There are other premium ice cream products as well as many lower-priced ice creams. A wide array of local pastry and candy with local Maine features compete for the consumer dollar.

Karl's products are highly regarded, and many vacationers look forward to their summer purchases. Grocery store sales remind buyers of their time at the ocean or lake. Also, the vacation population continues to grow, and the rising prices of recreational properties attest to the growth of the size and affluence of summer populations. In addition to the growth in tourism, there is substantial growth in the number of retirement communities, and the luxury home market reflects the growing appeal of Maine to live, retire, and recreate.

Karl and the Firm

Karl's father, Helmut, began the business in 1951. Karl began working for the firm after graduating from the business school at the University of Maine in 1966. After eight years of experience at all levels of the firm, Karl was appointed vice president. He spent three years working under the tutelage of his father before assuming management control.

Karl, age fifty-eight, is eager to pass the business to his two sons: Nicholas, twenty-seven, and Thomas, twenty-five, and be able to pursue his passions for fly fishing and hunting. Like his father, Karl has been teaching his sons the business after their graduation from university.

Their employees are hardworking and enthusiastic. Their north-country traditions assure that they will work even in adverse conditions. They have mechanical skills that are part of the experience of small farms and orchards and working in the woods.

Table C6.1 **Sales and Earnings Data**		
	Percent growth, sales (%)	Percent growth, earnings (%)
1998	7.5	4.2
1999	6.6	3.3
2000	6.7	3.1
2001	6.2	2.9
2002	6.0	2.2

Karl is the only member of the family engaged in the business, except for his sons. Over the period from 1980 to 1990, Karl purchased the equal shares of the business held by his two sisters. Both have professional careers and families, and they both have moved away from Maine. They were happy to sell their shares to Karl, given his interest and commitment to the business.

Over the last five years, Karl has transferred 25 percent of the firm to his workforce in a profit-sharing plan. The shares are not publicly traded, but each year the directors vote a draw for Karl and a contribution to the profit-sharing plan.

The firm's recent sales and earnings history is shown in Table C6.1. The data indicate that the firm has continued to grow at modest rates, despite declines in the stock market and a sluggish national economy. But the growth in earnings has been modest, and the earnings growth lags the growth in sales.

Table C6.2 shows a synopsis of the firm's financial highlights, and balance sheet data are shown in Table C6.3.

The Family and the Challenge

Looking forward, Karl gathers his sons, accounting and legal service providers, and long-term associates to discuss the future of the firm. The following summarizes their observations and suggestions:

- I think this business is very attractive. The family has enjoyed more than sufficient income, and it has allowed us to enjoy a very balanced lifestyle. We work hard, but have had chances to enjoy a unique homestead and family life. We don't need to share with family any more, and we continue to be generous to our employees. Those who vend our products also do well. We have been able to contribute generously to our church and to needs of social and civic groups. There is nothing on the horizon that threatens our collective well-being. Let's proceed as usual and simply enjoy our good fortune. We are truly blessed.

- Let's not think small. We have attractive opportunities to expand. We have limited debt and a great reputation. Our name is widely recognized and the brand could be placed on an array of products that are "country fresh." Though we lack experience with these products, we could purchase and brand soaps, cosmetics, personal care products, and food items.

- We could increase marketing, including buying advertising in the state's many tourist brochures. We can also collaborate with many tour groups and leave advertising materials at area resorts and hotels.

- Let's make our shops and restaurants more attractive by adding game areas such as miniature golf, expand the gift shops, and consider leasing some of our space to attract antiques outlets.

End-of-Case Exercise

Prepare a memo to Karl. Help him identify competing goals and objectives, and help him understand alternative corporate-level strategies.

Table C6.2 Income Statement Data ($ millions)					
	1998	*1999*	*2000*	*2001*	*2002*
Net sales	$17.00	$18.10	$19.30	$20.50	$21.70
COGS[a]	$11.90	$12.80	$13.90	$15.00	$16.10
Gross profit	$5.10	$5.30	$5.40	$5.50	$5.60
S & A expenses[b]	$3.40	$3.60	$3.90	$4.10	$4.30
IBT[c]	$1.70	$1.70	$1.50	$1.40	$1.30
Income tax	$0.70	$0.60	$0.60	$0.60	$0.50
Net income	$1.00	$1.10	$0.90	$0.80	$0.80

[a]COGS = cost of goods sold
[b]S & A expenses = selling and administration
[c]IBT = income before taxes

Table C6.3 Balance Sheet Data ($ thousands)			
	Working capital	*Total assets*	*Long-term debt*
1998	$391	$9,000	$300
1999	$395	$9,100	$300
2000	$370	$9,100	$300
2001	$350	$9,200	$300

Dr. Timothy Ryan is the chairman of the Department of Business at a midsize, private Catholic university situated in the suburbs of Chicago. The school has a strong religious heritage and commitment to a humanities-based undergraduate education. It offers undergraduate majors in the arts and sciences and selective professional disciplines, and three graduate degrees.

Dr. Ryan is at the final stages of recruiting a new instructor in management. The position is a result of the impending retirement of Professor John R. Hoope, a highly regarded member of the faculty. Professor Hoope came to the university after a successful business and consulting career. His background includes a Ph.D. from the University of Southern California and several years teaching Leadership Studies at the U.S. Army War College. During his civilian career Dr. Hoope has authored three management books. He has been teaching in both the undergraduate and MBA programs, and his experiences outside of academe have enriched his courses.

Dr. Ryan's Challenge

As is customary in the university's hiring process, Dr. Ryan appointed a three-person search committee. The committee's responsibility included the solicitation and screening of résumés, interviews at professional meetings, and invitations to the three finalists to visit the campus. The entire department plus administration meet the finalists and collaborate in making the final selection.

Though the recruiting process is clear, the university often finds it difficult to hire new faculty.

There are many external forces to overcome, and these include a seller's market and the university's salary range. Compared to the region's state universities and prestigious private colleges, the pay scale is below market. The teaching load is heavy, and tenure requires a record of successful teaching, service, and scholarship.

The newly hired professor will join a departmental faculty of eighteen, all of whom are male and Caucasian. The student population is 55 percent female and 20 percent African-American, Hispanic, and Asian.

The recruiting challenges also involve personalities. Choosing a three-person search committee was sensitive because there are several factions within the faculty. Some believe that the university's religious heritage influences hiring; others believe the heritage defines a commitment to a strong humanities-based instruction; others focus on academic credentials, and others think that practical real-world business experience is most important.

Given the factions, Dr. Ryan struggled to select a committee that could work together. He did not want to appoint a biased committee. The balanced committee, not surprisingly, was contentious from the beginning, but the committee produced the following job description.

Job Description

The University seeks an Assistant or Associate Professor of Management to teach undergraduate and MBA courses. Candidates must be able to teach at least one specialty area, including Human Resources Management, Operations/Management Science,

Business Policy, or Leadership. The teaching load is six courses per year. Ph.D. preferred but not required. Minority candidates are urged to apply. The successful candidate must demonstrate promise as a teacher, have a research agenda commensurate with earning tenure, and be prepared to serve as an active member of the University community.

A number of applications were received. After much discussion, three finalists were selected, and their résumés are shown below:

Linda Yonkers, Ph.D.

Education:
B.A. (1996): University of Notre Dame, Notre Dame, IN
  Major: Sociology
  Awards and Honors: Summa Cum Laude M.A. and Ph.D. (2002). University of Illinois at Urbana-Champaign, Champaign, IL
  Dissertation Topic: *Sex, Race, and Merit: An Empirical Study*

Experience:
Research Assistant 1998–2000
Teaching Assistant 2000–2002 (Introduction to Management)

Research:
"Women in a Culturally Diverse Workplace," Mid-West Management Association, June 2002.
"Sex Differences in Tasks and Behaviors," submitted to *Journal of Applied Psychology.*

Richard Brocade

Education:
B.A. (1972): New York University, New York, NY
  Major: Mathematics
M.B.A. (1982): The Wharton School of the University of Pennsylvania, Philadelphia
  Concentration: Operations Management

Experience:
1972–1980: Global Life Insurance Company of America
1982–1995: Merchant's Bank
  Assistant Vice President for Operations: Credit Card Division

(Continued)

1995–Present: First Bank and Trust
  Vice President for Operations: Credit Card Division
2000–Present: Adjunct Instructor of Management (University of Nebraska–at Omaha)
  One course per semester:
    Principles of Management
    Operations Management (MBA)

Research:
"Applying the Balanced Scorecard to Credit Card Operations," *Journal of Operations,* May 1996, pp. 12–19.
"Quick Response Technologies for Service Industries," *American Management and Operations Quarterly,* May 1998, pp. 31–38.
"Systems Thinking: Maintenance, Operations, Upgrades, and Process Management," *Journal of Quality Control*, September 2001, pp. 42–50.
"Modeling Continuous Improvement in a Data Management Environment," *Statistical Quality Review*, December, 2002, pp. 9–21.

David Loye, Ph.D.

Education:
University of Kansas, Lawrence, KS
  B.A. (Psychology) 1980
  M.B.A. (Management) 1982
  Ph.D. (Management) 1986

Experience:
1986–1989: Kansas State University, Manhattan, KS
  Assistant Professor of Management
1989–Present: St. Olaf College of Minnesota
  Assistant Professor of Management (1989–1993)
  Associate Professor of Management (1992–)

Teaching, Evaluation, and Service:
  Classes Taught:
    Principles of Management
    Business Communications
    Human Resource Management
    Principles of Leadership
    Seminar in Management (case studies for seniors)
  Evaluations:
    Average Course Rating = 4.3 (on 5-point scale)
    Department Average Rating = 3.76

(Continued)

Service
>   Adviser to Management Club
>   (1991–present)
>   Committees: Admissions (1990–1996),
>   Library (1994–1998), Student Life
>   (1995–present)

Research:
"Managing Change," presented at Central States
    Management Association, May 1989.
"Developing Executive Skills," *Training and
    Development Review,* June 1992, pp. 34–39.
"Teaching Managers about Ethics," presented at
    St. James College Symposium of Corporate
    Social Responsibility, March 1996.

End-of-Case Exercise

Build a weighted, strategy-specific hiring grid.
Discuss your assumptions, selecting the criteria
and the weights. Which one do you recommend
hiring?

Discuss the importance of strategy-specific
hiring. How will the school and its students
benefit?

Bibliography

Berry, Leonard. *Discovering the Soul of Service.* New York: Free Press, 1999.

Bossidy, Larry, and Ram Charan. *Execution: The Discipline of Getting Things Done.* New York: Crown Business, 1988.

Bounds, Gregory, Gregory Dobbins, and Oscar Fowler. *Management: A Total Quality Perspective.* Cincinnati: South-Western Press, 1995.

Capstone: A Business Simulation. Northfield, Ill.: Management Simulations, 2003 (www.capsim.com).

Certo, Samuel, and J. Paul Peter. *Strategic Management.* New York: Random House, 1988.

Collins, James C., and Jerry I. Poras. *Built to Last.* New York: Harper Business, 1994.

Covey, Stephen. *Principle-Centered Leadership.* New York: Summit Books, 1990.

De Kluyver, Cornelius. *Strategic Thinking.* Upper Saddle River, N.J.: Prentice Hall, 2000.

Drucker, Peter. *Management: Tasks, Responsibilities, and Practices.* New York: Harper Collins, 1974.

Epstein, Mark J., and Robert A. Westbrook. "Linking Actions to Profits." *MIT Sloan Management Review* 42, no. 3 (Spring 2001): 39–50.

Forgang, William G. *Competitive Strategy and Leadership: A Guide to Superior Performance.* New York: Rowman and Littlefield, 2001.

Grant, Robert M. *Contemporary Strategic Analysis,* 4th ed. Malden, Mass.: Blackwell Publishing, 2001.

Hamel, Gary, and C.K. Prahalad. "Strategic Intent." *Harvard Business Review* 67 (May–June 1989).

Heskett, James, Earl Sasser, and Leonard Schlesinger. *The Service Profit Chain.* New York: Free Press, 1997.

Hill, Charles W.L., and Gareth R. Jones. *Strategic Management Theory: An Integrated Approach,* 5th ed. Boston: Houghton Mifflin, 1999.

Hitt, Michael, R. Edward Freeman, and Jeffrey S. Harrison, eds. *The Blackwell Handbook of Strategic Management.* Oxford: Blackwell Publishing, 2002.

Hunger, David J., and Thomas L. Whalen. *Strategic Management.* New York: Addison-Wesley, 1993.

Juniper, Dean. *Making Decisions.* Oxford: How to Books, 1998.

Kaplan, Robert S., and David P. Norton. *The Balanced Corporate Scorecard.* Cambridge, Mass.: Harvard University Press, 1996.

Kotler, Philip. *Marketing Management,* 8th ed. Englewood Cliffs, N.J.: Prentice Hall, 1994.

Maister, David. *True Professionalism.* New York: Free Press, 1997.

March, James. *A Primer on Decisions: How Decisions Happen.* New York: Free Press, 1994.

Martin, Chuck. *Managing for the Short Term.* New York: Doubleday Books, 2002.

McCarthy, Dennis. *The Loyalty Link.* New York: Wiley and Sons, 1997.

Nelson, Reed. *Organizational Troubleshooting.* Westport, Conn.: Quorom Books, 1997.

Porter, Michael. *Competitive Advantage.* New York: Free Press, 1985.

Porter, Michael. "What Is Strategy?" *Harvard Business Review* 74 (November–December 1996): 61–98.

Niven, Paul R. *The Balanced Scorecard Step-by-Step.* New York: Wiley and Sons, 2002.

Pearce, John A., and Richard B. Robinson Jr. *Strategic Management,* 4th ed. Homewood, Ill.: Irwin Press, 1991; 8th ed., New York: McGraw Hill, 2002.

Price, William, and O.F. Farrell. *Marketing Concepts and Strategies,* 8th ed. Boston: Houghton Mifflin, 1993.

Rackham, Neil, and John DeVincentis. *Rethinking the Sales Force.* New York: McGraw Hill, 1999.

Russo, Edward, and Paul J.H. Schoemaker. *Decision Traps: 10 Barriers to Brilliant Decision-Making and How to Overcome Them.* New York: Fireside Press, 1999.

Rust, Roland, Valerie Leithaml, and Katherine Lemon. *Driving Customer Equity.* New York: Free Press, 2000.

Turner, Colin. *Lead to Succeed.* London: Texere Press, 2002.

Weston, J. Fred, and Eugene F. Brigham. *Managerial Finance,* 7th ed. Hillside, Ill.: Dryden Press, 1981.

Index